Martin Butler, Albrecht Hausmann, Anton Kirchhofer (eds.)
Precarious Alliances

Cultural and Media Studies

Martin Butler, Albrecht Hausmann, Anton Kirchhofer (eds.)
Precarious Alliances
Cultures of Participation in Print and Other Media

[transcript]

Published with generous support from the Carl von Ossietzky University, Oldenburg

Bibliographic Information published by the Deutsche Nationalbibliothek
The Deutsche Nationalbibliothek lists this publication in the Deutsche Nationalbibliografie; detailed bibliographic data are available in the Internet at http://dnb.d-nb.de

© 2016 transcript Verlag, Bielefeld

All rights reserved. No part of this book may be reprinted or reproduced or utilized in any form or by any electronic, mechanical, or other means, now known or hereafter invented, including photocopying and recording, or in any information storage or retrieval system, without permission in writing from the publisher.

Cover design: Bernd Ganser-Lion, based on Leonardo da Vinci,
 »The Lady with the Hermine« (wikimedia commons)
Printed in Germany
Print-ISBN 978-3-8376-2318-5
PDF-ISBN 978-3-8394-2318-9

Contents

Introduction:
Participation and Precarious Alliances, Now and Then
Martin Butler, Albrecht Hausmann, Anton Kirchhofer | 7

MARKETS
Martin Butler | 15

Net-Works: Collaborative Modes of Cultural Production
in Web 2.0 Contexts
Martin Butler | 19

Participation: It's Complicated (A Response to Martin Butler)
Henry Jenkins | 33

The History of the Booker Prize as a History of Problems
and Precarious Alliances
Anna Auguscik | 47

Socialist Realism in a Capitalist Context:
Marketing Strategies in the Russian Book Market
Ulrich Schmid | 63

The New Circumstances of Content Innovation
in the Digital Book Value Creation Network:
Precarious Guarantee of More of the Same?
Christoph Bläsi | 77

AUTHORSHIP, AGENCY, AND VALUE
Albrecht Hausmann | 99

Whose Intentions? The Posthumous Careers
of F. Scott Fitzgerald and William Styron
James L. W. West III | 103

Precarious Alliances: The Case of Arno Schmidt
Sabine Kyora | 117

Touched by an Author: Books and 'Intensive' Reading in the Late Eighteenth Century
Geoffrey Turnovsky | 135

Authorship, Participation, and Media Change: Perspectives from Medieval Studies
Albrecht Haüsmann | 157

POLITICS, INSTITUTIONS, MOVEMENTS
Anton Kirchhofer | 177

The War of Systems: Print Capitalism and the Birth of Political Modernity in Britain, 1789-1802
Wil Verhoeven | 183

'Success' and 'Failure' of Literary Collaboration between Authors in Belarus in the 1920s
Gun-Britt Kohler | 207

Profession and Ideology: Cultural Institutions and the Formation of Literary Circles in the Soviet Occupied Territory and the Early GDR
Arvi Sepp | 241

Precarious Alliances between Literature and Law: A Tentative Account of the Case of Australia
Ralf Grüttemeier | 257

Literary Movements as Precarious Alliances? Observations and Propositions on Movement Discourse and Cultural Participation
Anton Kirchhofer | 281

Notes on Contributors | 311

Introduction:
Participation and Precarious Alliances, Now and Then

MARTIN BUTLER, ALBRECHT HAUSMANN, ANTON KIRCHHOFER

In recent years, participatory forms and practices of cultural expression have increasingly been paid attention to in public and scholarly discourses. Both a wide media coverage of the implications of new digital technologies on our ways of creating and distributing cultural knowledge and a steadily growing number of academic publications and projects, especially in the field of popular cultural studies, give ample proof of the dramatically increased fascination with participatory cultures. Participation, it seems, is *en vogue*, both as a mode of cultural production that has especially gained ground with the advent of what is commonly referred to as social media and as an analytical category employed for the examination of the processes and results of exactly this mode of production.

However, both the public debate and the scholarly discussion in the field tend to exclusively focus on contemporary practices and forms of expression and explore their participatory potential within present day social, cultural, and political contexts. Moreover, whether it is the participation of fans in the writing, or rewriting of their most famous narratives online, or the creation and dissemination of amateur clips on Vimeo or YouTube, the subject matter of the discourse on participatory cultures, more often than not, limits itself to the ways and channels of participation provided by Web 2.0 environments (e.g., Ackermann/Boroffka/Lersch; Apprich/Stalder; Delwiche/ Jacobs Henderson; Greif et al.). And, to be sure, there are good reasons for doing so, as the increase in what Axel Bruns has labeled "produsage," i.e., the convergence of production and consumption through interactive online media, is certainly due to the most recent technological developments in this area.

What might be a legitimate choice in popular cultural and media studies, then, i.e., focusing on different modes of participation in contemporary mediascapes, has only rarely been turned into a perspective of analytical inquiry when it comes to the examination of *past* modes and practices of cultural production. More often than not, we indeed tend to forget that the concept of participation might also help shed light on *historical* phenomena, and that its application is not restricted to the most recent trends and developments. What seems to be an obvious insight, however, has not manifested itself in projects and publications so far—still, scholarship as well as the public discourse are predominantly concerned with participatory cultures since the advent of Web 2.0. In other words, starting from the theoretical, conceptual, and analytical insights that the study of contemporary participatory cultures has already brought forth, we should allow ourselves to look back and ask, first, whether or not we can identify and describe specific historical settings and/or constellations which might be approachable via the concept of participation, and, second, whether or not the concept of participation could not lend itself to a fruitful revaluation of some of our central ideas on cultural production both in historical and contemporary print and other media cultures. In other words: It might well be that established notions of 'text,' 'author,' or 'originality' appear in a different light once reconsidered through the conceptual lens of 'participatory cultures,' which may thus prove to be a fruitful concept for the analysis of both past and present phenomena.

This book sets out to contribute to answering these questions by investigating into past and present modes of collaborative cultural production, approaching them as 'cultures of participation,' in which a number of different—historically and culturally specific, and sometimes highly unlikely—actors, such as authors, printers, agents, critics, scholars, fans, readers, audiences, cooperate and interact in a range of different and highly complex ways which have not been described and analyzed systematically and in full detail yet. In so doing, the present volume probes the adequacy of the concept of 'participation' for the scholarly examination of historical forms and practices of cultural expression and might thus add to the critical revaluation of a number of received notions and ideas about historical processes of cultural formation and transformation.

We assume that the ways of cooperation and interaction between actors in these processes lead to the formation of what we would like to conceive of as 'precarious alliances,' i.e., particularly fragile agreements of collaboration through which all participating individual and/or institutional actors at least temporarily benefit from. Admittedly, this definition remains as vague as the term 'alliance' itself. Moreover, it bears only a limited analytical potential, as it leaves open many questions, such as: How many actors have to be involved to form an alliance? Do these actors have to know that they are part of an 'alliance' to make the collaboration work? What kind of relationship do the participants have (symbiotic, parasitic, hierarchical, balanced)? How does the term 'alliance' relate to other terms that are employed to describe phenomena of collaboration (e.g., cooperation, network, movement)?

Against the backdrop of this list of unsolved issues and open questions, one could well drop the term for good. However, we deliberately decided to keep it exactly *because* of its vagueness: We would like to argue that the term 'alliance'—due to its very *un*specificity—invites a discussion of the questions listed above (among others), a discussion which will eventually contribute to further sharpening our understanding of what it is that constitutes an alliance in the realm of cultural production. Luckily enough, then, the contributions to this volume accepted the invitation and added to this discussion, tested the applicability of the term and thus contributed to shedding light on its many dimensions and implications as well as on alternative terms and concepts.

To conceive of historical and contemporary cultural forms of expression as results of participatory practices, which, in turn, foster the formation (and transformation) of a range of alliances between a variety of individual and collective actors, of course questions the notion of the author as an autonomous creator of original content and value, an idea which, for quite a considerable amount of time, has informed literary historiography as well as literary criticism. To be sure, this romantic notion has been demystified to a great extent by literary and cultural criticism and scholarship anyway (though, surprisingly, it has remained quite powerful both within scholarly debates and in public discourse). Most sustainably, perhaps, the works of Pierre Bourdieu have fostered the proliferation of the idea that authors as well as their writings are embedded in a network of a range of individual and collective actors which impact on literary production, distribution, and reception, and have thus significantly contributed to deconstructing the myth of the solitary genius. So, after the 'death' of the author (Barthes) and the recently proclaimed 'rebirth,' or return, in literary and cultural studies (cf., e.g., Jannidis et al.), there is certainly no need of declaring the author obsolete once again. Yet, what remains to be done is to identify and analyze in much closer detail (and from a number of different theoretical and methodological perspectives) the complex entanglements of individual actors and institutions in the realm of literary and cultural production, in which 'the author' (among other usual and unusual suspects) might be conceived of, conceptualized as, even constituted as a historical person, a public persona, a category, or a concept.

It is among the goals of this book to highlight the collaborative nature of this kind of 'cultural work' which can be observed in both past and present contexts, and which, through diverse kinds of interactions, results in the formation and transformation of print and media cultures, their institutions, and—not to forget—the very terms and concepts employed to describe exactly these formations and transformations. To pursue this endeavor, we believe that the notions of participation and precarious alliances provide fruitful conceptual coordinates for an analytical framework that indeed allows us to trace and describe both the specific nature of the interactive modes of production, dissemination, and reception, as well as the (changing) roles, functions, and intentions of diverse actors involved therein.

Thus examining both past and present modes of cultural collaboration, this volume also sheds light on the many complexities attached to the concept of participation itself, among them, for instance, its highly normative usage in recent (and not so recent) debates on processes of democratization and in-/exclusion, in which participation usually turns out to be something 'good.' Indeed, if we set out to discuss cultures of participation in print and other media, we also need to reflect and be constantly aware of the context-specificity of the concept and the values ascribed to it. To be precise, the discourse on participation (at least in western democratic societies), more often than not presupposes a functionally differentiated society complemented by a specific idea of justice, according to which every individual's option of participation is a desirable norm. Under these premises, then, participation turns out to be a core concept in these societies—and a highly normative one at that. Starting from here, one might argue that *cultural participation*, understood as an important asset in processes of education and identity formation, and, consequently, as a basis for the accumulation of social prestige, has become a central demand as well, especially for those who, for various reasons, have been excluded from it so far.

In one way or another, then, the contributions to this volume add to a theoretical discussion that has only begun to take shape very recently; a discussion which needs to be led exactly because the rhetoric of participation and participatory cultures has become so pervasive and, thus, incredibly powerful. "Our understanding of participatory culture," as Henry Jenkins argues in his contribution to this book, "is evolving rapidly at a time when there are many emerging kinds of relationships between media producers and audiences, when there are many loose or broad claims being made about the value of participation, when there is an ongoing theoretical project—both within and beyond the academy—to refine our understanding of the concept of participation." It is exactly this "ongoing theoretical project" that this volume sets out to advance by drafting what Jenkins calls "a more nuanced vocabulary" for the description and analysis of participatory cultural production, without, however, mystifying the concept of participation the very moment the concept of authorial autonomy has been disqualified as a romantic invention. What this book offers, then, is an alternative perspective on print and other media cultures through the centuries, which, in the process of developing critical terms and concepts, is (or shall be) aware of its own blind spots, shortcomings, and contingencies at all times.

In order to structure the analyses of the forms and functions of precarious alliances now and then, we decided to cluster the contributions to the present volume according to what we identified as important dimensions in the complex fabric of participatory cultural production (of course, being fully aware of the contingency of our choice and the overlaps between the dimensions). Resulting from this are three sections ("Market," "Authorship, Agency, and Value," "Politics, Institutions, Movements") framed by short introductory notes, which illustrate the interrelatedness of the sections' contributions and their relevance in the discussion of the central questions this volume sets out to address.

Starting from the analysis of contemporary forms of participatory cultures, the first section ("Markets") is dedicated to the many intricate relationships of literary and cultural production to market-related processes and developments. As the contributions reveal, print and media cultures in different cultural and historical contexts are—in one way or another—shaped by economic parameters, e.g., by calculations of cost and benefit, by strategies of marketing, or by processes of commodification and commercialization, all of which, in turn, involve a number of individual and institutional actors that are collaborating (but also, at times, antagonizing) in a range of different ways in order to achieve their goals.

The second section ("Authorship, Agency, and Value"), then, returns to the category of the author, which, as hinted at above, still plays a dominant role, especially in public debates on questions of authorship and, closely attached to this, questions of ownership, agency, and the 'value' of literary and cultural production. The contributions in this section take a close look at the intricate processes of creating the author as a subject position, which is not seldom charged with a set of particularly normative assumptions that, in turn, allows the participants involved in this process to harvest different kinds of material and immaterial benefits. The topics dealt with in this section range from the making of posthumous careers of authors and strategies of self-fashioning to the repercussions of media change and the investments of readers on the state and role of the author.

Finally, the contributions to the third section ("Politics, Institutions, Movements") open up the view on the political contexts of print and media cultures and both analyze and theorize the different practices of collaborative cultural production with particular regard to their embeddedness in institutional frameworks and in specific constellations of political power. Covering different historical periods ranging from the late 18th to the 20th centuries as well as different cultural, economic, and ideological environments, the essays in this section show in how far and to what extent cultural production in print and other media both is shaped by and contributes to shaping larger societal and political patterns and structures.

* * * * *

The contributions to the present volume are based on papers given at a symposium held at the Hanse-Wissenschaftskolleg (HWK) in Delmenhorst in June 2012, in which a range of scholars from a variety of disciplinary and cultural backgrounds met for two and a half days to discuss cases of precarious alliances and cultures of participation in different fields of literary and cultural production. The symposium was held as part of an HWK Associated Junior Fellowship awarded to Martin Butler in December 2011.

We owe gratitude to a number of people who helped turning this project, i.e., both the symposium and this book, into what we had hoped it would be: a lively and productive dialogue, a space to exchange ideas, to initiate debates, to link up with colleagues, and—finally, and in the most productive sense—to become aware of the limitations and shortcomings of one's own approach. First of all, we would like to thank the scholars we invited to join the conversation. In their contributions to the symposium, they all engaged with the notion of 'precarious alliances' which we had introduced in our conceptual draft for the event, and thus contributed to weaving a central thread, while, at the same time, adding new and insightful perspectives to add further precision to the debate. Fortunately, they kept up the dialogue with us even after the symposium and added, with their articles, to the coherence of this volume.

We would also like to thank the staff at the HWK for their generous financial and organizational support, first and foremost Dr. Susanne Fuchs and Sabine Friedrichs for their commitment before, during, and after the event, which has been extraordinarily helpful and productive. In general, as an Institute for Advanced Study, the HWK served as the ideal setting and provided the necessary infrastructure for our interdisciplinary dialogue—we are very grateful that we had the opportunity to use these resources for our symposium. We also thank the President's office of the University of Oldenburg, which provided financial support for the printing of this volume. Last but not least, we owe gratitude to our student assistants, who neither lost their patience nor their politeness in handling the all-too-busy editors of this volume: We are particularly grateful to Katharina Bieloch and Almke Ratjen for their translations as well as for their general support in proofreading the manuscript, as well as to Britta Kölle, Thomas Hühne, Patrizia Striowsky, and Lara Brünjes who also invested an incredible amount of energy into the editing and formatting of this volume.

Works Cited

Ackermann, Felix, Anna Boroffka, and Gregor H. Lersch, eds. *Partizipative Erinnerungsräume: Dialogische Wissensbildung in Museen und Ausstellungen*. Bielefeld: transcript, 2013. Print.

Apprich, Clemens, and Felix Stalder, eds. *Vergessene Zukunft: Radikale Netzkulturen in Europa*. Bielefeld: transcript, 2012. Print.

Barthes, Roland. "The Death of the Author." *Image / Music / Text*. Trans. Stephen Heath. New York: Hill and Wang, 1977. 142-47. Print.

Bourdieu, Pierre. *Die Regeln der Kunst: Genese und Struktur des literarischen Feldes*. Frankfurt/Main: Suhrkamp, 1999. Print.

Bruns, Axel. "Towards Produsage: Futures for User-Led Content Production." *Cultural Attitudes towards Communication and Technology 2006: Proceedings of the Fifth International Conference on Cultural Attitudes Towards Technology and Communication, Tartu, Estonia, 28 June-1 July, 2006*. Ed. Fay Sudweeks, Herbert Hrachovec, and Charles Ess. Perth: School of Information Technology, Murdoch University, 2006. 275-84. Print.

Delwiche, Aaron, and Jennifer Jacobs Henderson, eds. *The Participatory Cultures Handbook*. New York: Routledge, 2012. Print.

Greif, Hajo, Larissa Hjorth, Amparo Lasén, Claire Lobet-Maris, eds. *Cultures of Participation: Media Practices, Politics and Literacy*. Wien: Peter Lang, 2011. Print.

Jannidis, Fotis, Gerhard Lauer, Matias Martinez, and Simone Winko, eds. *Rückkehr des Autors. Zur Erneuerung eines umstrittenen Begriffs*. Tübingen: Niemeyer, 1999. Print.

Jenkins, Henry. "Participation? It's Complicated (A Response to Martin Butler)." In this volume. Print.

Markets

The production, circulation, and reception of print and other media are in many ways shaped by a range of forces and actors who can be said to constitute what is often referred to as the literary and cultural marketplace. Be it books, comics, television series, computer games or even the seemingly unrestricted grassroots productions of Web 2.0 environments, the aesthetic make up as well as the distribution of cultural artifacts are not seldom the result of (or at least significantly influenced by) strategic considerations on how to address the right target audience, how to compete with other goods available to the recipient (or customer) and, consequently, how to increase economic benefits.

Seen in this light, the creation of literature and other medial formats turns out to be a collaborative endeavor which, to a considerable degree, follows the complex logic of the marketplace and thus stands in stark contrast to the romantic notion of autonomous authorship and unrestricted artistic freedom, which, though scholarship has long addressed this economic framing of cultural production, has been surprisingly persistent. Within this logic of the marketplace, then, a number of different individual and institutional actors, ranging from prize committees and publishing houses to independent filmmakers and internet users—become involved in the process of making, spreading, and consuming diverse forms of cultural expression in different media. In order to pursue their own specific agendas and reach their specific goals based on different motivations, these actors not seldom enter 'precarious alliances,' i.e., highly fragile, short-term forms of strategic cooperation and agreement.

The following section will focus on these alliances within the literary and cultural marketplace, on their different forms and functions, on their preconditions and outcomes as well as on moments of their stability and their precariousness.

Martin Butler is concerned with different modes of collaborative cultural production in Web 2.0 environments. He argues that, in very contrast to the notion that the internet serves as an unrestricted space of amateur creativity, these environments are not seldom designed to instrumentalize intellectual and financial resources through the proliferation of what he calls a 'rhetoric of participation.' This rhetoric, as Butler shows by referring to two case studies, explicitly celebrates the benefits of collaborative creativity and thus obliterates the implicit power structures that shape the interplay and the formation of alliances between actors in these very environments.

In his response to Martin Butler, Henry Jenkins distinguishes between what has become known as 'participatory cultures' on the one hand, which, as he suggests, "may in its purist form exist only as an ideal" and, as such, are characterized by balanced power relations, and Web 2.0 on the other, which provides platforms that can be used to implement new business models following a neoliberal logic through their harvesting of intellectual labor and the accumulation of capital via crowdsourcing. As both 'cultures' operate with the term 'participation,' though, Jenkins eventually argues for a more "nuanced vocabulary" which may both help to specify the normative implications of the term and add precision to the description and analyses of modes of participation in internet environments.

Anna Auguscik focuses her attention on the Booker Prize as another actor in the literary and cultural marketplace and scrutinizes the economy of attention that the Booker—or, to be more precise, the many controversial debates on the Booker, for instance on the constellation of judges, the shortlisted books and the winner—regularly generates. As Auguscik manages to illustrate, these debates on the 'problematicness' of the Booker Prize and its award impact both on the symbolic capital of novels as well as their authors and on the sales figures and market shares of publishing houses.

Focusing on two case studies, Ulrich Schmid examines the intricate relationships between the Russian book market and other sectors of the economy. Yet, for him, strategies such as product placement (in Daria Dontsova's novels) or the transmedia marketing of a literary text, e.g., through the proliferation of a computer game adaptation (as in the case of Glukhovsky's novel *Metro 2033*, which itself is based on a blog entry) do by no means contribute to what some have felt to be the "end of literature"

(Schmid, in this volume), but rather provide alternative models of cultural production based on the formation of precarious alliances between media and markets.

From a distinctly marketing-oriented perspective, Christoph Bläsi's contribution sheds light on the many actors and processes involved in the creation of innovation in the book industry. With his argument, which rests on the idea that innovation and familiarity have to be kept well-balanced in order to turn a book into a marketable commodity, he dismantles the romantic notion of innovation as something particularly creative and original, a notion which, as he shows, is substantiated, for instance, by the discourse on open source software and demand media production. His contribution thus adds another fruitful perspective to the section's overall focus on the complex entanglements between the production, dissemination, and reception of print and other media and the literary and cultural marketplace.

(Martin Butler)

Net-Works: Collaborative Modes of Cultural Production in Web 2.0 Contexts

MARTIN BUTLER

Cultures of participation, i.e., the active involvement of the recipient, the reader, the listener, the viewer, in the process of cultural production, are not a result of 21st century digital technologies. It would indeed be misleading to assume that participation in cultural production is only a recent phenomenon. Instead, the 'consumer's' active and creative use of cultural goods and materials, in other words: The appropriation of the culture industry's products in everyday-life contexts, has been an integral part, if not a defining characteristic of popular culture. However, in the history of popular culture, this form of participation through appropriation, more often than not, remained a highly private practice and was not, at least not as a rule, exposed to a public audience. The creative use of mass-produced cultural goods, as Henry Jenkins has it, "existed behind closed doors and its products circulated only among a small circle of friends and neighbors. Home movies never threatened Hollywood, as long as they remained in the home" (*Convergence* 140).

This, as Jenkins convincingly illustrates in his contribution to this volume, has changed dramatically in recent years, as there has been a significant increase in quantity and speed of networked communication in many fields of life, including that of cultural production (cf. 35-36). Indeed, with the emergence of new technological possibilities, participation in the production of cultural goods and artifacts has become a widespread option, its results—most frequently, in the shape of amateur productions and reproductions—at times spread at an unprecedented speed and become quite successful, not only in terms of distribution, but also as regards sales figures. Of course, this is not to herald the advent of a generally evolving creativity of the masses and, as David Gauntlett has remarked recently, "it may always be the case that people will spend more time as 'readers' than as 'writers,' which would make sense, otherwise there would be far too much original material in the world and nobody would be consuming it, simply because they wouldn't have time" (71).

Still, there is no doubt that participation in cultural production has been facilitated through Web 2.0 technologies and environments. And I would even go one step further: Participation—understood as a cipher for the belief in the democratizing potential of the Internet—is *en vogue*. In other words, it has become fashionable to participate, and participation, especially in and through social media, has become a value in itself, both for consumers and the media industries, as it works as an interface between producers and users of cultural materials and thus enables the formation of alliances between the two.

Against the backdrop of this assumption, my contribution sets out to take a closer look both at various modes of participation in Web 2.0 contexts, arguing that these contexts, more often than not, draw upon a particular rhetoric that exploits the normative dimension of the notion of participation, staging it as something wishful and desirable. With the help of a number of examples from various fields of cultural production (including film and popular music), the contribution also illustrates that the surplus value of this 'rhetoric of participation' for the actors involved and thus its potential to either foster or endanger alliances between them, depend on a range of contextual parameters that need to be taken into close consideration.

Yet, let me begin by coming to terms with the very term 'participation' or 'participatory culture' in times of Web 2.0., for which I come back to Henry Jenkins and his approach towards the term, which starts from distinguishing 'participation' from 'interactivity.' For him, this distinction (between 'participation' and 'interactivity') is a matter of degree. As he writes, "[p]articipation is more open-ended, less under the control of media producers and more under the control of media consumers" (*Convergence* 137). And he goes on: "Allowing consumers to interact with media under controlled circumstances is one thing; allowing them to participate in the production and distribution of cultural goods—on their own terms—is something else altogether" (137). Participation, in sum, is less regulated and less limited than interactivity, it seems. But, as we may infer from the quote, it still *is* regulated and limited. This notion would also be underlined by the phrase "*allowing* [consumers] to participate" (137, my emphasis) as it limits the often taken-for-granted democratic appeal of participatory cultures right from the start. "Allowing" indeed seems to suggest that there might be somebody who controls, regulates, gives and takes options of participation.

And there may indeed be some degree of control in participatory environments, as Elana Shefrin has shown with regard to the alliance between the producers of the *Star Wars* movies and their fans. In this case, participation in the 'production' of *Star Wars* spin-offs on the web was (and still is) regulated and framed by a set of restrictions and limitations. As Shefrin notes, "in the late 1990s, the StarWars.com official website began granting free web space to fans who desired to post their creations, but only if their submissions would become the studio's intellectual property" (275). Henry Jenkins has also hinted at the *Star Wars* producers' ways of 'allowing' participation to a certain degree, pointing out that George "Lucas (i.e., the mastermind behind the *Star Wars* universe) wants to be 'celebrated' but not appropriated. Lucas has opened up a space for fans to create and share what they create with others but only in his terms" (*Convergence* 154). Shefrin has also pointed to "Lucas's and Lucasfilm's flagrant commodification of participatory fandom" (276), which, though it "has not visibly eroded the general audience consumption of their franchise products, […] has clearly resulted in a loss of symbolic prestige among media critics and *Star Wars* fans" (276).

As regards the case of *Star Wars*, the alliances between producers and fans might thus become endangered, as the producers' highly restrictive 'politics of participation' stand in contrast to the fans' belief that the producers of *Star Wars shall* not limit creative expression among their true adherents. In the end, then, it is the fans' trust—and with it their romantic idea of a limitless universe of imaginary freedom they inhabit side by side with the movies' producers—which is severely shaken by this act of limiting creativity. Moreover, commodification of participation here quite literally means turning fan creativity into monetary benefit for the production company, as the fans' intellectual labor is automatically turned into Lucasfilm's property.

As Jason Mittell has shown, a similar case of commodifying online participation by drawing on the alliance between producer and fans (this time, however, in a camouflage way), appeared in 2007, when a short user-generated clip called "The Seven Minute Sopranos" was published on YouTube (cf. 95). As a "highly rapid recap of the previous five and a half seasons in advance of the (TV-series') final episodes, the humorous but affectionate fan-created video garnered over a million views and successfully promoted the final season" (95). Then, as Mittell continues to argue, "[p]roducers took note of the success, and enlisted marketers to create similarly glib online recaps, such as '*Lost* in 8:15' and 'What the frak is going on?' for *Battlestar Galactica*" (95), two other highly successful TV-series.

Here, the alliance between media industries and consumers could well be conceived of as a mutual give-and-take, with the consumers using the producers' 'raw materials' and the producers drawing on the user-generated content. Yet, money only flows in one direction. Nicolas Carr has pointed to the economic 'exploitation' of this alliance, arguing that

by putting the means of production into the hands of the masses but withholding from those same masses any ownership over the product of their work, Web 2.0 provides an incredibly efficient mechanism to harvest the economic value of the free labor provided by the very, very many and concentrate it into the hands of the very, very few. (qtd. in Gauntlett 68)

This variation of a Marxist argument might draw too dark a picture, as David Gauntlett has recently argued, pointing out that "the best-known Web 2.0 projects simply don't claim ownership in the way [Carr] asserts" (69). And indeed, Carr's argument sounds deeply fatalistic. However, I would not share Gauntlett's more optimistic view here either, as I believe that the economic or symbolic value attached to participatory practices as well as to their creative output still plays a central role in the formation and dissolution of alliances between producers and consumers.

Let me, at this point, draw on two other examples, a closer look at which is supposed to shed light on the many parameters that need to be considered when analyzing these processes of the formation and dissolution of alliances between producer and recipient through the interface of 'participation.' The first example is the film *Iron Sky*, in the production of which participation was a built-in-feature from the outset: *Iron Sky*, which was released in 2012 and which tells the story of Nazis that hid on the dark side of the moon for more than seventy years and attack earth in the year of 2018 to reclaim their territories. The film was a result of a collaboration between Finland, Germany, and Australia, and was partly financed through crowdfunding, i.e., the collection of money online. To be precise, when 'official money' ran out at the end of the film's making, crowdfunding was used to make sure that the movie could ever be screened. Moreover, a number of amateur Internet-filmmakers were involved in the production process, contributing ideas for the development of the plot, which were then taken up by the Finnish director Timo Vuorensola. For their collaborative efforts, these amateur filmmakers could use the online platform *Wreck-A-Movie*, which, according to the *Iron Sky*-website, "offers film creators a direct connection with their audience, and offers the fans a never-before-seen chance to interact with movie projects."[1]

To be sure, participating in the creation of the film on *Wreck-A-Movie* was also restricted by rules, and there was a director and a team of people who would be in charge of editing the sent-in materials. Nevertheless, Vuorensola is said to have always taken sensitive care of the interests of his collaborators, never forgetting—as one reviewer put it—"his old fans during the six years of production." "[O]ld fans," because Vuorensola is certainly among the most prominent Internet-filmmakers, whose prestige also made sure that enough monetary support could be crowdsourced for *Iron Sky*. Moreover, we have the German popband Laibach providing the soundtrack, and Götz Otto and Udo Kier (both not too famous, but still famous enough) being featured among the film's protagonists. All in all, what we witness here is a strange mixture of participatory practices and the conventional workings of the media industries relying on "big name actors," as the *Iron Sky*-website has it, and the usual marketing channels, which also becomes manifest in the following disclaimer we can read on the same site:

Iron Sky is on the forefront of a new wave of indie movies, where the filmmakers are in direct contact with the audience even before the movie is out, using the power of communities in both creating the movie and also to a degree in funding it. [...] This is your chance to take part in this groundbreaking movie project. We have been

---

1 <http://www.ironsky.net>. The details on the film and its production are also taken from this website.

successful in financing 87% of the budget, and to cover the missing 900,000 euros we are establishing an investment scheme for EES-based individuals and companies to invest and share the future profits from Iron Sky. Initial investments will start from 1000€ and they include extra perks, like a chance to meet the cast, etc. ("Crowdfunding")

Iron Sky, then, may be said to be a prime example of what Grant Patten has labeled a "Web 2.0 business model" (1) which relies on the alliance between the 'official' filmmakers and their fans, and in which so-called "indigenous knowledge" (1 et passim), i.e., user-generated ideas and content (cf. 1), are incorporated in a marketable movie production. Though the website constantly stresses the give-and-take nature of this alliance, the movie production is far away from being the result of a collaborative endeavor in an egalitarian sense; instead, it draws on a campy topic, the almost cult-status of its protagonists and, finally, the crowdfunding-model to shape a 'rhetoric of participation.' This rhetoric, then, is supposed to render the collaborate online practices of cultural production as part of the deeply political enterprise of inclusion, but actually operates to disguise a logic that may well be called prototypical of a new form of neoliberal entrepreneurship made fit for the 21st century, whose aim is to harvest intellectual resources without too much effort, both in an organizational and in a monetary sense (cf. Patten). And "produsers" (Bruns) of the *Iron Sky* universe had to realize this, when the German distributor of the film "threaten[ed] them with copyright infringement lawsuits for allegedly distributing the science fiction movie *Iron Sky* via file sharing networks. There was only one way not to get sued, the letter [they received] informed them: Sign a cease-and-desist notice and pay € 800 (about $1012)" ("*Iron Sky* Distributor").

It is moments like these that again complicate the distinction suggested by Henry Jenkins in the present volume "between participatory culture (which may in its purist form exist only as an ideal, but which many groups have struggled to achieve across the past few centuries) and Web 2.0 (which might be best described as a business model that seeks to capitalize on this long-standing desire for participation)." To be precise: A lawsuit may be a perfect example of the "struggle over the terms of our collective participation" (39) and, as such, it clearly illustrates that the characterization of a project such as *Iron Sky* either as a participatory project or as refined Web 2.0 business model is subject to constant negotiation between the 'parties' involved. In other words: The 'rhetoric of participation' inscribed into the project from the very beginning, then, is open to both appropriations, so I do not understand this 'rhetoric' as an "empty" (Jenkins) signifier in a negative sense, but rather as an 'open' or 'polyvalent' signifier, which can be read and interpreted in different ways and for a range of different purposes.

Thus, as much as there is a struggle on terms and conditions of participation, there is also a constant negotiation about the semantics of participation, which, of course, adds to the complexity of the issue. Consequently, as helpful as it is to distinguish between participatory cultures and Web 2.0 business models for heuristic reasons, I tend to believe that it is exactly the openness (or polyvalence) of the rhetoric of participation, i.e., its appropriability for different actors with different goals, that makes projects such as *Iron Sky* work, as they are based on what might well be labeled a 'participatory pact,' the precariousness of which is, time and again, epitomized by occasional lawsuits or other types of frictions that may threaten the alliance between producers and fans.

Another example of such a precarious alliance between producers and users is taken from the field of popular music: In the spring of 2012, the German pop-punk-band Kettcar released their fourth studio album called *Zwischen den Runden*, which, combining electronic popsounds with amplified electric guitars, could certainly be considered a step towards a broader popularity for the band. However, it is not so much the songs themselves, but the videoclips that were produced and published shortly after the album's release, which are of particular relevance for my argument: For *Zwischen den Runden*, the band decided to have one clip for each song, which amounts to twelve videos in sum. All of them were published online and, as regards their visual make up, are at least flavored with a particular 'do-it-yourself'-aesthetics—of course, 'do-it-yourself' in times in which even 'do-it-yourself' may look highly professional.

In this process of visualizing their album, Kettcar invited listeners to make their own videoclips to three additional new songs (cf. "Kettcar"). Through announcements online, fans were explicitly encouraged to 'use' these Kettcar-songs as the soundtrack to their very own and self-produced versions of what they thought would be the ideal visualization of words and music. Next to this, the band also encouraged fans to send in photos showing themselves for the production of the video clip to the album's first single called "Im Club" ["In the Club"] (cf. "Neues"). Both the video clip contest and the integration of photos of fans into one of the 'official' clips, I argue, work as prime examples of how participation (or at least its rhetoric) and the fostering of alliances between the band and its fans went hand in hand, as they serve to facilitate and to substantiate the identification between the band and its audience and, what is even more, contribute to the myth of authenticity in times in which this myth has largely been eroded.

Yet, the band's participatory project was limited by a set of regulations: The fan-produced videoclips had to be sent in on DVD and the users had to make sure not to upload them on YouTube or Vimeo first. Moreover, as already hinted at above, fans were only 'allowed' to create clips on the basis of the three bonus tracks to be found on the deluxe edition of the album—for clips to all other new songs had already been produced by the band. With the incentive of upgrading the contest's winner to the status of 'official video' to the song it was based on, the band's project also included an additional competitive dimension (cf. "KETTCAR").

I believe that the 'rhetoric of participation' established here, however, did not serve to harvest the economic surplus of fan creativity as was the case with *Star Wars* or the "The Seven Minute Sopranos," or, to a certain extent, with *Iron Sky*. In the case of Kettcar's video competition, it is rather the symbolic value attached to the notion of participation that is drawn upon here in order to sustain the band's credibility.

To back up my argument, let me briefly go back into the band's history: Kettcar were founded in 2002 as a follow-up project of the German punk band ...But Alive, which formed in the early 1990s, became a prominent representative of the German punk scene, and became known particularly for their deeply political, but at the same time highly sophisticated lyrics. After the dissolution of ...But Alive, three members of the band continued with a new project, i.e., Kettcar. Ever since then, Kettcar's concern has been to maintain the subcultural posture of protest and resistance, while being fully aware of the constant co-optation of subcultural practices through what is commonly referred to as 'the mainstream.' More often than not, they have done so by establishing—both through their lyrics and their music as well as through a number of paratexts such as CD-booklets or interviews—what I would call a highly self-reflexive 'narrative of authenticity' both based on and critically interrogating the ethics and ideals of punk rock at the very same time (cf. Baßler/Butler).

This 'narrative of authenticity' has also been regularly reproduced by the media. The German alternative music magazine *VISIONS*, for instance, featured the band in their March 2012 issue (i.e., shortly after the release of *Zwischen den Runden*). The issue includes a major feature on the band's history and development, the subtitle of which neatly epitomizes the feature's intention of establishing narrative coherence and closure: "Taking stock after 20 years of resistance"[2] indeed suggests ideological continuity and emphasizes that the band had never lost their 'street credibility.'

Against this backdrop, the agenda of 'do-it-yourself' that accompanied the release of the band's most recent album can be seen as part of this very narrative of authenticity (cf. also Baßler/Butler). The staging of participation (which, especially within the normative realm of punkrock as a subculture, is considered a central value) thus functions as a mode of self-fashioning for the band. And, once again, it seems as if it is not the economic gains that play the most significant role here. Rather it is the band's credibility which is at stake and emphasized with a vengeance, with the seemingly perfect match of the 'do-it-yourself'-ethics and aesthetics of punkrock and the opportunities of direct participation offered by Web 2.0 technologies serving this purpose well.

As a consequence, the alliances between the band and their fans enacted through this partially staged mode of participation might be put to the test. Some die-hard fans might take this faked authenticity as another symptom of a subculture gone mainstream, some others might not even consider this strategy of including the listeners as a problem, as for them, Kettcar is a pop band that is just taking care of its fans. To examine actual fan reactions to this videoclip contest which were posted in blogs or on websites would be one way of finding out about these ways of 'reading' the rhetoric of participation in this particular case and about the actual motivations and intentions of listeners to participate/interact or to not participate/interact. This, in turn, would give us a sense of how the 'terms of participation' were negotiated and understood in this highly specific and discrete case.

---

2   My translation. The German subtitle reads: "20 Jahre Widerstand: Die große Zwischenbilanz." The 'collaboration' between the band and the magazine in the construction of this narrative, by the way, could also be considered a precarious alliance, which might be worth looking at more closely.

To conclude, I would like to agree to Henry Jenkins in pointing out that there are a wide range of digital environments that "allow [consumers] to participate in the production and distribution of cultural goods—on their own terms" (*Convergence* 133). And it might well be true that these environments may contribute to foster grassroots creativity among Internet users (or vice versa), who use new technologies and media for their very individual, and at times highly subversive and politically motivated purposes. However, what my examples were supposed to illustrate is that this might not always be the case. I argued that, instead, the participation in cultural production in these environments is, at times, highly restricted and limited. And, coming back to the fine line between participatory cultures and Web 2.0 business models, one could even argue that in some cases the latter are disguised as the former through a specific layout suggesting little to no regulation where, in fact, there is a lot. It is in these environments, then, that the mere semblance of participation (often taken—or mistaken—as a term charged with the appeal of empowerment) can be used for a number of different purposes—not only to enhance financial bargains, but also to accumulate symbolic capital through the formation of alliances (cf. Butler).

Accordingly, an analysis of these alliances, which can be understood both as preconditions and as potential results of participation, has to be highly context-sensitive. To be precise, the examination of the formation and disintegration of alliances between 'the media industries' and 'the consumer,' first of all, has to take notice of the fact that there is not such a thing as 'the media industries' or 'the consumers.' As Elana Shefrin has argued, the ways in which production companies "forge strategic alliances" (275) indeed differ to a considerable degree and very much depend upon the specific "expectations of the fan base attached to a specific textual universe, and upon the pre-dispositions of the cultural producers, both personally and corporately" (275). The relationship between Lucasfilm and a first generation *Star Wars* fan, to come back to my first example, might be easily shattered by a restriction in the creative usage of the films, whereas a newcomer would not find that to be a problematic issue at all. And indeed, as Shefrin points out with regard to Lucasfilm's incorporation of user-generated content uploaded to the *Star Wars* website, "while some fans were appreciative, others have been highly critical of the policy, complaining that their creative designs are being co-opted by a corporate decision that violates fair-use laws and compromises their personal chances of profiting from their artistic practices" (90). Moreover, first-generation fans perhaps 'want to believe'—they want to believe in the creation myth of the *Star Wars* universe, with its mastermind George Lucas finding ways to realize his project in spite of adverse circumstances; they want to believe in a tale of 'do-it-yourself' creativity, which does not really fit to a restrictive policy that limits creative expression.

It is the fans' trust, then, both in the *Star Wars* example as well as in the case of the German band Kettcar, which is at stake. In the latter case, the video competition (with the winner clip becoming the 'official video') was potentially supposed to foster alliances; yet, this staging of participation might produce exactly the opposite effect, i.e., the band might lose first-generation fans who would surely be highly skeptical of this restricted form of participation—but this, as I have hinted at above, still needs to be examined in detail. The band's strategy of 'going DIY,' in turn, can only be understood against the backdrop of their history which has always been marked by the tight-rope walk between commercialization and political subversion; hence their need to (re)claim authenticity after their turn from punk to pop.

Going on from here, it becomes apparent that—in order to analyze alliances and their precariousness in Web 2.0 contexts—one also needs to consider the development of these alliances over time. Participation in *Iron Sky* had been restricted and prestructured right from its very beginning, resulting in a hierarchized form of collaboration between producers and users very early on. This, of course, does not exclude frictions and problems. Still, it seems as if users, or "producers" (Bruns), involved in the project were not at all worried about the restriction of creative participation, exactly *because* the production of the film was embedded in a narrative that, though it pushed participation to the foreground, also made clear that these forms of participation would be limited. So emotional investments, which, in the worst case, would lead to disappointment or disillusionment, were not made to the same extent as has been the case with *Star Wars*. Perhaps projects like *Iron Sky* work because they are based on alliances between producers and users who do no longer believe in the myth of Web 2.0 as an anti-hierarchical, democratizing force, but who, without any resignation and in a mood of constructive serenity, share Hakim Bey's observation that in the end, "participation in the commodity can only amount to a commodification of participation" (n.pag.).

Works Cited

"Crowdfunding—The New Way to Finance Movies." *Blind Spot Pictures.* N.pag., n.d. Web.

"*Iron Sky* Distributor Threatens File Sharers with Lawsuits." N.pag., 23 May 2012. Web.

Baßler, Moritz, and Martin Butler. "Doubt to Stand: Die Stimme von Marcus Wiebusch." *Performativität und Medialität Populärer Kulturen.* Ed. Marcus S. Kleiner and Thomas Wilke. Wiesbaden: Springer, 2013. 277-318. Print.

Butler, Martin. "Partizipation—Zum Einsatz eines Begriffs." *POP: Kultur und Kritik* 6 (2015): 162-76. Print.

Butler, Martin, and Arvi Sepp. "Punk's Not Dead: Erinnerung als Strategie der Abgrenzung und Neuorientierung einer (totgeglaubten) Subkultur." *Populäre Kultur und soziales Gedächtnis: theoretische und exemplarische Überlegungen zur dauervergesslichen Erinnerungsmaschine Pop.* Ed. Christoph Jacke and Martin Zierold. *Siegener Periodicum zur Internationalen Empirischen Literaturwissenschaft* 24 (2008): 285-96. Print.

Bey, Hakim. "The Utopian Blues." N.pag., n.d. Web.

Bruns, Axel. "Distributed Creativity: Filesharing and Produsage." *Mashup Cultures.* Ed. Stefan Sonvilla-Weiss. Vienna: Springer, 2010. 24-37. Print.

Gauntlett, David. "Creativity, Participation and Connectedness: An Interview with David Gauntlett." *Mashup Cultures.* Ed. Stefan Sonvilla-Weiss. Vienna: Springer, 2010. 65-78. Print.

Jenkins, Henry. *Convergence Culture: Where Old and New Media Collide.* New York: New York UP, 2006. Print.

---. "Participation? It's Complicated (A Response to Martin Butler)." In this volume. Print.

"Kettcar—Nie genug." N.pag., 24 Feb. 2012. Web.

"KETTCAR—Dreh' selbst ein Video." N.pag., 28 Feb. 2012. Web.

Mittell, Jason. "Previously On: Prime Time Serials and the Mechanics of Memory." *Intermediality and Storytelling.* Ed. Marina Grishakova and Marie-Laure Ryan. Berlin: De Gruyter, 2010. 78-98. Print.

"Neues aus dem Grand Hotel." N.pag., n.d. Web.

Patten, Grant. "Working without Pay: Toward Participatory Media Unions." N.pag., 2011. Web.

Shefrin, Elana. "*Lord of the Rings*, *Star Wars*, and Participatory Fandom: Mapping New Congruencies between the Internet and Media Entertainment Culture." *Critical Studies in Media Communication* 21.3 (2004): 261-81. Print.

Participation? It's Complicated (A Response to Martin Butler)

HENRY JENKINS

At their most excessive, digital advocates imagined a world where the mass media conglomerates would be totally displaced by cottage industries, artisanal and amateur cultural production, and niche content (a view expressed most prominently by Nicholas Negroponte and George Gilder). This Fantasy of the withering away of mass media existed alongside claims about new forms of political participation displacing the role of the nation state (see, for example, John Perry Barlow). The rapid and widespread embrace of networked computing, its clear and dramatic impact on many core institutions and practices, brought new urgency to these long-standing struggles to expand the communicative capacity available to average citizens and grassroots communities. What made the discourse of the digital revolution 'revolutionary' was a wide-spread recognition that things which seemed static and unchanging suddenly looked to be open to review and transformation.

As a faculty member at MIT from the early 1990s till the late 2000s, I was an eyewitness to what might be described as 'ground zero' for the 'Digital Revolution.' My own perspective was at once skeptical and welcoming. I was skeptical of the more excessive forms of technological determinism which drove some of the early digital advocates and skeptical of the idea that grassroots media was likely to displace mass media rather than exist alongside it and complicate or contest the power it had exerted during the Broadcast era. I was welcoming in that the promises of cultural and political participation addressed my own experiences (and my most heart-felt ideals) as an active participant in the fan culture that I documented in my 1992 book, *Textual Poachers: Television Fans and Participatory Culture* (written during my first year at MIT, during the same time when I was first gaining access to email and online forums). With *Convergence Culture: Where Old and New Media Collide* (published in 2006, written in 2004-2005), I was trying to offer a 'snapshot' of one moment in a much longer period of media transition, as the culture (especially the media industries) had started to absorb the initial impact of networked computing. I argued that all parties were recognizing that the culture was going to become more 'participatory' (broadly-defined) but the central struggles of the 21st century would have to do with the 'terms of our participation.' While many have read *Convergence Culture* through the lens of 'Web 2.0,' the earliest formulations of the Web 2.0 business model were taking shape in parallel to the writing of the book (cf. O'Reilly), and I only became aware of that framework as the book was being released to the public.

Looking backwards, it is clear that the model of participation offered in the book reflected my own point of entry into these debates—through the study of fandom. Focusing on fandom meant that my emphasis was on the ways that a community with a much longer tradition was seeking to negotiate the changes being brought about by digital media, as opposed to, say, focusing on the new kinds of relationships around and through media that were emerging as a consequence of networked computing. I was focusing on a community defined around shared interests as opposed to say the more ego-centric sets of relationships which operate within contemporary social networking platforms, such as Facebook or Twitter. I was focusing on activities which formed very strong senses of sociality and a fully articulated identity, whereas someone like James Paul Gee stressed forms of shared activity that do not result in strong social bonds, common interests, or shared identities. I was focusing on a group which is consciously seeking to participate in the creation and circulation of culture, as opposed to the kinds of 'implicit participation' (such as data-mining) which Mirko Tobias Schafer argues are even more central to the ways Web 2.0 companies operate. I was focusing on the intersection between consumers and mainstream media producers, as opposed to, say, the relations of citizens to governments, students to schools, or the publics which grow up around independent or state-sanctioned media producers. For me, the first proclamations of Web 2.0 looked like "fandom without the stigma," the mainstreaming of practices with a much longer history within fandom. I have learned to regret that phrasing.

Even if I had focused on fandom itself, I might have seen a range of different models for what ideal forms of cultural participation might look like. So, for example, science fiction fandom historically functioned as a gateway into the professional sphere, with most of those involved in the publishing of science fiction novels, say, getting their start within fandom. Here, fandom functioned as a recruiting ground for new talent and as a support system for professionals and amateurs alike. The female-centered fanzine culture I described in *Textual Poachers* has taken shape primarily around experiences of exclusion—these women were neither embraced by media producers (typically seen as surplus audiences for their properties) nor by the existing science fiction fandom (which had been historically male). As a consequence, their cultural production was oppositional and transformational—offering alternative pleasures and politics which they knew was never going to gain access to the mainstream. These fan practices were designed not so much to influence industry insiders as to protect themselves from discovery by those who might inflict harm on their community. On the other end of the spectrum, we might point to the much more generalized notion of the affirmational 'fan' often fostered within the industry itself, especially as the industry is increasingly governed by a logic of 'engagement' where the goal becomes to increase viewer loyalty to its property by intensifying affective relations with the content. A key distinction between 'transformational' and 'affirmational' fans (*obsession_inc*.) has been widely embraced both within the fan communities (where the terms originated) and among many fan scholars. So, a more precise parsing of different kinds of fan experiences would have resulted in some core contradictions about what might constitute ideal forms of participation in relation to media franchises—between, say, seeking to influence decisions within beloved franchises or seeking simply the freedom to explore one's own fantasies in a space alongside or outside the commercial mainstream.

If anything, the actual realization of this push towards expanded grassroots participation has both accelerated and diversified since *Convergence Culture* was published. In politics, as Manuel Castells notes, grassroots movements around the world have embraced networked computing (as both a technology and as a model of social relations) as a key tool for their struggles to change the world (see, for example, the Arab Spring movements, Occupy

Wall Street, the American Tea Party movement, the DREAMers, etc.) In the arts, a growing number of high profile artists have experimented with various forms of crowdsourcing or participatory design processes. In journalism, more and more traditional news organizations have sought to make their peace with 'citizen journalism' (i.e., blogging, Twitter, podcasting, video-blogging, user-generated footage). In education, the Digital Media and Learning movement has sought to reshape schools both to incorporate broadly defined concepts of participatory or connected learning and to insure that young people acquire the skills needed for meaningful participation in the changing culture around them. In health, there has been a movement to breakdown the monopoly over information long maintained by medical professionals and build online communities where patients can compare notes and both collectively and individually, assert greater control over their own treatment. And, the entertainment industry, the primary focus of *Convergence Culture*, has integrated notions of audience engagement and fan participation more deeply into its logics and practices.

We could continue, but I think the core point is made: The concept of participation has become central to many of the core debates of our time, but in the process, as it has been taken up by diverse groups for diverse purposes, it risks becoming an emptied signifier unless more steps are taken to clarify its meaning. I suspect this is part of what Martin Butler means when he talks about a generalized "rhetoric of participation"—often, involving "opportunities" for participation which do little to shift the balance of power, diversify the culture, or achieve any of the other democratizing effects I hoped for a decade ago when I wrote about a move towards a more participatory culture.

Martin Butler is right, then, to call here for more theoretical reflection and refinement of our concept of participatory culture, especially closer examination of a more diverse range of cases which suggest the unequal relations between grassroots and commercial media producers, and he is not alone in making such a call. For example, Christopher Kelty writes,

'Participating' in Facebook is not the same thing as participating in a Free Software project, to say nothing of participating in the democratic governance of a state. If there are indeed different 'participatory cultures' then the work of explaining their differences must be done by thinking concretely about the practices, tools, ideologies, and technologies that make them up. Participation is about power, and, no matter how 'open' a platform is, participation will reach a limit circumscribing power and its distribution. (29)

Kelty's own team at UCLA (Fish, Kelty, Murillo, Nguyen, Panofsky, In Progress) has begun this process, developing a rich typology for identifying different claims being made about participation and the ways they are being applied within concrete circumstances and the ways power gets negotiated at all levels, from the design of platforms to policies regarding their governance and use. My graduate student, Ioana Literat, has offered a similar typology for thinking about competing claims made about participation within collaborative and crowdsourced art projects, whereas Nico Carpentier has argued for the difference between Maximalist models of participation (which emphasize an active role in the governance of core institutions) and more minimalist models (which use the term to describe any and all forms of involvement and interactivity). It is beyond the scope of this current essay to try to fully work through my points of agreement or divergence with these important interventions, nor can I fully deal here with a range of theorists who have been more skeptical about the promises of participation, seeing it as a rhetoric that masks a neoliberal corporate agenda and the ongoing pressures to conform to dominant social norms. But, I felt it was important to signal this larger context as the backdrop for this somewhat more focused response to Butler's arguments here.

This "participatory turn" depends on what this book is describing as "precarious alliances" between participants with competing or contradictory interests, varying degrees of power, and different stakes in terms of the value of expanding or limiting participation. We might describe this situation through a range of other terms: I often talk about the current moment as one of prolonged transition, as we deal with the disruptive impact of this new communication capacity without a clear or shared sense of where this change may be leading. I also often talk in terms of negotiation, as various agents seek to rewrite the "moral economy" or "social contract" allowing them to do business with each other on the basis of trust and with a clarity about what the core terms of exchange look like. Mirko Tobias Schafer talks about "bastard culture," stressing what happens as "heterogeneous participants and practices are blended together." Sarah Banet-Weiser uses the term, "ambivalence," to describe the experience of operating within what she argues is always already a commercial context, even as the commercial sector has been forced to acknowledge some forms of popular participation in the construction of its brands. All of these suggest a sense of instability, fragility, and impurity about these new and emerging configurations. Whatever we are seeing right now is unlikely to last, as we are seeing one system evolve into something different, something that may or may not, depending on your perspective, be better, more diverse, more democratic, than what existed before.

These transitions look different depending on whether we are seeing them from a top-down perspective, describing the choices made by established authorities as they are ceding some degree of control over production and circulation in order to gain some desired benefit (whether understood in terms of audience engagement, user-generated content, or data-mining, to cite three wide-spread models) or whether we are thinking bottom-up, describing the choices being made by communities with long histories of struggle over cultural participation as they choose whether or not to move their traditional practices and relationships into Web 2.0 platforms. So, Schafer writes about user participation as an extension of the cultural industries (a model which places core emphasis on industries and technologies) whereas I write about the push towards "a more participatory culture" as grassroots communities seek to apply folk culture logics to mass culture content.

In fact, it might be more productive to think about different kinds of trade-offs which are being made by different participants as they struggle over the terms of our collective participation. So, for example, the entertainment industries want to intensify audience engagement and consumer loyalty, they are willing to tolerate some forms of grassroots cultural production as long as they can maintain some level of plausible deniability about its existence, but they are threatened by 'piracy' of their content, since these file-sharing practices more directly impact their bottom-line. Meanwhile, as I document in my 2009 essay, "What Happened Before YouTube?," different segments of the fan community are actively debating how much they want to become integrated into the logics of Web 2.0 and what price they are willing to pay to achieve their goals. Some of the stakes for the fans might include: different degrees of autonomy from corporate control, different degrees of control over the circulation of their content, different degrees of visibility in terms of which groups have access to what they produce, different degrees of privacy in terms of who has access to and control over data they shed in the process of their transaction, and different systems of value at the intersection between commodity culture and a contemporary form of the gift economy that has long governed fan production and circulation.

These are not simply debates within critical theory; these are debates occurring on the ground across many different sites that promise increased participation in return for various terms of service.

For me, then, a key to understanding these debates is to start from a distinction between participatory culture (which may in its purist form exist only as an ideal, but which many groups have struggled to achieve across the past few centuries) and Web 2.0 (which might be best described as a business model that seeks to capitalize on this long-standing desire for participation). Web 2.0 advocate Tim O'Reilly spoke about creating the "architecture of participation" or "harnessing collective intelligence," both terms which capture the trade-offs involved when participatory culture impulses take root within Web 2.0 platforms. So, on the one hand, an architecture is an infrastructure that supports certain desired activities, whereas on the other, this architecture represents a set of constraints which channel grassroots participation towards certain pre-designated locations. Collective intelligence sounds promising on its own, but the term, 'harnessing,' raises key questions about who is controlling the process and who will benefit from its outputs, questions that are becoming more urgent as we see the various ways that grassroots collaborative efforts are exploited and abused by corporate interests.

Web 2.0 companies have offered a series of affordances, many of which do materially benefit various forms of participatory culture, and the media companies are ceding certain degrees of control over what happens to their content in return for teaching the fans to "color inside the lines" (a phrase associated with a now defunct Web 2.0 company, FanLib) and in return for providing the means of monitoring and monitizing activities that once took place totally outside their control. In many cases, the materials participants share within Web 2.0 platforms legally belong to the corporations that operate them and not the consumers that produce them. This assertion of ownership over user-generated content makes it hard to reverse decisions, once made, to bring one's social networks and cultural practices to a given Web 2.0 site. If many grassroots communities first embraced Web 2.0's promises as a gift, they have since learned to look that gift horse in the mouth and every other orifice because there have been so many hidden costs, unintended consequences, and other kinds of strings attached to these transactions.

This is perhaps the best way to think about my use of the word, 'allow,' in the various passages from *Convergence Culture* Martin Butler is discussing here. On a most basic level, participatory culture is notoriously difficult to regulate or control. The media industries have very much experienced the growth of participatory culture as a loss of control at every stage—from their ability to determine what a brand means to their ability to control how content circulates across the marketplace or to even control what information is made accessible to the public. The music industry was severely damaged both by the growth of digital piracy and by the legal and rhetorical excesses of their own response to what they perceived as a crisis in their traditional ways of doing business. Yet, the media industries have also started to make their peace with grassroots efforts to appropriate, rewrite, remix, and to a lesser degree, recirculate their content. This is one of the ways these media producers have sought to negotiate new terms of participation with their consumers. In practice, they do not have the power to stop various forms of unauthorized production and circulation, but different policies may nevertheless help to shape the choices fans make about how public they want to make the materials they produce. So, let's return to the example of *Star Wars* and video producers.

What I was describing in *Convergence Culture* was one moment in a series of complex, evolving, and often contradictory responses of Lucasfilm to *Star Wars* fandom. George Lucas is a producer who has historically had control issues with his fans, seeking to exert much greater power over their fantasy lives than fans were willing to tolerate, seeking to police which forms of fan participation were appropriate or inappropriate in ways which the fans themselves have seen as grossly inappropriate. (See, for example, *The People Vs. George Lucas* for a representation of some of his conflicts with *Star Wars* fans.) At one moment, Lucasfilm sponsored an official fan film contest, where they were giving permission for fans to create works based on their properties, but only under terms which limited what forms of expression could be shared. I argued in *Convergence Culture* that, consciously or not, these rules had the consequence of being discriminatory against female fans, because they accepted video genres (parody, documentary) most often produced by men while excluding those (fanvidding) most often produced by women. Julie Levine Russo makes a similar point in her essay, "User-Penetrated Content," describing a competition around *Battlestar Galactica* where fans who wanted to participate in the competition (and implicitly be secure from legal harassment based on copyright infringement) were required to use the footage provided, which in this case focused on action scenes and not the character moments that interested female fans. So, in both cases, the terms offered for participation actively included some fan interests while excluded others—and we can debate whether this is by design or as a result to their indifference or ignorance to existing forms of fan participation.

But, of course, fans are not obligated to enter such competitions, and so they may choose to share their works through some other platform. For example, they might post their videos on YouTube, probably the most highly visible of the video-sharing platforms, and hope that they do not receive a take-down notice. Or, they may try another, less visible platform, such as Vimeo, or they might choose to friends-lock their content, so that they can share what they create with a more closed community of people they already know and trust. They could go even further underground—they can share their videos as email attachments, they can circulate them on DVDs, and those DVDS might be sold openly at fan conventions or more covertly through the mail. Finally, the artist might produce only one copy of their works and show it in their own living room, allowing them maximum security from the risk of an adverse response from the networks or producers, but also substantially decreasing the visibility of their work to the culture at large.

Fan culture began in the underground and it has periodically been forced to retreat back there when its traditions have come under increased scrutiny and threat, yet fans have also gained a great deal by being able to expand their community, get credit for the cultural work they do at a time when remix practices are fostering greater aesthetic prestige, and perhaps, for some fans, to influence the decisions of the franchise producers or shape the contexts within which others interpret this work. Sarah Banet-Weisser has stressed the ways that YouTube's ethos of 'broadcast yourself' has encouraged everyday people to embrace a logic of 'self-branding' which imbricates them more deeply into neoliberal ideologies: There's certainly much truth to this claim, but in the case of fans, as well as many other groups which are producing and sharing media through YouTube (activists groups, for example), there's more at stake here than 'self-branding.' Their actions are governed by a strong sense of collective expression and often by specific cultural-political objectives (such as expressing alternative views about gender and sexuality). For many female fans, for example, the efforts of male producers to 'regulate' or 'tolerate' their cultural production are seen as paternalistic, yet so are the tendency to write women's contributions out of the history of 'remix culture.'

So, it again comes down to a series of trade-offs: Are you willing, say, to trade visibility and security from legal risk in return for less control over one's content or less autonomy over what you produce? These choices might look different if you are a film student whose video is really simply a calling card for breaking into the industry, a fan whose tastes are closely aligned with hegemonic norms, or a slash fan whose fantasies are going to be much less acceptable to the Powers That Be. What the producers 'allow,' then, might include multiple levels of visibility, accessibility, and security. There's a 'gray zone' between what they facilitate and what they tolerate, for example, and perhaps also one between what they seek to legally constrain and what actually occurs in one or another obscure corner of the web.

Butler's *Iron Sky* example fits within newer models of participation which have been broadly identified under the category of 'crowdsourcing' or 'crowdfunding.' For the moment, let's bracket reservations about the use of the term, 'crowd,' here, as opposed to concepts such as 'collective,' 'collaborative,' or 'community-based,' each of which might imply different conceptions about the people who are contributing to this process and a different understanding of the value of their contributions. As we discuss in *Spreadable Media*, independent artists, including filmmakers such as Timo Vuroensola, are increasingly seeking to develop alternative models for funding, producing, and distributing their work, which depend on their ability to align with the interests of potential networks of supporters. Such examples, to some degree, blur the simple conceptual distinctions I made earlier between participatory culture and web 2.0. Rather than seeing fans as unpaid labor, these models seek fans as investors who can now claim a stake in the content they help to produce. Through crowdfunding models, such as that adopted by Kickstarter, these artists are courting potential audiences even at the pre-production phases, and they are continuing to tap their participation in getting their completed works out to a larger public. In some cases, fan contributions are understood as donations in support of the artists while other models see them as micro-investments in which the artist is obligated to provide some token payment back at the end of the production process for the assistance their fans have provided (Kickstarter's core model). In practice, independent artists have always been forced to barter a certain amount of creative control over their work in return for funding or distribution. In the past, this exchange was made with commercial investors or distributors and under this new model, they are much more beholden to their audience. Yet, as Butler notes, they are also seeking to draw limits in terms of how much control they cede over their work and what forms of participation are embraced or rejected.

Ioana Literat writes, "Artists and curators working in the tradition of relational art tend to see participation and sociability through an optimistic, micro-utopian lens, and their discourse often omits conflict or hierarchization" (2975). The same would be true of the fan communities who are drawn to a project like *Iron Sky*. These projects are most often supported by groups who have a clearly defined and shared set of interests (in this case, fans of a particular genre or style of filmmaking) who feel marginal or excluded from the mainstream media (see for example various kinds of racial, ethnic, sexual or political minorities) and who see supporting an independent production as a means of supporting content which aligns with their tastes, interests, beliefs, or lifestyles. They also want to feel a closeness or connection with the artists, and they may want to be able to make a creative contribution to the work.

These contributions may be substantive, but more often, in the current context, they are what Literat describes as "tokenistic," that is, they contribute some element which does not substantially alter the work as a whole but may allow them to feel a part of the larger creative project. As Literat notes, such projects also may have varying degrees of transparency, so that the contributors may or may not know what use will be made of the material they contribute (see Butler's Kettcar example), and may offer different degrees of control, such that the nature of their contributions are predetermined by the artist or may be open-ended. Literat identifies a range of different forms of artistic participation, from relatively passive reception on one end of the scale and co-designed projects where the artist grants far greater authority to the larger community in shaping the creative output or co-authored projects, where "participants' structural contributions are formally recognized and rewarded" (2978).

While Literat focuses on projects within the realm of high art, Butler's analysis here suggests that her distinctions might also be applied to various forms of pop culture creation, including the crowdsourcing of cult movies (*Iron Sky*) or the use of user-generated content within music videos (Kettcar). That Vuorensola found himself at war with his audiences over the unauthorized circulation of *Iron Sky* should not be a surprise given the lack of precision with which both artists and participants embrace these kinds of crowdsourced projects: The fans really did feel a sense of ownership over the finished product as a result of their invested funds and labor and the promise of participation raises expectations about how much control they will be able to exert over the finished product, whereas for the independent artist, such arrangements are often understood in terms of ceding a minimal amount of creative control in order to gain the resources they need to continue their work. Despite a rhetoric that suggests that the fans and the producers are brought together as collaborators, they still understand their relationship to each other in different terms; this gap can be consciously and transparently negotiated as participants spell out their expectations to each other, but just as often, the gap is never acknowledged with all parties acting as if they were in agreement about the terms of their participation.

As they say on Facebook, "It's complicated." Our understanding of participatory culture is evolving rapidly at a time when there are many emerging kinds of relationships between media producers and audiences, when there are many loose or broad claims being made about the value of participation, when there is an ongoing theoretical project—both within and beyond the academy—to refine our understanding of the concept of participation, and where there are legal and policy debates to define the terms of our participation. I would not describe any of this in terms of unlimited participation or 'cultural democracy,' since any system which supports participation also serves to direct or constrain it. More and more people are getting the chance to participate in the creation and exchange of media, but they are participating on an uneven playing field. Some forms of participation, some kinds of participants, fit more comfortably into the existing cultural and political system than others. Some still exist in the margins, some are forced to make unacceptable trade-offs in order to increase their visibility and gain greater security from copyright crackdowns. But, such struggles are not static: Ground has been gained month by month, platform by platform, as the culture has sought to come to terms with our collective push towards greater participation.

Butler closes his essay with the quotation from Hakim Bey, "participation in the commodity can only amount to a commodification of participation." Such alliances should, indeed, leave us 'uneasy,' and there is certainly a high risk of commodification when fans and commercial producers end up interacting with each other. But, the question we will need to decide in the years ahead is whether this is the 'only' outcome of such exchanges. Like Butler, I believe we need a more nuanced vocabulary for identifying and critiquing different forms of collaboration and participation, but as we do so, we need to recognize the stakes for all participating parties, and that includes respect for what grassroots communities and individuals hope to gain by entering into such arrangements. These gains may be immaterial, social, affective, as opposed to the fiduciary gains that corporate producers hope to achieve through their efforts to control the platforms and the circulation of their content, yet they are nevertheless real.

WORKS CITED

"Affirmational Fandom vs. Transformational Fandom." *obsession_inc.* N.pag., 1 June 2009. Web.

Banet-Weiser, Sarah. *Authentic (TM): The Politics of Ambivalence in a Brand Culture.* New York: New York UP, 2012. Print.

Barlow, John Perry. "A Declaration of Independence in Cyberspace." N.pag., 8 Feb. 1996. Web.

Carpentier, Nico. *Media and Participation.* Bristol, UK: Intellect, 2011. Print.

Castells, Manuel. *Networks of Outrage and Hope: Social Movements in the Internet Age.* London: Polity, 2012. Print.

Delwiche, Aaron. "The New Left and the Computer Underground: Recovering Political Antecedents of Participatory Culture." *The Participatory Cultures Handbook.* Ed. Aaron Delwiche and Jennifer Jacobs Henderson. New York: Routledge, 2013. 10-21. Print.

Fish, Adam, Luis F.R. Murillo, Lilly Nguyen, Aaron Panofsky, and Christopher M. Kelty. "Birds of the Internet." *Journal of Cultural Economy* 4.2 (2011): 157-87. Web.

Gee, James Paul. *Situated Language and Learning: A Critique of Traditional Schooling.* New York: Routledge, 2004. Print.

Gilder, George. *Life after Television: The Coming Transformation of Media and American Life.* New York: W.W. Norton, 1994. Print.

Jenkins, Henry. *Textual Poachers: Television Fans and Participatory Culture.* New York: Routledge, 1992. Print.

---. *Convergence Culture: Where Old and New Media Collide.* New York: NY UP, 2006. Print.

---. "What Happened Before YouTube?" *YouTube: Online Video and Participatory Culture.* Jean Burgess and Joshua Green. Cambridge: Polity, 2009. Print.

Jenkins, Henry, Sam Ford, and Joshua Green. *Spreadable Media: Creating Meaning and Value in a Networked Culture.* New York: New York UP, 2013. Print.

Kelty, Christopher M. "From Participation to Power." *The Participatory Cultures Handbook.* Ed. Aaron Delwiche and Jennifer Jacobs Henderson. New York: Routledge, 2013. 22-32. Print.

Literat, Ioana. "The Work of Art in the Age of Mediated Participation: Crowdsourced Art and Collective Creativity." *International Journal of Communication* 6 (2012): 2962-84. Web.

Negroponte, Nicholas. *Being Digital.* New York: Alfred A. Knopf, 1995. Print.

O'Reilly, Tim. "What is Web 2.0?: Design Patterns and Business Models for the Next Generation of Software." *O'Reilly Media*, 30 Sept. 2005. Web.

Russo, Julie Levin. "User-Penetrated Content: Fan Video in the Age of Convergence." *Cinema Journal* 48.4 (Summer 2009): 125-30. Print.

Schafer, Mirko Tobias, ed. *Bastard Culture!: How User Participation Transforms Cultural Production.* Amsterdam: Amsterdam UP, 2011. Print.

Turner, Fred. *From Counterculture to Cyberculture: Stewart Brand, the Whole Earth Movement, and the Rise of Digital Utopianism.* Chicago: U of Chicago P, 2008. Print.

The History of the Booker Prize as a History of Problems and Precarious Alliances

ANNA AUGUSCIK

> Geraldine Byers now knew her literary destiny; she would win the Booker Prize. […] Because of her sense of destiny, [her] level of excitement about the award of the first Booker Prize was probably higher than that of most of the literary establishment.
>
> SIMON BRETT, THE BOOKER BOOK: A NOVEL, 1989.

In Simon Brett's novel *The Booker Book* (1989) the news of a new literary prize to be inaugurated in 1969 is not greeted with much fanfare among London's literati. Apart from Geraldine Byers, the protagonist and author of one slight debut novel, who sets out to pen her follow-up book in the hope of winning this new Booker Prize, the award fails to incite excitement. Geraldine's ambition and her plans to style her next novel after each winner may be a caricature of authorial responses to the promise of awards or other such competitions, but the description of the initial response to the Booker is spot on. Apart from its founders, nobody could or would foresee the Booker's potential. And even they were hard pressed in its initial years. The sponsors wanted to quit the whole undertaking when things began to change drastically in the 1980s after the Prize managed to draw the interest of national newspapers and TV broadcasts. By the end of the decade, the Booker had become a major force on the book market—driving everyone "mad":

> The Booker, after 19 years, is beginning to drive people mad. It drives publishers mad with hope, booksellers mad with greed, judges mad with power, winners mad with pride, and losers (the unsuccessful short-listees plus every other novelist in the country) mad with envy and disappointment. (Barnes 21)

Ever since, the Booker Prize (since 2001 known as The Man Booker Prize for Fiction), has had a roller coaster history of immense influence on sales and careers, heated annual debates, even controversy, and—due to different expectations and agendas—close if somewhat tense relationships with other participants in the game of literary fiction: publishers, retailers, critics, and not least authors. This contribution aims at describing this chequered history of problems and (potentially) precarious alliances, which are inherent to any literary prize, but which the Booker—now in its fifth decade—has managed to negotiate exceptionally well, if not always to everyone's desire.

RELATIONSHIP CHECKLIST: ALLIES AND THEIR AGENDAS

In 1987-88, the Hannah Arendt professor of sociology and political science at Rutgers University, Irving Louis Horowitz, pronounced the following checklist for desirable characteristics of a book prize, or, in other words, a list of questions a publisher needs to ask before handing in a manuscript. According to Horowitz, the publisher needs to determine the size or scope of the award and its compatibility with the book, the potential market benefit, the status of the award-giver in terms of age and respectability, its judging panel or selection committee, its transparency concerning rules, criteria of eligibility and dates, as well as its willingness to promote the chosen book both with prize money and by creating a broader public and further exposure (cf. 19-20). This specialist checklist was designed in the context of the U.S.-American book market, for awards given to non-fiction books, and from the perspective of an academic publisher,[1] but it shows just how much is expected from an association awarding prizes and how much is at stake for the publisher.

In this checklist that documents a range of potentially precarious relationships, Horowitz also hints at where the pressures for and from authors might materialize in the game of appreciation: "The concerns of authors—for honor, glory, and tenure—are such that they may strongly wish to see their publishers waive on all of the above points, rather than give up a chance at an award or prize" (21). In order to minimize risk on the publisher's side, Horowitz recommends persuading the author into a more participatory position, "a cost-sharing arrangement": "This can serve as a protection for the publisher against undue pressures, and no less, give the author an opportunity to share in the joys of high risk and high cost awards" (21).

This notion of actual capital investment on the part of the author is not one which is easily translatable into the marketplace for fiction. In fact, the position of the author vis-à-vis the publishing industry, the media and other mediating institutions is often described as a battle between a creative vs. an exploitative force, in which the author hardly ever ends up on top. In an article condemning literary prizes, Christopher Hitchens, in his role as contributing editor for *Vanity Fair*, vehemently objected to "the alliance that the racket represents—an alliance among publishers, booksellers, big-name critics, prestige reviewers, and dorsal-finned literary agents," an alliance which "is beginning to be a real insult to the creative process" (20). Indeed, the power relations and hence the nature of the alliance behind the production, distribution and reception of (literary) fiction is a game with different rules and logic.

Around the same time as Horowitz, though on the other side of the Atlantic, Martyn Goff, then administrator of the British Booker Prize, put his thoughts and experience in the world of cultural prizes on paper. He chose to introduce a volume of writing samples by past winners entitled *Prize Writing* (1989),[2] a manifesto in celebration of the Booker's 21st birthday,

---

1 Horowitz was also the founder of Transaction Publishers, one of the largest independent social science book and journal publishers in the U.S.

2 The volume is one of many instances in which the Booker makers sought to write their own history of the Prize. Apart from this volume and several other articles written by Goff for *Logos* and *The Bookseller*, the Booker Prize Founda-

by asking what exactly constituted its success. By then, the Booker had become one of, if not the most powerful literary award for novels written in English. Goff provides reasons for this achievement which to a certain degree recall the checklist pronounced by Horowitz—and yet differ decisively:

> 1. "The amount of the prize" (Goff 11): The Booker was first awarded in 1969 and came with a comparatively large sum of £5,000, which was gradually augmented to £15,000 in the late 1980s. As the competition among prizes rose, however, the Booker lost to other prizes when it came to the extent of the immediate reward. Only with the new sponsor in 2002 did it regain this position when the prize money rose to £50,000 and "outstripped inflation for the first time in its history" (Todd, "How Has the Booker Prize Changed" 12).
> 2. "Scandal" (Goff 11): From authors who raged against the Prize and its sponsors at the award ceremony to judges declining to continue the process of reading and selecting books on behalf that they found the entered books "too sexy," the Booker produced many a potential scandal to be picked on by the press (16).
> 3. "Careful choice and balance of judges" (11): The Booker operates with an annually changing judging panel (in contrast to the French Prix Goncourt, for example, which initially stood as its role model).
> 4. "Structure of the management" (12): Over the years and not least with the changes of sponsorship, the Prize has become an institution with an intricate set of committees, a system of checks and balances. It is this structure in the background, rather than the more visible panel of judges which creates continuity.
> 5. "Dramatic timing" (12): The Booker is awarded in an Oscar-like ceremony, with the judges making their last choices only hours before the actual award. Also, the timing between the announcement of the longlist in July to the announcement of the shortlist in September and finally the award in October creates a long period of tension, speculation and bet-placing.

---

tion was responsible for another anniversary issue, *The Man Booker Prize: 35 Years of the Best in Contemporary Fiction 1969-2003* (2003).

To this list, Goff adds "that stroke of luck or timing" (12) as well as the making of the Booker myth, a point which ought to be remembered despite the easy lending of its nature to the creation of conspiracy theories.

There are two important points which I hope to draw from a comparison of Horowitz's checklist for publishers and Goff's reasons for Booker's success. One is the different perspective on what a prize can and should achieve. Publishers have a different agenda than prize makers and each have in turn a different interest than the authors and their agents. The second point is the discrepant perspective on scandals. Although Goff at first makes every attempt to play down the influence of scandal as a distinguishing characteristic of the Booker Prize—claiming that other awards have in fact brought up much bigger scandals—he then proceeds to tell the Booker history based on this very aspect, making it the most relevant ingredient in the creation of the Booker myth.

Although other reasons have been put forward—shifts in book trade and publishing industry (cf. Todd, *Consuming Fictions*) and the government's withdrawal from funding the arts (cf. Norris) in the 1980s—scandal does, in fact, feature high on the list of reasons for Booker's success as put forth by scholars and journalists. James F. English described how critics came to acknowledge the "simple fact of complicity or convergence of interests between the more or less lofty and disdainful cultural commentators and those who have a direct stake in promoting the prize and enlarging its cultural role" ("Winning the Culture Game" 115). Such "playful and reflexive commentary," a "new rhetoric of amused complicity in the manufacture of scandal," "an instance of what Bourdieu calls a 'strategy of condescension'" (117) emphasized that scandal is in fact the best publicity for the Booker. More so, English understands that while "scandals invariably sort out into just a handful of basic and well-established types" all of them "ultimately derive from the scandalous fact of the prizes' very existence, their claim to a legitimate and even premier place on the fields of culture" (*The Economy of Prestige* 190). Hence, "[e]very new prize is always already scandalous. The question is simply whether it will attract enough attention for this latent scandalousness to become manifest in the public sphere" (192).

Just how did the Booker manage for so long and still manages to ensure this attention? Or to put it in context of a wider literary communication, how does the Booker despite or—as we may by now suspect—because of the scandalous potential, keep up the potentially precarious alliances with other participants in the game? If, as Julian Barnes observes, the Booker drives everyone "mad," why bother? If, as Horowitz writes, there is much to risk for authors and publishers, why then do these representatives along with booksellers, critics, and, not least, readers participate in the process or public appreciation? What sustains this communication? Could it be that the media-prone scandal is only the tip of an iceberg? Is scandal only a very explicit type of problem, while the actual reason for the success, the reason for a strong positioning of the Booker amidst other participants in literary communication rests with the Booker's constant offer of problems or incentives to debate?

PAST AND PRESENT PROBLEMS ON THE INSIDE AND OUTSIDE OF THE LITERARY FIELD

Martyn Goff's take on the history of the Booker Prize and its scandals is also a story of how the Booker management reacted to such disturbances, at times trying to solve problems by changing its own rules, and in doing so often creating new problems. From a questionable and questioned set of 'founding fathers' to its rules of eligibility, to the criteria of selection and the use of the literary calendar's cycles of attention, the history of the Booker seems problematic, and, more often than not, fruitfully so, if not always for everyone to the same degree.

In 1968 Tom Maschler and Graham C. Greene, publishers at Jonathan Cape, approached Booker-McConnell, with whom they had worked before already, and came together in laying the foundations for the Booker Prize—with possible advantages for each party. This alliance was later reported to have been a wish-come-true for both sides as they had been cherishing some sort of expectations in this direction for some time already.[3]

The publishers had been thinking about invigorating the UK book market with a prize which would instigate debate. This wish was made concrete at a meeting of the Society of Young Publishers in 1964 at which Maschler took a leading role and where a first set of criteria for a possible prize was

---

3   A comprehensive history of the Booker Prize can be found in Richard Todd's *Consuming Fictions*.

sketched.[4] Preferably, it was to come with a large sum of money attached, reward books published in Great Britain, attract publicity (not least with a spectacular award ceremony), be judged in a way which would grant objectivity, and be sponsored in a way which would guarantee autonomy. The authors present at the meeting requested that the criteria for winning the award should not be coupled to book sales and that the atmosphere should be kept worthy. The critics—represented by the literary editor of a daily newspaper—were in agreement with the propositions made so far, emphasizing the hitherto lack of publicity for prizes, the need for autonomy from sponsors, and additionally calling for a possible tie with universities. This ideal, multi-perspective take on what a prize should accomplish is interesting as it allows for two comparisons: first, as a third 'checklist,' to Horowitz's and Goff's catalogues, and second, to the actual rules which make up the current Booker Prize.

The final partner in the deal, Booker plc—a wholesale company with past interests in the sugar industry in Guyana—had shortly gathered their activities in the UK in consequence of the post-independence movement, and, in an attempt to diversify, had made fresh experience in the book world.[5] Booker's newly established "Author's Division" had bought the rights from several authors forming a tax-shelter for, among others, James Bond creator Ian Fleming, and crime icon Agatha Christie. Hoping for better publicity and more inside expertise to the trade, the company was happy to sponsor a prize which would carry its name.

Administered by the Publishers Association and sponsored by an outsider with inside profit, the product of this win-win situation, the Booker Prize was first awarded in 1969. Critics soon perceived the bond as problematic. The colonial and capitalist involvement of the Booker Prize, which was not seldom felt to be a 'handicap,' came to be understood as insurmountable at certain times and by different agents, but it also turned out to be one of its advantages, precisely because of the need to intervene. In order to make up for this disequilibrium between aesthetics and money, moral high standards and political and economic realities, the Booker needed a

---

4 Cf. "Unnoticed Literary Prizes" 1966-70. See Norris for a detailed account of a pre-history of the Booker with an emphasis on the publishers' side.

5 The sponsor's motivations were critically described by Graham Huggan ("Prizing Otherness").

way to find a more balanced representation. A glimpse at the organization of the Prize allows for a better understanding of the intricate process to obtain legitimacy *vis-à-vis* these structural problems.

The Publishers Association withdrew one year into the Prize, making room for new management. This change provided a much needed institutional framework for a literary prize which had been prone to be criticized for its sales-oriented 'industry' background. The critics of the Prize could forthwith concentrate on the other side of the 'dowry,' its corporate ties to an organization with a past of colonial exploitation. When John Berger was awarded the Prize in 1972, his acceptance speech lay open just how sensitive the literary scene would be towards a money-lender with a colonial past. The author did not accept his laurels without pointing out the exploitative past of the Booker and disclosing his plans to give away half his prize money to the Black Panthers movement. Berger's reaction also pointed to the difficult situation writers found themselves in having to publically accept the appreciation by an institution which did not fulfil their ideal characteristics.

The new management, "representing all parts of the book world" (Goff 14), gave insight into who was prepared to join the alliance and whose representatives were needed in order to establish widest possible legitimacy. The Management Committee consisted of an author, two publishers, a bookseller, a librarian, the Booker chairman, another Booker representative, and the administrator of the prize, the previously quoted Martyn Goff. Its main responsibility was to appoint the annually changing judges and—if necessary—amend the Prize's rules.

When Booker plc merged with Iceland and formed the Big Food Group in 2000, there was much speculation about the Prize's future. After three decades of sponsorship, Booker plc announced their withdrawal and transferred the award to a new registered charity, the Booker Prize Foundation, "which will in future be responsible for its organisation and operation and for the securing of a new commercial sponsor."[6] The new sponsor, Man Group, a British alternative investment management business with a focus on hedge funds came with new (and more) money, with new rules and new

---

6   Cf. "The Booker Prize: New Developments." *The Booker Prize*, 24 Apr 2002. Web. Internet Archive. 25 May 2012. <http://web.archive.org/web/2002102-2052541/http://www.bookerprize.co.uk/latest.htm>.

gossip. Old suspicions of hegemony gave way to new anxieties such as the fear of Americanization.[7]

The contemporary structure of the Man Booker Prize is an even more intricate framework of checks and balances in which all participants are carefully represented. The three bodies—the Foundation, the Advisory Committee, and the judges—represent members from different institutions who are involved in the public discussion of literature and those who are interested in it. The even spread of politicians, businessmen, publishers, booksellers, critics, and writers is an attempt on the part of the Prize to live up to the high standards of objectivity and balance out the investment on the part of the diverse groups which it takes on board.

The Foundation consists of the former chairman of Booker plc and seven other members, two of which are authors. Martyn Goff is the president of the Booker Prize Foundation. The names of the other members and their titles make instantly clear just how much Booker's profile has risen (cf. "FAQs"). The Foundation appoints the members of the Advisory Committee: the literary director of the Man Booker Prizes, Ion Trewin, as well as 13 other members: an author, two publishers, a literary agent, two booksellers, a librarian, two literary editors, one of whom also organizes the Man Booker International Prize, and representatives of the two sponsors. The Advisory Committee is responsible for changing the rules and the selection of the judges.

Finally, the annually changing panel of judges is, too, under the obligation to represent as many interests as possible and each of the participating groups has an interest in being represented, too. Since 1977 it is set as a five-headed organ consisting of "an academic, a critic or two, a writer or two and the man in the street" (Goff 18). These days the Booker website

---

[7] The rumours according to which the Man Booker Prize was supposedly going to open up its rules of eligibility in favor of the hitherto shunned U.S.-Americans accompanied the change of sponsorship and peaked in May 2002. After much protest and debate, the initial plans were not realized but the decision was put back on the agenda in 2013 when it was announced that the Man Booker Prize would expand globally as of 2014 (cf. "Man Booker Prize announces global expansion." *The Man Booker Prizes*, 18 Sept 2013. Web. 29 Nov 2013. http://www.themanbookerprize.com/press-releases/man-booker-prize-announces -global-expansion).

specifies "a literary critic, an academic, a literary editor, a novelist and a major figure."[8] The Chair of judges is already appointed towards the end of each calendar year; the other four members are then assembled so as to ensure the heterogeneity and mix of personalities. It is with the judges where the actual responsibility of the Prize lies. Each year, the panel chooses "the very best book," or more specifically, "the best novel of the year written by a citizen of the United Kingdom, the Commonwealth or the Republic of Ireland."[9]

A three-fold presumption can be uncovered in the Booker's short statement on eligibility: (1) the best book of the year is in fact a best novel;[10] (2) there is such a thing as a best novel; and (3) a prize which is situated in the UK and judged by a set of British judges makes a selection among authors from around the English-speaking world, excluding the Unites States of America, and does so on the condition that their books are published with a UK publishing house. Graham Huggan is perhaps the most prominent scholar to have spotted a problem here (cf. "Prizing Otherness"). While some have seen the Booker's interest in so-called postcolonial fiction positively, or at least as a form of compensation for the first sponsor's exploitative past, Huggan elaborated on the ironies of picking authors and their writing (instead of sugar or other resources) from around the former empire whilst the money and infrastructure remains in (mostly) London: "The Booker might be seen [...] as remaining bound to an Anglocentric discourse of benevolent paternalism" ("Prizing Otherness" 111).

From the perspective of the Prize, however, this area of conflict ensures an annual check of forces, not dissimilar to a cricket championship or a

---

8   "How the Prize Works." *The Man Booker Prizes*. Web. Internet Archive. 29 Nov 2013. <http://web.archive.org/web/20120531093357/http://www.themanbookerprize.com/prize/about/how-the-prize-works>.

9   "About the Prize." *The Man Booker Prizes*. Web. Internet Archive 29 Nov 2013. <http://web.archive.org/web/20120504014616/http://themanbookerprize.com/prize/about>.

10 Claire Squires goes even further in claiming the direct marketing consequences of the Prize's category for "the best novel" for the positioning of "literary novels" above any other genre and for the self-positioning of the Booker as more important award in comparison to a genre award such as the Arthur C. Clarke Prize (98).

wider version of The Ashes, and positions the Booker as a state-of-the-empire-prize. In addition to the annual speculation about gender or genre, this *inter*national debate is one which secures circulating media coverage from Ireland to South Africa, from Canada to Australia. Mostly, however, it puts the other nations in question under pressure: Should they rejoice in case 'their' representatives win, or withdraw attention to such a renewal of imperial imposition?[11]

Against this backdrop, the problematic alliances which are at stake here are both on the outside and the inside of a theoretically defined literary field. The twofold tensions on the outside of the traditional participants in literary communication have been described above. For one, there are the ties to the corporate world of sponsors—be it a wholesale company (Booker plc) or an investment business (Man Group, who has taken over sponsorship since 2001). Secondly, there are tensions on a national, or inter-national, level. The UK book market—with the Booker Prize as their tool—intervenes into other national book markets by appropriating their creative talent. The tensions between participants on the inside of a literary communication circuit—from author to reader via publisher, printer, distributor, retailer, and critic[12]—will concern us in the following.

One of these internal tensions, i.e., the potential accusation of the Booker Prize as an industry, can be said to have been avoided quite early. With the withdrawal of the Publishers Association, and the representative composition of its managing bodies of publishers, retailers, critics and authors, the Booker has gained much legitimation. Yet, the Booker's aim at promoting literature and boosting sales continues to incite concerns of commercialization and commodification of fiction. This 'inside,' then, also seems divided: into a core-inside, core-literary position, a realm of aesthetics, and a pecuniary side of the literary endeavor, the publishers and retail-

---

11 In 2008, for example, after the Indian-born Aravind Adiga won the Booker with his novel *The White Tiger*, an Indian critic found himself in that very position between national pride and the feeling of British usurpation and, somewhat reluctantly, decided to accept with anxious pleasure: "The Brits have chosen and who are we to cavil at that? An Indian novelist has won the Man Booker. We can rejoice in the Indianness and ignore the novelist for the moment" (Menon).

12 See Squires (51-53) for a discussion of Robert Darnton's communications circuit and its development by Thomas R. Adams and Nicolas Barker.

ers, in short, the industry. Martyn Goff makes clear how tricky these relationships are:

> The judges' biggest problem [...] is [...] the definition of the 'best novel of the year.' It is very flexible and each set of judges will give their own interpretation. It is not, of course the only aim of the Prize. Booker plc want to reward merit, raise the stature of the author in the eyes of the public and increase the sale of books. The rub probably comes in the third aim. Booksellers in any case regard the choice of the winner as good if the book sells well and bad if it does not. [...] To find a book that passes the tests of literary critics and academics, and pleases the booksellers is not easy. (17)

The pressures which Goff describes and the attempts to please several parties at once, publishers and booksellers on the one hand, and critics and academics on the other, are somewhat relieved by bringing justice to either set of criteria by rotation—but they can never be fully resolved to the satisfaction of all participants. The Prize may have created "a new genre—the 'literary-novel-as-bestseller'" (Norris 25), but it has also called for fears of standardisation, of the 'literary' novel becoming less innovative, pandering to the market, to the demand for readable, i.e., saleable goods.

The Booker's annual attempt to overcome such "dualist structures" (English, *The Economy of Prestige* 220) is media-worthy material: James F. English emphasizes media attention as means to this goal. Not only does the Prize convert symbolic into economic capital, it has a history of establishing what English calls "journalistic capital" (208). It has the ability to cause a second wave of reviewing for the winning title as much as for the nominated books.[13] Apart from such additional coverage for the individual books, the Booker offers itself for the debate throughout the year and invites the commentators and their audiences to accompany any of its decisions from the selection of the Chair of judges in November to the announcement of the longlist in July, the shortlist in September and the final winner in October. This coverage ranges from individual book-related topics to specific group dynamics of nominations in a given year, to recurring annual discussions which can be applied to any long- or shortlist, such as quota and tokenism or reports on betting odds.

---

13 Richard Todd described this phenomenon as "double publication" (*Consuming Fictions* 72).

What the Booker offers is a legitimation for all participants to engage in the process and to actively comment on problems which the Booker presents to others in the game: usual suspects (gender, nation, genre) and questions concerning the relevance of these aspects for literary quality, considerations just what it is that makes "the best novel" and if that is something one can ask in the first place, questions concerning the criteria and the makers of these criteria, as well as their legitimation to pronounce such criteria, to appreciate, to select, i.e., questions regarding the participants and their relationships, market formation and power structures.[14]

The Prize not only offers something for each of its alliance partners—be it sales, attention, or prestige—but also an opportunity of problematizing the alliance between the different people and institutions acting in the literary marketplace. As the Booker interacts with other interlocutors in literary discourse, it allows for a discussion of forms of participation and processes of appreciation, thus making the whole constellation of allies and their diverse agendas visible.

THE POWER OF PROBLEMS

Where are literary prizes to be placed in a literary communication circuit as proposed by Robert Darnton (1982)? Are they part of the production, distribution, or reception of literature? Do they participate, and if so how, in the *prises de position* within a literary field model as defined by Pierre Bourdieu (1983)?

According to communication scientist Wouter de Nooy, literary prizes take a "central position in the literary field, since they are related to many of its institutions" (199). In fact, in the course of a heightened academic interest from the late 1980s onwards, predominantly if not exclusively based

---

14 One of the commentators of Aravind Adiga's 2008 Booker success seized this very opportunity to pinpoint the dimensions of these structures: "Wannabe entrants should steel themselves to the fickle tyrants of this undemocratic realm—editor and agent, publisher and promoter, reader and critic. And you haven't even exhausted that list yet—there's the jury too, midwife of prize and prejudice. Aravind Adiga is probably best able, at the moment, to convey the sensations of baptism into Bookworld—at once beatific and blistered" (Thakur).

on Bourdieu's sociology of literature, literary awards have been placed in different positions in processes of literary communication. De Nooy, for instance, propagated their close relations with "the institution of criticism":

Reports of juries are similar to reviews and other types of criticism in that they contain statements on the qualities of texts, their literary value and the legitimate ways of discussing these texts. In short, they contain statements meant to contribute to the harmonization of opinions on literature. (De Nooy 199-200)

Prizes in general and the Booker in particular have been understood as consumer guides and parts of a new culture of consumption (cf. Todd, *Consuming Fictions*), as a continuation of the commodification of a perpetually created exotic periphery (cf. Huggan, *The Postcolonial Exotic*), as part of a wider economy of prestige (cf. English, *The Economy of Prestige*), or as one of the manifestations of literary marketing (cf. Squires).

In his 2002 proclamatory essay James F. English called for a new model of communication, which would incorporate Bourdieu's concepts but also transcend them, and which would be adequate to our postmodern age:

We need a new model of the field of cultural production in terms of which these very dispositions can themselves be scrutinized and transformed. The sort of model I have in mind would owe much to Bourdieu, certainly, but would resist any division of social space into two preexisting sides, two proper positions or placements, between which the originary 'double discourse of value' plays out its ostensibly permanent antagonisms. ("Winning the Culture Game" 128)

Can such a differentiated, specific model be glimpsed in the Booker's own exertions to guarantee representativeness? The complex arrangement of participants in the annual award of the Booker Prize may guarantee representation from all sides of the communications circuit but it does not guarantee harmonious negotiations. Instead, it guarantees—or rather, offers, as it cannot replace other participants—a reason for negotiations. The annual media coverage of the Booker comprises discussions of ethics in the marketplace, questions of literary quality, and problems of canon formation. Most of all, it puts gate-keepers and their institutions into a competitive race for the authority to pronounce future literary history.

The Booker Prize does not prove an uncontroversial mediator between pure art and its contaminating elements, between the literary marketplace and the forces of economy. Rather, its main interest—and one which may hint at a possible explanation for the collaboration, the participation in a potentially precarious alliance—seems to arise from its offer of problems which may not be necessarily solved but which can be debated.

WORKS CITED

Barnes, Julian. "Diary." *London Review of Books* 9.20 (12 Nov 1987): 21. Print.

Bourdieu, Pierre. "The Field of Cultural Production, Or: The Economic World Reversed." *Poetics* 12 (1983): 311-56. Print.

Brett, Simon. *The Booker Book. A Novel*. London: Sidgwick & Jackson, 1989. Print.

Darnton, Robert. "What is the History of Books?" *Daedalus* 111.3 (1982): 65-83. Print.

De Nooy, Wouter. "Literary Prizes: Their Role in the Making of Children's Literature." *Poetics* 18 (1989): 199-213. Print.

English, James F. "Winning the Culture Game: Prizes, Awards, and the Rules of Art." *New Literary History* 33.1 (Winter 2002): 109-35. Print.

---. *The Economy of Prestige. Prizes, Awards, and the Circulation of Cultural Value*. Cambridge, Mass.: Harvard UP, 2005. Print.

Goff, Martyn. "Introduction." *Prize Writing: Original Collection of Writings by Past Winners to Celebrate 21 Years of the Booker Prize*. London: Hodder and Stoughton, 1989. 11-23. Print.

Hitchens, Christopher. "These Glittering Prizes." *Vanity Fair* (Dec 1992): 20. Web.

Horowitz, Irving Louis. "Publishing and Prizing." *Book Research Quarterly* 3.4 (Winter 1987-88): 18-21. Print.

Huggan, Graham. "Prizing 'Otherness': A Short History of the Booker." *Studies in the Novel* 29.3 (1997): 412-33. Print.

---. *The Postcolonial Exotic. Marketing the Margins*. London and New York: Routledge, 2001. Print.

Menon, Suresh. "Keep Your Socks On." *Mumbai Mirror* (24 Oct 2008): n.pag. Web.

Norris, Sharon. "Recontextualising the Booker." *Fiction and Literary Prizes in Great Britain*. Ed. Wolfgang Görtschacher, Holger Klein, and Claire Squires. Vienna: Praesens, 2006. 20-36. Print.

Squires, Claire. *Marketing Literature. The Making of Contemporary Writing in Britain*. Basingstoke: Palgrave Macmillan, 2007. Print.

Thakur, Sankarshan. "The Hero India Doesn't Want." *The Telegraph, Calcutta* (16 Nov 2008): n.pag. Web.

Todd, Richard. *Consuming Fictions: The Booker Prize and Fiction in Britain Today*. London: Bloomsbury, 1996. Print.

---. "How Has the Booker Prize Changed since 1996?" *Fiction and Literary Prizes in Great Britain*. Ed. Wolfgang Görtschacher, Holger Klein, and Claire Squires. Vienna: Praesens, 2006. 8-19. Print.

"Unnoticed Literary Prizes: Plea for a New Major National Literary Award." *The Bookseller* (7 Nov 1964): 1966-70. Print.

Socialist Realism in a Capitalist Context: Marketing Strategies in the Russian Book Market

ULRICH SCHMID

For a long time, Russians have prided themselves to be the most-reading nation in the world. However, this self-assessment suffered a serious blow after the breakdown of the Soviet Union. In a survey from 2008, Russia ranked only eighth with an average of seven hours of reading per week. The global winners were India, Thailand, and China, and little has changed ever since ("Samye čitajuščie" n.pag.).

Yet, book production is still impressive in Russia. In 2011, nearly 123,000 titles were produced, with an overall print run of more than 612 million copies. The two biggest publishers, Eksmo and AST, each produced around 9,000 titles in 2011, with a print run of 65 million copies each (cf. table 1).[1]

	Number of titles	Print run in 1,000 copies	In % of all titles	In % of the print run
Total	122,915	612,506.3		
Print run up to 500	54,861	13,291.7	44.6	2.2
Print run up to 1,000	11,332	10,811.5	9.2	1.7
Print run up to 5,000	33,946	112,685.5	27.6	18.4

---

1 These numbers are based on the data provided by the Russian book chamber (cf. "Knigoizdanie v RF v 2011 godu").

Print run up to 10,000	11,983	96,739.9	9.8	15.8
Print run up to 50,000	8,933	195,803.2	7.3	32.0
Print run up to 100,000	897	66,153.2	0.7	10.8
Print run up to 100,000	522	117,021.3	0.4	19.1
No indication of print run	441		0.4	

Table 1: Titles and print run in the Russian book market 2011

One important feature of the Russian book market is the fact that only one percent of all titles account for around 30% of the whole book production. In other words, the Russian book market is dominated by very few bestsellers. And these bestsellers do not just appear coincidentally; they are created with the help of a set of special marketing strategies. The most important of these strategies is branding. Books and authors have to be recognizable in order to secure a sustainable commercial success. If an author functions like a brand, readers will exactly know what to expect from the purchased book. In bestsellers, literary style, plot organization, and choice of protagonists are no longer aesthetic categories that form a fictional world, but features of a product that guarantees the renewal of a pleasant reading experience without boring repetition.

Branding is not new in the realm of literature. Authors of all epochs have sought to acquire a distinct image that would shape their name into a brand. At the beginning of the 21st century, however, things seem to have become more complicated. The sheer number of active writers has reduced the chances of fame for a single author significantly. Publishers therefore have to decide very carefully about advertising strategies for their authors. Prominence is no longer the *result* of literary success, but its *presupposition*.

In Russia, a bestselling author has little prestige among the reading intelligentsia. Books that are distributed in a huge number of copies are considered to particularly cater to the demands of rather unsophisticated readers. To be sure, such print runs remind most readers of Soviet times when ideologically 'correct' literature was printed in enormous quantities—these books were usually called '*makulatura*.' The very moment they were delivered to book shops, it was clear that nobody would buy or even read them. Conversely, forbidden books containing dissident texts circulated in hand typed copies—often readers were given just one night to read the book before they were supposed to hand it along to the next reader. It was precisely the shortage of time and paper that made those books precious in the readers' eyes.

Today, such a secret success is not possible anymore. Still, a difference is made between 'highbrow' and 'lowbrow' literature, but there are no authors anymore who would exist outside the market. In contrast to this significant change, another line of tradition has been preserved. Official soviet literature had to follow the aesthetic principles of Socialist Realism. In 1934, all writers' associations were dissolved and united in the Soviet writers' union. During the first congress, the style of Socialist Realism was imposed upon Soviet literature. Novels had to "represent the Soviet reality in its revolutionary development" (Gutkin 49). Though this implied that Soviet literature was allowed to portray negative phenomena, the depicted problems had always to be solved by a 'positive hero,' striving for realization of the ultimate goal, i.e., the construction of a socialist and eventually communist society—a goal which had to be made visible throughout the entire text.

One main feature of Socialist Realism is the claim for 'clarity' and 'comprehensibility,' which was pushed forward through the concept of '*massovost*.' Characters, plot construction and narration had to be kept simple so that every worker and farmer could follow and understand the literary production in the Soviet Union.

The ideology of Socialist Realism died a sudden death in 1989, but its narrative and stylistic clichés have indeed survived until today and have made their way into bestselling literature. There is both a historical and a structural explanation for this phenomenon: first, creative writing in the Soviet Union was taught in a Socialist Realist key, and readers were educated at schools and universities that included the canon of Socialist Realist literature in their curricula. Second, the structure of the Socialist Realist text still bears the potential to attract a more Westernized readership. As Katerina Clark explains in her study of the Soviet novel, the Socialist Realist text is structured according to a scheme that, to a considerable degree, resembles Western narratives: The positive hero arrives in a microcosm, receives a task, sets out to resolve this task, falls behind, talks to a mentor, and finally overcomes all obstacles (cf. 256-60). Indeed, one may argue that this scheme does not solely apply to Soviet literature, but also to a great deal of Western, especially American popular fiction. Many Hollywood productions rely on a similar pattern of plot as well. The genre is of secondary importance—dramas, Western and animated films often depict the overcoming of a difficult situation (cf. Buck-Morss 134-151).

This structural similarity between Socialist Realist texts and Western narrative patterns allows for the survival of Socialist Realism in a capitalist context: Russian bestselling authors reanimate the clichés of Soviet literature and deploy them in their own novels. At the same time, just as in the Soviet cultural hierarchy of distinction, these writers are present in TV shows, in the new media and in newspapers. In Soviet times, the official culture was responsible for the construction of a 'successful' author. Today, the big publishers push their authors into the literary arena and carefully define their strategies as to whom they single out and whom they leave in the background.

Product Placement in Daria Dontsova's Bestsellers

The writer Daria Dontsova certainly belongs to the former group. In absolute numbers, she is Russia's largest-selling author. On her website she proudly states that she has authored 144 books with a total print run of 5.4 million copies so far. Her success builds on a specific aesthetics that is combined with a sophisticated marketing strategy.

Her preferred genre is the so-called 'ironic detective novel' which was invented by the Polish bestselling author Joanna Chmielewska (born in 1932). In her home country Chmielewska has a total print run of six million copies, in Russia she sold as many as eight million copies. She defines her favorite genre as "humorous thrillers," ("Joanna Chmielewska Passes Away" n.pag.) which is basically a mix of comedy and action. Chmielewska's heroines find themselves willy-nilly in a dangerous criminal case. However, even in dangerous situations they do not transform themselves into skirt-wearing James Bonds, but remain average people whose struggle with their role in the criminal case serves as the basis for a range of comic effects. In Russia, Joanna Chmielewska became famous in the late Soviet period. Her novels scored print runs of half a million copies—the cover of one publication even featured Agatha Christie alongside Chmielewska, which created a strong marketing effect and thus turned out to be a successful sales strategy, which, by the way, is widely used by internet platforms such as Amazon or iTunes today:[2] A famous, almost iconic representative of a genre (Christie) is used to promote a newcomer (Chmielewska).

Daria Dontsova copies Chmielewska's formula of success. As a female protagonist, she does not choose an astute analyst, but a harmless housewife who has many pets and does not work—at the utmost she teaches some private language lessons. It is especially the naiveté of Dontsova's characters that serves to entertain the readers of her texts.[3]

Dontsova's novels follow a model which can be described best in the terminology of Vladimir Propp who authored a famous book with the title *The Morphology of the Folktale* in 1928. Repetition is a key feature of Dontsova's work. She herself divided her 100 novels into four series with different protagonists: *The Amateur of the Private Investigation Dasha Vasil'eva, Evlampiia Romanova—The Investigation is Conducted by a Dilettante, Viola Tarakanova—In the World of Criminal Passions*, and finally, *The Investigating Gentleman Ivan Podushkin*. Already the wording of the series' titles makes clear that heroines and situations are almost exchangeable. The protagonists only have a limited range of acting options, the plot is a sequence of adventure scenes that may be permuted and combined according to predetermined narrative principles (cf. Lipovetsky 233-50). Moreover, the happy end is a recurring feature in all series. In her interviews, Dontsova always stresses the fact that her readers may trust that not one single hero is going to die. Dontsova does not present complex

---

2   Agata Kristi: Pjať porosjat. Joanna Chmelevskaja: Prokljatoe nasledstvo. Moskva: Raduga 1990.

3   Dontsova takes her cue not only from Chmielewska, but also from Rex Stout who is being alluded to in many of her works (cf. Iščuk-Fadeeva 112-31). In the past, Dontsova has been accused of plagiarism at several occasions. However, the allegations that had some literary relevance pointed to narratives that are quite common in Russian folk tales or to the name of a place of action. There is only one quite obvious case of plagiarism that she committed in one of her two cookbooks. In this text, she copied entire sections from a cookbook that was published in 1967 in the GDR and appeared in a Russian translation in 1973 (cf. Iguana n.pag.). Dontsova herself preferred not to comment on this affair.

characters—the fairytale distinction 'good' vs. 'bad' is simply substituted by the detective novel's categories 'just' vs. 'criminal.'

Daria Dontsova has a very bourgeois style—both in her self-presentation as an author and in her fictional texts. In 2010, she showed her living room in a televised home story. Her almost baroque house with the clumsy furnishing corresponds to the ideal dreams of the average Russian citizen: A 'cottage,' as the style of her detached mini castle is called in Russian, equipped with a fireplace and a salon with several heavy armchairs and a chandelier. Interestingly enough, Dontsova's taste corresponds with Soviet ideas of cosiness and decency. In the 1930s, the Soviet culture, which had initially propagated a proletarian aesthetics, turned to an ideal of '*kulturnost*,' which can be translated as 'cultural refinement' (cf. Volkov 210-30). Until the end of the Soviet Union, party leaders wore ties and suits; and private homes became carefully furnished fortresses against the gray tristesse of the public space. As paradoxical as it seems: The official propagation of '*kulturnost*' turned the workers' and farmers' state into a society with bourgeois preferences of taste (cf. Mehnert 87).

Even Dontsova's official website (cf. Ill. 1) is structured along the lines of a home story. The items of the menu correspond to different rooms in her house: hall, living-room, kitchen, library, study, winter-garden, dog's room and children's room. The website tries to establish a personal relationship between the reader and the author. The reader is given the impression that he knows his favorite writer intimately and is a guest in her private home.

Dontsova's literary style is a continuation of Soviet aesthetic traditions as well, as she takes up the Socialist Realist scheme.[4] The main change in

---

4   Dontsova was well acquainted with Socialist Realism through her family ties. Her father Arkadi Vasiliev belonged to the nomenclatura and was a prominent member of the Soviet writers' union. He wrote in a satirical key, he attacked Soviet vices like bureaucracy and toadyism in a politically very correct manner. Vasiliev was a staunch communist hardliner and even testified at court against the dissident writers Andrei Siniavski and Juli Daniel, who were sentenced to seven years in a prison camp in 1966 for the production of non-conformist literature. The writer Kornei Chukovski was so appalled by Vasiliev's vile accusation that he forbade him in his testament to attend his own funeral (cf. Oksman 148).

Ill. 1: Screenshot from Dontsova's website www.dontsova.ru

comparison with the Soviet tradition concerns the positive hero who becomes a female hobby sleuth (The *Podushkin*-series is the exception to the rule, but Dontsova's only male protagonist is rather effeminate and may be seen as a disguised variation of a female investigator). The protagonist's high moral standards are preserved in Dontsova's fiction—the reasons for the ethical behavior vary: In the Soviet tradition, the positive hero is ideologically highly conscious, Dontsova's heroines are rather naïve and do not question or even legitimize their own values.

Dontsova does not write purely Socialist Realist prose, but enriches it with elements and features that can also be found in Joanna Chmielewska's 'ironic detective novel.' This genre became most popular in Russian popular culture after 1990, which is probably due to the low profile it kept during Soviet times for ideological reasons. As a matter of principle, crimes were unthinkable in 'developed Socialism,' as the Brezhnev era was officially called by the regime. The success of the detective novel in the 1990s testifies to the fact that there was a huge demand for ideological compensation. Moreover, Dontsova's stylistic emulation of Chmielewska's books becomes obvious in the design of her book covers, which employ a strikingly similar visual make-up.

Ill. 2: Cover illustration from Joanna Chmielewska, *To Drive out a Wedge with a Wedge*

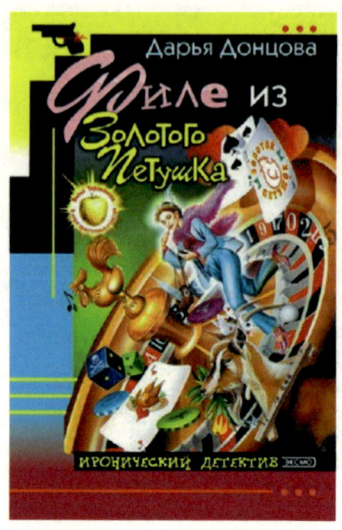

Ill. 3: Cover illustration from Daria Dontsova, *A Filet from the Golden Cockerel*

The set of marketing strategies to promote Dontsova's books also includes product placement in literary texts (cf. Berezkina 120). In fact, Dontsova is a pioneer in this field. Her protagonists drink Lavazza coffee, sport a Cartier watch, wear Chanel costumes and use Dior perfume. A prominent case in point is her novel *A Filet from the* Golden Cockerel, with "Golden Cockerel" being a food brand selling frozen chicken.

Dontsova inserts an advertisement scene into her novel and even incorporates the brand name into the title of her book. Insiders estimate that such a prominent product placement costs about 50,000 dollars. The advertising scene does not even try to disguise itself:

This is the *Golden Cockerel*, said the young girl with a smile.
I hesitated.
　No, thank you.
　　Try it!
　　I know chicken very well. Over there, in the fridge, there is plenty of it.
　　Yes, but you have to cook it first.

> And your meat can be eaten raw?
>
> No, of course not,—the girl smiled,—but it is very easy, just throw it in the frying pan and that's it. We have something for every taste. Would you like a tender breast filet? Or winglets with spices? I personally prefer the legs, they are the juiciest.
>
> Mechanically, I ate a bite, then a second, a third ...
>
> Do you like it?—the girl asked.
>
> Yes, it is very good.
>
> Take a box for dinner.
>
> I have cutlets.
>
> Put it in the fridge, you may need it.
>
> The girl was nice, the *Golden Cockerel* seemed to be fresh, and I decided not to sadden the student girl who earned some money doing advertisement. Probably, she was paid *pro rata*.
>
> And it is not expensive,—the promoter brought in her final argument.—The kilo is only 69 Rubles. The same product from Germany costs 140.
>
> Give me a breast filet,—I decided,—although I do not like deep fried food, but once in a while we can do it.
>
> If you come back, do you want a tip?
>
> Which one?
>
> Do not mix us up: we are the *Golden Cockerel*.
>
> I got that.
>
> There is still the "Brave Hen," don't take that, there is only chemistry in that.
>
> (*File* 38)

After this scene, the protagonist goes home and cooks a meal for her father. Of course, the father is very happy with the food: "You began to cook very good, my daughter,—said my father, sprawling just like a cat enjoying the warmth in a sunny spot" (39).

This scene anticipates the emotional reward any reader may earn by buying products from the "Golden Cockerel." Basically the scene in the supermarket functions as a textualised TV-advertisement: The advantages of a product are explained in a short dramatic scene. The text even goes beyond the possibilities of a short video clip. For the protagonist, the acquisition of the "Golden Cockerel"-box is not only an economic, but also an ethical act. She helps the young promotor to finance her studies. Practical considerations (easy to cook), economic rationality (as good as the German product, but half the price), family values (the happy father) and moral behaviour (indirect financial support for a working student) form a whole array of marketing arguments that eventually leads to the purchase of the frozen chicken meat.

Dontsova does not only advertise the "Golden Cockerel" in her novel, she also participates in the "Golden Cockerel Clubs" and shares her favorite recipes with her female readers who are supposed to buy products from the "Golden Cockerel." The combination of a bestselling novel and a frozen food-product is a win-win situation for both market participants. Luckily enough, the target audience coincides, as a marketing report from the "Golden Cockerel" indicates:

The brand The Golden Cockerel is geared towards people with an average income, between 25 and 45 years old, mainly women, professionally and privately established, with family. They like quality and diversity in food products, a quick and easy preparation. [...] The restyling of the brand The Golden Cockerel concentrated on specific elements of the logo (typography and color) and corrected the color, which makes it more appealing and attractive. The combination of yellow and read highlights the emotional component of the brand and symbolizes activity, zest for life and optimism. ("Пресс-релизы")

This precarious alliance between a bookshop and the frozen food section in a supermarket indeed seems to satisfy both market participants—and Daria Dontsova has at no point in the deal hesitated to put her literary talent at the service of a commercial company.

DMITRI GLUKHOVSKY'S METRO 2033-SERIES

Another case in point is the bestselling series *Metro 2033* by the young journalist Dmitri Glukhovsky. He created a dark world in a post-apocalyptic setting. His assumptions are the following: In 2013, a worldwide nuclear war broke out and turned the earth into a radioactive desert. There is no sunlight anymore, almost all human beings were killed; the only other existing species are mutants and dinosaurs. Only around 70,000 people survived in Moscow—those who happened to be in the metro during the nuclear strikes. Twenty years after the devastating war, several communities exist in different metro stations, and they fight each other for water, food and other supplies.

Glukhovsky, too, follows the Socialist Realist model in his plot construction. As in the Soviet novel, Glukhovsky deploys a positive hero who is a one-dimensional character. The remaining characters in the novel are not so different from those in Socialist Realist texts either: The positive hero has to find out who is a friend and who is an enemy. And just like in the Soviet novel, the enemy has to be destroyed—there are no moral considerations about killing a hostile human being. Against this backdrop, some critics even maintained that his novel is a literary version of an ego shooter computer game.

The main difference between Socialist Realist conventions and Glukhovsky's fiction is the open ending of the latter. There is no happy end in the *Metro 2033*-world, and there cannot be one, because there is no historical teleology in Glukhovsky's universe as there was in the Marxist utopia of Soviet communism.

Ill. 4: Post-apocalyptic Moscow, screenshot from www.metro2033.ru

Glukhovsky employs a number of marketing strategies for his prose as well. He started off as an internet author publishing portions of his texts on his live journal blog and on several literary websites in Russia. He went as far as to recommend specific music to his readers, which they were supposed to listen to while reading his novel. By doing so, he set out to influence the mood of his audience and, at the same time, hoped to gather their feedback through the interactive interfaces that the internet provided him with.

In 2005 a book edition came out with Eksmo, a little later Glukhovsky explored the possibilities of selling fan products on the internet. He set up a poll asking his readers if they would order such items or if they thought that the world of *Metro 2033* may not be corrupted by commercialization.

Today, *Metro 2033* is a commercial empire with many authors writing novels within its post-apocalyptic universe. In 2006, even a computer game was created (cf. Ill. 4). Thus, *Metro 2033* is an excellent example of a fictional text that began as a blog entry, then turned into a novel and finally served as a base for the creation of a video game.

THE BOOK AS MERCHANDISE

Dontsova and Glukhovsky are two examples of writers who do not just write literature. They engage in a greater project that creates a lifestyle—be it the bourgeois cosiness of Dontsovas ironic detective novels or the postapocalyptic world which is basically an exaggerated metaphor for surviving in the postcommunist Moscow of the 21st century. Moreover, both Dontsova and Glukhovsky employ marketing strategies that transgress the boundaries of the book market—they boost their bestselling books by expanding the brand into other realms of lifestyle accessories. In this situation, the book is not an end in itself, but only a means that serves other goals.

In the capitalist context, the simplistic plot model of the Socialist Realist novel does not carry a political ideology, but works as a sales strategy. The fictional scenes contain a behavioral script that should be appropriated by the readers. If the "Golden Cockerel" sponsors Dontsova's novel, the food company aims at the same target group as the publisher. Ideally, eating frozen chicken and reading ironic detective novels should coincide in a coherent lifestyle. Eating, drinking, dressing up in the fictional world prefigures eating, drinking and dressing up in the real world. The readers do not only identify with the protagonists, but with her entire lifestyles. In a way, product placement in prose fiction is advertisement that is not recognized as direct progaganda. If Dontsova's heroine constantly drinks Lavazza instead of just coffee, readers may come to the conclusion that drinking coffee in real life should also be synonymous with drinking Lavazza.

Similarly, Glukhovsky considers his novel *Metro 2033* only as an intermediary stage in an ongoing marketing project. He aims at a constant expansion of his transmedial fictional world in further novels, in computer games and, as the ultimate goal, in a blockbuster movie. In this project, *Metro 2033* has become a brand that does not just designate the title of a single novel, but evokes an atmosphere of dark aesthetics, action scenes and science fiction. Glukhovsky borrows the positive hero from the Soviet novel. By doing so, he significantly adds to the 'comprehensibility' of his fiction for a broad readership, which, in turn, guarantees commercial success.

What some may call 'the end of literature,' then, arguing that literature has eventually depraved into a servant of larger commercial projects and has thus lost its (alleged) autonomy, I would rather like to understand as an impulse for other writers or writings to emerge. I believe indeed that other books will react to literary phenomena like Dontsova and Glukhovsky. Especially in the Russian context, writers have proved to be able to cope artistically with challenges such as bestselling prose. In the near future, we will thus witness the emergence of novels that analyse the conflation of literary style and lifestyle. The marketing strategies of bestselling authors will be turned into narrative strands. And then the textual nature of the commercialization of literature will become visible and produce a new kind of art.

WORKS CITED

Berezkina, Olga. *Product Placement. Technologija Skrytoj Reklamy*. St.Petersburg: Let Me Print, 2012.
Buck-Morss, Susan. *Dreamworld and Catastrophe. The Passing of Mass Utopia in East and West*. Cambridge, Mass: MIT P, 2000. Print.
Chmielewska, Joanna. *Čto skazal pokojnik*. Moscow: Raduga, 1989. Print.
---. *Prokljatoe nasledstvo*. Moscow: Raduga, 1990. Print.
Clark, Katerina. *The Soviet Novel: History as Ritual*. Bloomington: Indiana UP, 1981. Print.
Dontsova, Daria. *File iz Zolotogo Petuška*. Moscow: Eksmo, 2005. Print.
---. *Ivan Podushkin*. Moscow: Eksmo, 2003. Print.
Glukhovsky, Dimitri. *Metro 2033*. München: Heyne, 2008. Print.

Gutkin, Irina. *The Cultural Origins of the Socialist Realist Aesthetic: 1890-1934*. Evanston: Northwestern UP, 1999. Print.
Iguana, Donna. "Sekrety masterstva—D. Dontsova." *Livejournal.com*. 10 Mar. 2010. Web.
Iščuk-Fadeeva, Nina. "Ženskij detektiv kak zerkalo russkoj perestrojki." *Voprosy literatury* 9.10 (2010): 112-31. Print.
"Joanna Chmielewska Passes Away." *The Polish Book Institute*. N.pag., n.d. Web.
"Knigoizdanie v RF v 2011 godu." *bookchamber.ru*. N.pag., n.d. Web.
Kristi, Agata. *Pjat' porosjat*. Joanna Chmelevskaja. *Prokljatoe nasledstvo*. Moskva: Raduga, 1990. Print.
Lipovetsky, Mark. "Introduction to Part III: Fairy Tales in Critique of Soviet Culture." *Politicizing Magic: An Anthology of Russian and Soviet Fairy-Tales*. Ed. Marina Balina, Helena Goscilo, and Mark Lipovetsky. Evanston: Northwestern UP, 2005. 233-50. Print.
Mehnert, Klaus. *Der Sowjetmensch. Versuch eines Porträts nach zwölf Reisen in die Sowjetunion 1929-1957*. Stuttgart: Deutsche Verlags-Anstalt, 1958. Print.
Oksman, Julian G. *K.I. Čukovskij: Perepiska 1949-1969*. Ed. A.L. Grišunina. Moskva: Jazyki slavjanskoj kult'ury, 2001. Print.
"Пресс-релизы." *Kompanija Produkty Pitanija*. N.pag., 23 Sep. 2005. Web.
"Samye čitajuščie strany mira. Spravka." *ria.ru RIA Novosti*. N.pag., 11 June 2008. Web.
Volkov, Vadim. "The Concept of 'Kulturnost'." *Stalinism: New Directions*. Ed. Sheila Fitzpatrick. New York: Routledge, 2000. 210-30. Print.

The New Circumstances of Content Innovation in the Digital Book Value Creation Network: Precarious Guarantee of More of the Same?

CHRISTOPH BLÄSI

INTRODUCTION

This paper deals with a specific kind of innovation in the book industry. In times of a rapidly evolving ebook market, technological innovations, such as those in the technology used to distribute books and book content, might be the first innovations to come to mind. In this paper, I take a new perspective on the question of innovation within the book industry. More specifically, I focus on the consequences of the digitization of the book industry on the *content* of books.

In order to do so, I follow a book studies approach to literary communication and book communication respectively. The argument of this paper is based on the assumption that book content, and thus content innovation in the book industry, is brought about not just by a single (genius) originator (i.e., the author), but is also the result of processes controlled by an entire set of actors along the industry's value chain—to make use of a view and of concepts from economics and management that have become popular also in media studies. Against this backdrop, I argue in this paper that over the last years—especially since the advent of online bookshops and the rise of the ebook following the success of Amazon's Kindle and Apple's iPad—there have been ground-breaking transitions in the book industry, affecting the very structure of its value chain. Consequently, both book content and processes of content innovation in the book industry have certainly also changed to a considerable degree. I will address this transformation in the following sections, and focus more specifically on changes in book content innovation in the case of fiction books.

What is Book Content Innovation?

Before I go into detail and discuss the processes of book content innovation in the fiction book industry, it is important to clarify two basic concepts that I will refer to throughout this paper.

Since this paper is about innovation in the book industry, the concept of the 'book' is a central concept here—although in the digital era, it is by no means a self-evident one. Books are artifacts (printed books) or immaterial phenomena (digital books) that transport predominantly textual information and are characterized by specific features (length, argumentative complexity, aesthetic style, etc.). They can also be complemented by images or other entities from different sign systems like audios or videos. These artifacts or immaterial phenomena fulfill certain functions, which include, but are not limited to, working as a medium of individual or collective memory, for publicly articulating a particular perspective, or serving as a form of entertainment, education, information, or edification.[1]

The second concept I would like to clarify is that of 'innovation.' Since this concept has predominantly been shaped by economics and management, it is strongly connected to the concept of utility, which denotes the actual usefulness of a new feature or element (see below). Hence, innovation and utility go hand in hand. Habann (19, drawing on Schweizer) explains the link that exists between utility and media products:

The granting of utility [...] is ensured by the elements of the media product, i.e., its immaterial content and its material carrier and transmission technology, which are interdependently interlocked. Schweizer states that more precisely by dividing the content up into a 'core', i.e., the message, and the 'inner form', i.e., the style of the

---

[1] This is based, among others, on Rautenberg (82-86).

presentation. The style is a specific design variable that features a utility component with goods with an aesthetic product dimension.

Thus, though the central semantic component of 'innovation' is the feature of being new, i.e., of not having been seen, heard, or experienced before, it is important to be aware that in the economic discourse, a second, equally important and constitutive feature of innovations lies in the actual usage of these innovations.[2] Indeed, Habann points out that "[o]nly the usage of an invention (something new, different from previous inventions, C.B.) in the sphere of the economy makes it an innovation in the economics and management context" (15). In conclusion, an innovation is something *new* and, because it is useful, is *actually used* in the economic sphere.

Building on Schweizer's insights into the utility component of a media product, I will now explain the specific aspects of content innovation in the book industry, and more particularly in the case of fiction books. In recent years, digitization has triggered a fair amount of game-changing innovations in the book industry. These innovations have appeared not only in the area of production (e.g., desktop publishing, content management) and distribution (e.g., online bookshops), but also in the shape of the products themselves, by affecting the material 'carrier' of the content (ebooks vs. printed books). Using Schweizer's concepts, I will focus on yet another kind of innovation that the digitization of books has triggered: *content* innovation, i.e., innovation with regards to the story, or 'core' message of the book on the one hand, and the narration, or 'inner form,' of the product on the other hand, which is especially important in the case of fiction books.

Content innovation can thus be seen as a process that provides new and useful features to the story[3] ('core,' or message) and its narration ('inner form').

---

2   "A central consequence of the numerous debates about the phenomenon of the innovation is the semantic plurality of what can be conceived as an innovation. [...] Notwithstanding the plurality of existing definitions of 'innovation' as well as of the perspectives taken for defining it, there are two criteria that occur explicitly or implicitly in all definitions: the criterion of being new and the criterion of the economic use of this novelty" (Polster 50-51).

3   From a narratological viewpoint, "story [...] has been defined as a mental image formed by four types of constituents: (1) a spatial constituent consisting of a world (the setting) populated by individuated existents (characters and objects);

WHO ARE THE TRADITIONAL AGENTS OF BOOK CONTENT INNOVATION?

A book as an economic good is the output of a series of processes that typically ends in a bookstore, where the customer/reader buys the product. If this book is or is considered new or original with regard to its 'core' and/or its 'inner form,' the following questions arise: How exactly did the new or original features come about, and at what stage of the book value chain did they appear? There are a number of possible entities within the traditional value chain of the book industry that could be involved in content innovation, and they are all linked to one another.

The specific chain links of the book industry value chain are often mapped onto the more abstract 'value steps' of media industries in general. For example, in one model, the chain links of the book industry value chain can be seen as consisting of the following three basic steps: creation, bundling, and distribution (cf. Schumann/Hess 11-12; 53-54). The entities involved in these steps of the book industry are: the authors (involved in the creation step); the editorial and production departments of publishing houses (involved in the bundling step); the marketing and distribution departments of publishing houses as well as the printing houses, logistics companies, and retailers (involved in the distribution step).

Against this backdrop, the traditional agents of book content production and dissemination, and thus also of potential content innovation, consist of a) people that create content; b) people that bundle this content, i.e., people who process it editorially (including filtering and refining) and manage its production; and c) people that distribute this content, not least by communicating its utility and hence propagating its actual use. These people are respectively the authors, the individuals working in the editorial, production and marketing departments of publishing houses, and the indivi-

---

(2) a temporal constituent, by which this world undergoes significant changes caused by non-habitual events; (3) a mental constituent, specifying that the events must involve intelligent agents who have a mental life and react emotionally to the states of the world (or to the mental states of other agents); (4) a formal and pragmatic constituent, advocating closure and a meaningful message" (Ryan, paragraph 22).

duals working in downstream book marketing, for example as booksellers in book stores (who complete the physical distribution, or propagation, of the content). Within this value chain, publishing houses and booksellers serve as the gatekeepers between authors and readers (I will not be tackling the case of book wholesalers here). In addition to these gatekeepers situated in the value chain, there are other gatekeeping entities outside it: the media (which provides reviews), institutions of literary education and literary criticism, etc.; these entities also contribute to the propagation of content innovation and are interesting topics for future research.

Among the entities mentioned, publishing houses play a particularly significant role within the book chain since they are the institutions that turn cultural goods into economic goods. This means that especially decisions taken in publishing houses are influenced by economic considerations. Indeed, the primary goal of a publishing house is to find enough customers for a book so as to cover its production costs (from the author's royalties to the book's printing, transport, and dissemination), and to satisfy the profit goals of the company's owners, be they families or shareholders (in the case of a public company). Otherwise the survival of the company cannot be guaranteed.

Typically, manuscripts are sent in by an author or his or her agent. The publishing house can, however, also commission a specific author to write a book, basing this request on prior market research carried out on the procurement market (authors) and/or the sales market (readers). On this level of observation we can record: Whether the manuscript is sent in or commissioned by the publishing house, the authors' interests and aspirations (and issues of innovation and originality in general) play only a marginal role in the publishing house's decision-making processes.

AUTHORS & GATEKEEPERS

The traditional model of the book industry suggests that the flow of content through the value chain is initiated by an author who provides native content, which is accepted and then processed and handled in the subsequent steps. However, this traditional model appears to be an over-simplification of what actually happens, since it provides only one quintessential path for the flow of content. Indeed, content has always also flowed along a number of bypasses, shortcuts and atypical paths that do not correspond to the vision of unidirectional flow provided by the traditional model.

In addition, this model is based on a romantic conceptualization of the author as an original genius who primarily considers writing as a means of self-expression (and to communicate ideas). In contrast to this model, I argue that many authors primarily set out to enhance their probability of economic success, and therefore, that the content they produce is (at least also) geared towards the readers' expectations. Indeed, the downstream value steps seem to explicitly encourage authors to meet these expectations.

Consequently, if an author wants his or her texts to be published, he or she is forced to rely on the other players of the book industry—players of a market-driven game that is based primarily on economic considerations. Publishers and booksellers as the main gatekeepers of the book industry are the ones who decide on the assumed attractiveness of an author's manuscript, thereby opening or closing the doors to a broad readership. The primary gatekeepers in the value chain are thus continuously balancing between the artistic, expressive and communicative freedom of authors on the one hand, and market demands on the other—with an inevitable bias towards the latter. This reality of the institutions in the book industry might be considered as negative to some; however, publishing houses seem to also contribute to content innovation processes in an explicitly positive way. I will address these contributions in detail in the following section.

OCCASIONALLY MORE THAN JUST GATEKEEPERS: PUBLISHING HOUSES AND THEIR EDITORIAL DEPARTMENTS

A fundamental requirement for the propagation of content innovation is that books with innovative—or more precisely, at that stage: inventive—content get published. Indeed, the decision of whether or not to publish a manuscript lies in the hands of the publishing houses, which fulfill a central gatekeeping function, as we have seen. In terms of content innovation, publishers need to be willing to publish content that is innovative. Certain types of publishers, such as the German publisher Kurt Wolff, do indeed show proactive support of innovative/inventive content created by authors, even if it does not directly match expectations. Indeed, he once pointed out that "[e]ither you publish books, which you think people should read, or books, which you think people would like to read" (14). Kurt Wolff considers himself as a publisher of the former kind: a publisher who publishes books people *should* read.[4]

It is important to note here that, beyond controlling the physical production process etc., publishing houses *can* indeed influence the content of books, they are not unescapably dependent on the initial qualities of a manuscript. However, the role of editorial departments in publishing houses in general has been gradually shrinking. Editorial departments no longer get as involved in the content production and refinement of a text; rather, they increasingly tend to give only a market-driven thumbs-up or thumbs-down. There is, however, scattered evidence that editors still play an important role in content innovation processes, beyond just deciding on the publication. To illustrate this point, I will look into the perspectives of literary critics and scholars, who judge content innovation using primarily philological criteria, on the subject of Raymond Carver, the famous American writer, and his editor. This will provide interesting insights into an editor's influence on content innovation. I will also briefly mention ongoing research into Herta Müller, the Romanian-German literature Nobel laureate, and her editor. Moreover, I will present a more general academic account that deals with the role of editors in the literary process.

Raymond Carver

Raymond Carver's editor, Gordon Lish, always claimed to have had a decisive role in the success of Carver's *What We Talk About When We Talk About Love*. This claim has been under scrutiny since the publication of the unedited version of Carver's 17 stories under the title *Beginners Uncut*. Indeed, the German literary critic and journalist Paul Ingendaay compared the unedited version of the text to the edited version. This is his conclusion:

In some stories, Lish axed 40 percent, in two cases even four fifths, of the original. He changed the plot, simplified the vocabulary, shortened the dialogues, eliminated reflections, digressions and integrated stories; three quarters of the stories got a new

---

4   Such a posture can of course only be a guideline, never a strict principle—after all, Kurt Wolff was himself an entrepreneur who had to sell books in order to keep his company in business.

ending created by him. His homogenisation work is a masterpiece. [...] As a minimalist, he [Carver, C.B.] acquired worldwide fame; at the same time he was much softer in truth and wrote texts bordering on sentimentality [...]. (Ingendaay)

On the whole, this view was endorsed by the scholar of literary studies Enrico Monti:

All things considered, Lish's editorial strategy comes across as a mix of sheer perception of Carver's talent and crafty understanding of what groundbreaking, innovative [!, C.B.] fiction should be at that time. Lish was undeniably a major (and mostly beneficial) influence in Carver's writing [...]. And indeed his influence on Carver's prose, through fifteen years of exchanging and editing manuscripts, may well go beyond the traces that are left for us to examine and speculate on. (Monti 70)

Herta Müller

One of my Mainz colleagues is currently researching the unique specimens of Literature Noble Prize winner Herta Müller (and her publishing house at the time, Rotbuch) located in the Mainz Publishers' Archive. His ongoing research suggests that, similar to the case of Raymond Carver, the characteristic laconic style of Herta Müller is to a considerable degree the result of extensive discussions with her editor, Gabriele Tietze. The case of Raymond Carver and that of Herta Müller both show that the editors have not only just opened the door for the authors' way of expressing themselves (and their ideas), but that the intervention of the editors made the texts more 'innovative' and 'original.'

An Academic Account

Ute Schneider has presented one of the few comprehensive academic accounts of the history and role of the editor in literary publishing houses, in her book *Der unsichtbare Zweite*. In her introduction, she writes:

There are only very few academic accounts of the history of the 'editor' profession as well as of the editorial department as an institution in the [...] literary publishing house [...]. This is especially hard to understand, since it can be assumed that editors have a decisive influence on the writing process of an author, on the development of literature and on the general literary judgment. (9)

The assumption in the second part of the quote, that editors strongly influence the content of books, supports the observations made about Raymond Carver and Herta Müller and their editors. This assumption is actually generalized later on in the book as follows: "[T]he role of the editor is not limited to the process of evaluating a manuscript with regard to its printability; its role is essentially more complex" (29). The significance of the editor is again supported by Ute Schneider when she quotes a generalizing view from a prominent editor, J. Hellmut Freund, who argues "that the programs [of publishing houses, C.B.] resemble each other more and more. The identity of the publishing house must be shaped, literature must be 'made'" (244). This statement substantiates the idea that literature (and, hence also more specifically, content innovation) is an output parameter that cannot only be influenced by the author as the originator, but also to a significant degree by the editorial departments of publishing houses.

THE EVOLVING VALUE NETWORK OF THE BOOK INDUSTRY—SHORTCUTS, BYPASSES AND NEW PLAYERS

As exposed earlier, the traditional value chain of the book industry consists of the author, the publishing house, the wholesaler, and finally the bookseller. It has been mentioned that—as natural and undisputable as it might look—this view is perceived as a rather recent economics and management one. Given the cultural studies approach taken in this volume, it is interesting to note that a very similar model has been used for quite a while in book studies, more specifically in book history. This model was actually outlined long before economists started talking about value chains. Indeed, Robert Darnton proposed the "communication circuit (of the book)" (68) decades ago, based on an explicitly non-economic culture-centered perspective. However, the nodes of his graph are basically the same as the ones we know from media economics. There are only a few differences between Darnton's model and the media economics view: Darnton did not differentiate between book wholesalers and book retailers, and gave the service providers of publishers, such as printers and shippers, a role of their own. His model, which used rather generic names for its various steps, was abstract enough to fit more or less all book industries, or at the very least, those in developed countries. Robert Darnton went even further in arguing, that "[w]ith minor adjustments, it should apply to all periods in the history of the printed book" (67). This bold statement shows just how much and how unpredictably the current developments have changed the book industry: After only a few decades, Darnton's all-encompassing model can no longer be applied to the industry, at least not to evolving parts of it. And there is one more major difference to models in media economics: Using a humanities-based approach, which focused on acts of communication rather than on the circulation of economic goods, Darnton considered that the book follows a circuit (rather than a chain, as in media economics), where the two ends, author and reader, are connected. He underpins this idea in the following observation: "The reader completes the circuit, because he influences the author both before and after the act of composition. Authors are readers themselves. […] So the circuit runs full cycle" (67).

In the wake of the progressing digitization of the book business and, since around 2007, of the book itself, the traditional value chain (or communication circuit) has been undergoing a phase of rapid transition. Among other things, the transition has contributed to creating a number of shortcuts and bypasses that undermine the traditional value chain. The most radical of these shortcuts allows authors to directly access their readers, with no publisher, or trade stage, being involved. This is the case of Wikipedia, for instance. In Janello's discussion of this transition, he suggests replacing the idea of the book value chain with the notion of a book value *network*, in which there are not only shortcuts and bypasses (as compared to the 'traditional' situation), but also players new to the industry, such as software/ hardware companies (e.g., Apple) or search engine companies (e.g., Google), can be included.

NEW REALITIES FOR THE PROPAGATION OF INNOVATION

Against the backdrop of digital developments in the book industry, it is important to ask how the transformation of the value chain into a value network has influenced content innovation processes. In order to shed light on this particular consequence of the 'digital turn,' I will, in this section, briefly examine the inner workings of digital self-publishing and online bookstores.

I will begin by focusing on the subject of self-publishing, and more specifically, by contrasting two marked cases of content flow between an author and a reader: In the case of traditional publishing, the textual outcomes are the result of the traditional value chain, i.e., which includes a publishing house; in the case of self-publishing, the textual outcomes are the result of a path through the evolving book value network, where no publishing house is involved.

In the examples for the first case, the following set of books were not only produced within the traditional value chain; they were also prominently featured, namely by being chosen to be on the shortlist of the German Book Prize 2011, which consisted of six books. Here are excerpts from the official blurbs of these books:

- "In a village in Eastern Frisia, cows graze on the meadows; behind the thuja hedges of the developing area, flowers bloom; in the driveways, new cars shine. Daniel Kupfer was born here in the mid-seventies. A cagey boy [...]" (Jan Brandt, *Gegen die Welt*)
- "In the summer of 1964, young Moritz Schoppe spent 10 distressed weeks in the small Upper Franconian town of Wunsiedel—his engagement with the yearly Luisenburg pageant had turned into a fiasco. [...]" (Michael Buselmeier, *Wunsiedel*)
- "Big, yellow, and relaxed, a lion lies in the study of the philosopher Blumenberg one night. His limbs are stretched out on the carpet, his eyes on the man of the house. With some effort, Blumberg is able to maintain his demeanor. [...]" (Sibylle Lewitscharoff, *Blumenberg*)

For the case of self-publishing, I will focus on a set of books (in the sense of book-like digital files) that reached the reader by bypassing a value creation step formerly thought to be constitutive (the publisher), namely by using Bookrix (www.bookrix.de), a German self-publishing platform. These books were featured by the platform users as three of the ten best-ranked books on the platform on May 15th, 2012. Here are excerpts of the book descriptions found on the platform, as well as the keywords attributed to them by their authors:

- "Christiy Piersen is a student with a side job as a waitress. One night, against her will, she gets kissed, abducted, [...]"

Keywords: vampires, love, and hot bottoms ("pauline," *Vampire sind auch nur Männer*)
- "Cat is a vampire hunter with heart and soul. She does not waste time on her enemies. But when they abduct her, the tide turns. [...]"
Keywords: vampires, love, fate, eroticism (Vivian Angelique, *Gegen das Schicksal*)
- "Alley Adlers' has a life with all the fixings: a move to another place, a gay best friend, various conflicts, a whole lot of vampires and of course a heart-breaking love story. [...]"
Keywords: vampires, love, humor, romance (Liz Ehrlich, *Midnight Serenade*)

It is important to know that at the time I looked over Bookrix for this article, in June 2012, four of the twenty best-selling books for adolescents in Germany according to the Spiegel Bestseller List of May 19th, 2012 ("Bestseller" 34) were about vampires (*Die Welt von Bella und Edward* by Stephenie Meyer, *Ungezähmt* by P.C. & Kristin Cast) or similar creatures (*The Riding Hood, Beastly*).

In spite of the fact that online bookstores are perceived as the most serious immediate threat to the book industry by many traditional players in the field (especially booksellers), these online bookstores in themselves are not manifestations of a transformation of the book business.[5] Indeed, structurally, they are just a new type of bookstore, namely one without physical outlets and with a web-based ordering process. However, online bookstores still have a huge effect on the book industry and, at least potentially, also on innovation within the book industry.

Booksellers are gatekeepers that have an influence on the propagation of innovation. Indeed, they compose specific assortments of books, decide how to present their books and, of course, they discuss books with customers, either recommending them or dissuading customers from buying or reading them. Ideally, and typically in the case of independent bookstores, the booksellers' assortment and presentation decisions as well as their inter-

---

5 Notwithstanding, some of, e.g., Amazon's more recent additional business activities go far beyond online bookselling and have of course huge transformational potential.

actions with customers are based on their familiarity with customers' preferences, a broad knowledge of the books on offer and their contents, as well as general book 'connoisseurship' and taste. Many online bookstores, and Amazon (the most important online bookstore on many national markets) in particular, have created mechanisms that imitate the service of face-to-face recommendations, which is recognized as very important in the interactive communication between bookseller and customer.

The algorithms used to implement these services of 'virtual' recommendation are called 'recommender engines' (cf. Klahold). These algorithms either carry out what is called 'collaborative filtering,' i.e., they produce recommendations on the basis of users' past behaviors (views/clicks, ratings, previous purchases), or they carry out content-based filtering, which means they produce recommendations based on the features of these products, i.e., the books' genre, subject area, publisher, author, etc. In the case of collaborative filtering, the recommender engine will suggest books that other individuals with a similar 'profile' (i.e., primarily the interaction history) have looked for, have previously bought and/or have positively rated. In the case of content-based filtering, the recommender engine will suggest books that are similar to those the customer has previously bought and liked or showed interest in. This similarity can be based on the author, the subject area, or other factors. When both content-based filtering and collaborative filtering approaches are combined, this is called 'hybrid filtering'; this kind of filtering brings together customer-oriented considerations and product-oriented considerations.

Many customers find these recommendations helpful, sometimes even frighteningly accurate. If customers convert these algorithm-based recommendations into a purchase, it is probable that they will continue to buy books that they and/or other 'similar' users have been exposed to, and/or that they will buy books that are similar to books they have purchased or showed interest in earlier.[6]

---

6 However, it would be interesting to know if the concrete algorithms used by online bookshops are in fact uniquely based on the past behavior of individuals or groups of individuals, and on the products' features. Given the economic interest of the operators of these online bookstores, it is possible that the recommendations are also influenced by factors such as the availability of a book, the number of copies in stock, the expected margin obtained when selling it (based on

Unsurprisingly, this system of 'guiding' people in their book purchases has stimulated severe criticism, and 'recommender engines' have been considered as symptomatic of a more general problem. To be more precise, digital algorithmically-derived guidance that is based on the past behaviour and/or past judgements of an individual or a cluster of individuals is considered to be a threat to the emergence of non-mainstream thoughts, news, and judgements. The most prominent example of such an algorithm is PageRank, the core algorithm of Google's search engine, which ranks a search hit higher if a large number of other websites link to it. People such as Schirrmacher or Meckel point to the fact that such algorithms implement what is often called the 'Matthew principle.' This labelling refers to Matthew 25:29 in the New Testament: "For unto every one that hath shall be given, and he shall have abundance: but from him that hath not shall be taken away even that which he hath" (KJV), and is meant to express that such algorithms reinforce past developments rather than giving chances to new and potentially original ideas and developments, which are considered necessary for progress in open societies.

Online bookstores and self-publishing can be seen as the two most significant phenomena of the digitized book industry. Although online bookstores account for almost a quarter of book sales already and are on a steady upward trend, self-publishing as a much more radical manifestation of the evolving value network is only gaining major economic significance. That Amazon is also offering self-publishing opportunities to its customers will certainly help. Self-publishing has the potential of opening up financially viable publishing opportunities to an increased number of authors. And some of the resulting content might have been misjudged by editors before and indeed be original. However, the collection of texts presented earlier, which were published on one of the most popular self-publishing platforms in Germany, seems to indicate that unsupervised publication opportunities tend to reinforce trends in an obviously, and almost ridiculously, uniform

---

the business deal with the supplier/publisher), and so on. However, due to the lack of transparency of these algorithms as well as to their personalization, it is hard to gather evidence for an assumption such as this one. The dispute between publishers and Amazon in 2014 suggests strongly that there are business strategic parameters for Amazon's recommender engine.

way. The observations made earlier regarding online bookstores also seem to point in this direction: If customers rely only on the recommendation algorithms of this type of book retailing, they will end up with book recommendations that can be considered, in a slightly simplified manner, as being just 'more of the same.'

GENERAL SUCCESS FACTORS OF INNOVATION AND CONTENT INNOVATION

After having looked at the contributions of certain value steps (publishing houses, booksellers) in a particular industry (book industry), I will now relate this to general 'success factors' for content innovation and innovation in general. Such factors have been identified by preceding research.[7] The rationale behind looking at these factors is that I would like to verify if and to what extent the identified innovation contributions of the book value chain links are in line with more general findings.

First, I will look at which corporate factors are thought to foster innovations in the media industry in general. As a reminder, innovation is, as described earlier, something new and actually used in the economic sphere. Habann, in his book *Erfolgsfaktoren für Medieninnovationen*, identified in the literature the following key success factors for media innovations: the design of the product development process and the organisation of the entities involved. In addition, his own empirical research yielded two further key elements that contribute to successful content innovation. The first success factor he found was recipient interaction, the amount of interplay between a media company and its customers. The items Habann used in his survey to identify this success factor included the "integration [of recipeents, C.B.] into idea generation" and the "integration [of recipients, C.B.] into idea evaluation." The second success factor Habann identified was project manager control, the degree of decision-making power on the side of project managers. The items Habann used to identify this success factor included the "solving of organisational-administrative problems [by the pro-

---

[7] It is of course important to keep in mind that such more general factors might not do justice to every specific situation, development and/or context.

ject manager, C.B.]" and "leadership with empathy competencies." Indeed, organizational-administrative support, leadership and empathy are certainly characteristics that constitute a good editor, and lead to a productive author-editor relationship.

As far as the integration of the recipients is concerned, however, Habann's findings are not in line with what I have been arguing so far: Recipient ratings on Bookrix seem to have strongly supported mainstream trends and have apparently not fostered processes of innovation. This aspect could be an interesting topic for future research. Among other things, it would be worthwhile to ask whether this difference in results can be linked to the different structures and processes of the broadcast industries, on which Habann's study is mainly based.

In a second step, I will look beyond the media industries. Habann's findings concerning the success factors for innovation in the media industry are at least partly compatible with cross-industry findings, e.g., those of Govindarajan. Indeed, Govindarajan claims:

[F]or game-changing innovation it's the opposite [namely, there are no metrics as with incremental innovations, C.B.]. The strategy is fuzzy, and traditional metrics can't be applied early in the process, because that which is truly new has no frame of reference nor benchmark. So Stage-Gate models [i.e., models in which the next stage of operations only gets initiated if certain criteria are met, C.B.] can unintentionally kill potentially big ideas. The pursuit of game-changing innovation only works when the person who can say yes to big spending visibly sponsors and participates in the work and provides air cover to the work team. [...] It's not about metrics; it's about 'the educated gut.' Old models don't work. Autocratic decision-making fails to engage all of the critical stakeholders, while consensus sinks every decision to its lowest possible common denominator. It doesn't work without a passionate champion who can make decisions and engage the team to support those decisions. [...] Willingness to take risk and see value in absurdity. Albert Einstein once said, 'If at first an idea doesn't seem totally absurd there's no hope for it.' Innovators understand that you have no choice; you must take risks, often big ones, by moving toward the absurd, the 'seemingly' irrelevant, in order to create pre-emptive competitive advantage while competitors move in the 'obvious' direction.

Thus, an editor who is supportive of an author, who supports or fights for an author's project, who escorts it through the value steps of the publishing house and, last but not least, who actively participates in the work by editing it, is someone who is very much in line with Govindarajan's general points. In this respect, a good editor seems to share the characteristics of a general propagator of innovation. With respect to the work of Habann, the analogies are not quite as strong and explicit as with respect to the ones of Govindarajan.

A FEW LATERAL OBSERVATIONS: ANALOGIES AND DISTENSIONS

In this section, I will be looking at two phenomena from outside the book industry, phenomena, where intellectual property is also produced by more or less individual originators and assessed and refined by gatekeepers in a corresponding value chain. The first of these phenomena is Open Source Software; the second is web content made to order on demand by members of the crowd of web users (e.g., as organized by the US company with the telling name Demand Media). These phenomena are linked to certain paths through the evolving value network of the book industry by the fact that value steps of gate-keeping and quality assurance do not exist and issues of originality and innovation have been explicitly raised.

Open Source Software

Open Source Software is software developed in communities. It is not commercially traded; rather it is made available to users or downstream exploiters under predefined licencing agreements, typically without payment. To make this a feasible 'business model,' zero earnings must correspond to zero expenditures—which is achieved if the software developers come from outside the software industry or use their spare time to contribute to a distributed software development process, organized with the help of digital means of communication. This model is sometimes called the 'bazaar model' of software development, as opposed to the proprietary top-down model, which is often called the 'cathedral model' (cf. Brügge). Examples of software products developed along the lines of the bazaar model are Mozilla Thunderbird (a browser), Apache (a web server), or mySQL (a relational database management system). When the risks and limitations of Open Source Software are discussed, the possibility that this kind of software could drive traditional software companies out of business is raised. However, comparative research on the two fundamental ways of developing software and on their outcomes has yielded a different picture: "The community-based open source development process has proven itself primarily in the construction of [...] systems, 1. the function of which is known [...] (Cloning) or 2. that have [...] a design that can be deduced [...] from the source code [...] " (Brügge 171). That means "that the community-based bazaar development model [...] is very suitable for incremental improvements, whereas for extensive [...] new developments the classic proprietary approach ('cathedral model') seems to be suitable. Open source software [...] tends rather to imitation [...]" (171).

Thus, in terms of software development, it seems that the creation of original (and complex) software is typically brought about in contexts with top-down planning, controlling/'gatekeeping,' and project management. If this is not provided, the newly developed products are merely imitations or ameliorations of previously developed products. In this sense, Open Source Software is typically producing just 'more of the same' (albeit slightly improved 'more of the same'). This is a clear analogy to what had been said concerning the features of texts published on a self-publishing platform without quality control.

Demand Media
Demand Media is a US company that identifies potentially attractive topics, based on an evaluation of the search queries run by users on search portals. Attractiveness is equivalent to attention, and thus corresponds to advertisement potential. Many of the topics identified are linked to how-to questions. Following this identification and using a web-based process, Demand Media commissions freelance authors to write content that corresponds to the identified topics, i.e., content that is meant to satisfy the user needs, allegedly expressed by the query. Finally, it publishes these made-to-order texts on user-generated content platforms (in the case of video content, e.g., YouTube) and on its own websites (such as eHow), and generates revenues by selling advertising space next to this content. Demand Media "is the largest contributor to YouTube, uploading between 10,000 and 20,000 new videos per month, and gets about 1.5 million page views per day on YouTube" ("Demand Media"). With the niche Google query "how can I repair a hair dryer," the search result on priority position three is a content

chunk from eHow, a Demand Media site, that explains how to repair a hair dryer—with more or less relevant online adverts next to it.[8] In the case of Demand Media and other companies that follow the same model, the interest of the public is not just anticipated; rather, it is directly deduced from actual search queries. For this reason, the relevance of the content to the readers' queries is high, and surprises appear to be impossible 'by design.' Content created along this model cannot be original or innovative: Indeed, it corresponds to what readers expect—hopefully not less, but certainly not more. I would call this a distension of the concept, since with its outright made-to-order content production it goes beyond uncurated user generated content as in the case of the self-publishing portal.[9]

CONCLUSIONS AND DISCUSSION

In terms of innovation in the book sector, it seems as if the traditional institutionalized value creating steps have in fact had a verifiable impact on bringing about new, original content. In cases where the content originators' desire to create something new and original is not supported by the bundling and distribution institutions (since they no longer exist), and where it is systematically overridden by the anticipated demands of customers, content innovation will likely be hampered. Ways to make use of the potential of these institutions also in the evolving value network of the book industry will have to be and are being developed. Observations in the software and web publication sectors support the view that an unfiltered addressing of recipients by originators is not the best way to bring about inno-

---

8 A communication approach based on a rather narrow view of users' interests is, however, not automatically one that bypasses editorial departments, as the following example shows: with *Chip*, a German computer magazine, online editors have monitors hanging from the ceiling that display in real time the traffic flow on their website and search queries on their site (as well as on Google). This is to encourage website journalists to orient their online posts to the interests of their readers.

9 There are indications, though, that the feed-back generated by e-reading devices on how the reader has traversed content is used in instructions for authors by cloud e-reading platforms.

vation in media and IT; rather, it seems to hinder innovation by homogenizing products.

However, several factors can put this observation into perspective. Indeed, in an era of increasing egalitarianism with regard to the question of who is or is not entitled to expressing him- or herself publicly, new channels that allow people to disseminate their literary works are not in themselves a 'bad' thing just because they go off outside the traditional book value chain. Indeed, the book value chain has its own limitations: Looking back on the innovation 'merits' of the book industry in its traditional setup, the decisions (and interventions) of traditional gatekeepers sometimes turned out to be (editorial, assortment or recommendation-oriented) misjudgments afterwards, especially *sub specie aeternitatis* as it were. Indeed, books evaluated and presented as new and original are not always necessarily perceived as such (and the other way round). Moreover, the editorial departments of publishing houses sometimes even try to monetize identified trends by intentionally coming out with often overtly unoriginal 'me-too'-products.

In contrast, processes under the label of open innovation, where stakeholders of a future product get involved in a dialogic development process, could constitute a different, supervised form of crowd participation. This might possibly expand the possibilities for content innovation rather than narrow them down. New types of products, especially enhanced ebooks, might also trigger a reappraisal of the situation in the book industry. As opposed to a movie, a typical book can easily be made available to readers by bypassing institutions such as publishing houses (and booksellers), since advance financing is not essential in this process and there is usually no need to manage teams. This is particularly true for most of today's digital books, the ebooks that contain only text and possibly images. However, the interactivity and multimediality of enhanced ebooks, ebooks that, for instance, contain videos, audios, or gaming elements, add such complexity to the products and the processes needed to create them that a 'producer architecture' might be required to finalize their creation. The 'producer architecture' is a management and production infrastructure that transcends what is available to a single originator. It would in this context be composed of one or more originators and a team of people with various capabilities, managed and pre-financed by someone that could be called an enhanced ebook producer. This would not least correspond to the 'cathedral model' of development, which—as I demonstrated by contrasting it to the Open Source Software development process—is more likely to lead to successful innovation.

WORKS CITED

Brügge, Bernd, Dietmar Harhoff, Arnold Picot, Oliver Creighton, Marina Fiedler, Joachim Henkel. *Open Source Software: Eine ökonomische und technische Analyse.* Heidelberg: Springer, 2004. Print.

"Bestseller/Der Spiegel: Jugendbücher." *Buchreport Express* 18 (2012): 34. Print.

Darnton, Robert. "What is the History of Books?" *Daedalus* 111.3 (1982): 65-83. Print.

Davis, Fred D. "Perceived Usefulness, Perceived Ease of Use, and User Acceptance of Information Technology." *MIS Quarterly* 13.2 (1989): 319-40. Print.

"Demand Media." *YouTube.com.* N.pag., n.d. Web.

Govindarajan, Vijay. "Innovation's Nine Critical Success Factors." *HBR Blog Network.* N.pag., 5 July 2011. Web.

Habann, Frank. *Erfolgsfaktoren von Medieninnovationen: Eine kausalanalytische empirische Untersuchung.* Baden-Baden: Nomos, 2010. Print.

Ingendaay, Paul. "Sein Lektor machte ihn zum Markenartikel." *Frankfurter Allgemeine Zeitung* 28 April 2012: 33. Print.

Janello, Christoph. *Wertschöpfung im digitalisierten Buchmarkt (Gabler Research: Markt- und Unternehmensentwicklung).* Wiesbaden: Gabler, 2010. Print.

Klahold, André. *Empfehlungssysteme: Recommender Systems—Grundlagen, Konzepte und Lösungen.* Wiesbaden: Gabler, 2009. Print.

Meckel, Miriam. *NEXT. Erinnerungen an eine Zukunft ohne uns.* Hamburg: Rowohlt, 2011. Print.

Monti, Enrico. "Il Miglior Fabbro? On Gordon Lish's Editing of Raymond Carver's What We Talk About When We Talk About Love." *The Carver Review* 1 (2007): 53-74. Print.

Polster, Tilo. *Innovation in Beratungsunternehmen: Eine managementorientierte Perspektive.* Wiesbaden: Gabler, 2012. Print.

Porter, Michael. *Wettbewerbsvorteile: Spitzenleistungen erreichen und behaupten.* Frankfurt/Main: Campus, 1986. Print.

Rautenberg, Ursula, ed. *Reclams Sachlexikon des Buches.* Stuttgart: Reclam, 2003. Print.

Ryan, Marie-Laure. "Narration in Various Media." *The Living Handbook of Narratology.* Ed. Peter Hühn et al. Hamburg: Hamburg UP. N.pag., n.d. Web.

Schirrmacher, Frank. *Payback. Warum wir im Informationszeitalter gezwungen sind zu tun, was wir nicht tun wollen, und wie wir die Kontrolle über unser Denken zurückgewinnen.* München: Blessing, 2009. Print.

Schlohmann, Knut. *Innovatorenorientierte Akzeptanzforschung bei innovativen Medientechnologien.* Wiesbaden: Gabler, 2012. Print.

Schneider, Ute. *Der unsichtbare Zweite: Die Berufsgeschichte des Lektors im literarischen Verlag.* Göttingen: Wallstein, 2005. Print.

Schumann, Matthias, and Thomas Hess. *Grundfragen der Medienwirtschaft.* 3rd ed. Berlin: Springer, 2006. Print.

Wolff, Kurt. "Vom Verlegen im Allgemeinen und von der Frage: Wie kommen Autoren und Verleger zusammen." *Autoren, Bücher, Abenteuer: Betrachtungen und Erinnerungen eines Verlegers.* Ed. Kurt Wolff. Berlin: Wagenbach, 1965. 13-25. Print.

Authorship, Agency, and Value

According to the emphatic notion of the author that has been prevalent ever since the 18th century, an author is conceived of as a more or less autonomous creator of 'his' or 'her' own works. Authorship has thus become a highly prestigious value in the literary field and can be almost directly converted into symbolic (and also, though less easily, into economic) capital (Bourdieu). Consequently, to this day, the literary scene is still viewed as being characterized by the dichotomy of the author as the original producer, on the one side, and the numerous reproducing and receiving agents such as editors, readers, critics and so on, on the other.

Although literary theory has regularly announced the death of the author (Barthes) ever since the 1960s, we still primarily conceive of literature as the product by a particular author. The author's name remains a crucial marketing tool in the commercialization of literature. Accordingly, anonymous works are difficult to shelve and classify in bookselling and library catalogues and tend to remain of second rank; double authorship is rare and evokes the question of who has authored what. Still, in some areas of literary production authors become of minor interest in favor of the genre or subject, for instance in the field of crime novels or in fan fiction. Interestingly, however, the author's fading from the spotlight then often ties in with a devaluation of such products as 'cheap literature' which, more often than not, has remained neglected by traditional literary criticism and has only recently been given scholarly attention.

Yet, this author-centered, binary model does not, of course, describe the actual conditions and practices of production and distribution of literature accurately, as there are, in fact, no clear-cut boundaries between production and distribution/reception. Rather, the boundaries are fluid as numerous agents in the literary field are involved in the production process of literature without being given the credit and enjoying the privilege of authorship. At the very same time, however, it seems that these very agents (who are not considered as 'authors' in the traditional sense), can use the emphatic concept of authorship in order to gain influence in the market and even secure a (text)productive participation. In this way, authorship becomes a function (in the sense of Foucault) and can potentially serve as a means of (self)positioning in the literary field, especially for those who, according to the traditional notion, would not be regarded as an author.

The question of who has 'created' Franz Kafka's 'oeuvre,' for instance, is thus not easily answered. Undoubtedly, Franz Kafka himself accounts for his body of work. But his friend Max Brod is certainly no less part of the product as he has administered Kafka's literary legacy, produced an edition and made crucial interventions and stylizations which, as one could well argue, created the Kafka-myth in the first place.

A similarly precarious alliance also exists between medieval authors and their modern editors, who, driven by their emphatic and somewhat anachronistic concept of authorship, used to make considerable changes in traditional texts in order to get closer to what they imagined to be the original—an original which, they thought, had been spoiled by medieval scribes through their textual intervention. This somewhat paradoxical instance once again both highlights the power of the emphatic notion of authorship and exemplifies the productive participation of an agent, who does not otherwise conceive of himself as an author.

The second part of this volume deals with such practices of productive participation. James L. W. West III focuses on a particularly insightful form of alliance between 'authors' and other agents, investigating the ways in which friends, editors, publishers, and heirs (among others) participate in the authorship of deceased authors and how, in the Bourdieuesque sense, they acquire symbolic capital through their participation. His analysis of the 'posthumous careers' of F. Scott Fitzgerald and William Styron indeed reveals that authorship is not necessarily linked to the actual author but can very well be produced and utilized in the literary marketplace by a range of highly influential people. West's own engagement in the case of Styron is certainly a remarkable aspect of his contribution: He is not only Styron's biographer but is simultaneously involved in the publication of Styron's works. Therefore, his contribution can be considered both a case study and a self-reflection on the production of authorship from the position of a participating agent.

Geoffrey Turnovsky's contribution deals with the early period of the emphatic author concept and further develops Engelsing's distinction between intensive (premodern) and extensive reading, which Engelsing describes as emerging around 1750. The development he outlines is characterized both by a shift from oral to visual reading and by a dematerialization of reading: Reading, in other words, turns into an internal process of seeing. In the second part of his contribution, then, Turnovsky takes on the metaphor 'touched by the author' and reads it as a compensation for this very process of dematerialization. By taking into account numerous fan letters which attest to the fact that readers have been 'touched by the author,' Turnovsky considers the 'being touched' as a highly active form of participation (despite of its passive construction) because readers use the 'touch' of the author to communicate their own reading as legitimate and to thus (potentially) impact on literary production itself.

The emphatic notion of the author and the associated concept of the autonomy of literature also played a significant role in post-war Germany. The case of Arno Schmidt, explored by Sabine Kyora, shows how a particularly distinct concept of autonomy can be utilized by an author in order to gain access to the literary field and to position himself within this very field. Arno Schmidt's alliances during the 1950s are noticeably motivated by economic reasons and secure him access to the market; based on Bourdieu, Kyora's analysis very convincingly shows how flexible Schmidt applies his autonomy concept in order to define his role within these very alliances, which, as Kyora's contribution demonstrates, were often decidedly precarious and at times even paradox. At the same time, there were also programmatic alliances (with other authors) which primarily served the positioning in the literary field and played a significant role in times of economic rivalry on the book market.

The final contribution of the section provides insights into premodern, medieval conditions of the production and distribution of texts. As Albrecht Hausmann illustrates, the absence of a functional differentiation between authors and recipients (primarily due to traditions of oral or handwritten communication) allowed a range of agents to participate more easily in the production of texts. In literary company, different members of the courtly society could become authors; the audience could effectively exert influence on the literary production during oral performances; finally, scribes could alter literature in the process of transmission. As the emphatic notion of the author is not yet developed and disseminated in Medieval Ages, the audience has a variety of options to participate, which, as one could argue, bears some resemblance to new forms of participation in Web 2.0 environments.

(Albrecht Hausmann)

Whose Intentions? The Posthumous Careers of F. Scott Fitzgerald and William Styron

JAMES L. W. WEST III

A good many students of literature have had a go at defining the concept of intention. For our purposes here, I'd like to start with a definition proffered by the 19th-century American journalist, short-story writer, and misanthrope Ambrose Bierce. This definition appeared in *The Devil's Dictionary*, a compendium of Bierce's efforts in the lexographic line that he published, in several successive editions, beginning in the 1870s. "Intention," according to Bierce, is "the mind's sense of the prevalence of one set of influences over another set." Further, intention is "an effect whose cause is the imminence, immediate or remote, of the performance of the act intended by the person incurring the intention." The language is approximately circular. Bierce, a thoroughgoing skeptic, appears to be saying that if fate should decree that things turn out as you hoped they would (more or less), then you can claim that this was your intention all along.

Bierce seems to have doubted that anyone could develop a satisfactory definition of intention, and probably he was right. Still, we must talk about the concept if we are to discuss what happens after an author dies and the posthumous reputation of that author begins to gather and solidify. Many varieties of intention can be found at this juncture, and they operate within several "precarious alliances." They include the intentions of the deceased author (so far as these can be known), of the author's heirs, of friends and enemies, allies and rivals, fellow authors, publishers, literary agents, biographers, bibliographers, book collectors, book dealers, librarians, and critics. The intentions in play include the desire to consolidate the author's copyrights, locate and assess unpublished writings, gather the literary remains into clothbound collections, develop a narrative of the author's career, form an estimate of the author's importance, give shape to the oeuvre, engender assessments by book reviewers of the author's achievement, and (not least) make money for the estate—which is to say, to do what almost any author wishes to accomplish in life: produce literary works that critics will praise and people will buy. None of this will happen by accident.

All of these elements fall within Pierre Bourdieu's definition of cultural capital—an elastic and capacious term. In "The Forms of Capital" (1986), Bourdieu defined cultural capital as "goods," both material and symbolic, that are thought to be desirable, even precious, by members of a particular social formation or "field." Bourdieusian taxonomy helps in analyzing the behavior of those who maneuver to manage an author's posthumous career. Cultural capital leads to economic and social capital. It generates *embodied* capital (for the author's heirs, most obviously); *objectified* capital (for libraries and book collectors); and *institutionalized* capital (for biographers, critics, editors, bibliographers, publishers, and literary agents). In this paper, I will identify and discuss these forms of intellectual capital.

We are talking here about 'keepers of the flame,' all of whom have their own intentions, and all of whom are probably convinced of the rectitude of their efforts. These acolytes must form an 'alliance' and agree upon a course of action for the author, who is now absent. Much depends upon the author's reputation at the time of death. Has the author, like Ralph Waldo Emerson or Walt Whitman or Mark Twain, become an *eminence grise*? Or has the author's name and reputation faded from view, as was the case with Herman Melville? Is the audience for the posthumous publications already in place, or must that audience be discovered and created—as, in an extreme case, was the situation with Emily Dickinson's poetry? Have the author's papers been placed in a library or other institution, or are they in private hands? Are they available for study or on restriction? Is there an established publisher with financial muscle who is keen to issue the literary remains and keep in print the earlier works? Is there a literary agency with records of the author's publications and financial career? Is this agency willing to continue handling the author? Do surviving family members know what rights have been sold and what rights retained? Does anyone know where the signed contracts are, not only for books but for subsidiary rights such as cinema, television, and stage versions?

Another important matter: Has a biographer been appointed? Alternately, has someone already published an authorized (or unauthorized) version of the life? Is a corrective biography needed? Did the author leave behind a compelling memoir—something as memorable as Theodore Dreiser's *Dawn* (1931) or Gertrude Stein's *The Autobiography of Alice B. Toklas* (1933) or Ernest Hemingway's *A Moveable Feast* (1964)? Memoirs of that kind are both a blessing and a curse: They reveal much about the life but are difficult for biographers to disagree with. Are there others—children, lovers, spouses, friends, amanuenses—who are poised to publish their own memoirs about the author? Can any of this be controlled?

The two authors I'll discuss here are both American novelists: F. Scott Fitzgerald, who flourished in the 1920s and 1930s and died in December 1940; and William Styron, whose best fiction was published from the 1950s to the 1970s, and who died in November 2006. Both of these writers began their careers with highly praised first novels: Fitzgerald with *This Side of Paradise* in 1920 and Styron with *Lie Down in Darkness* in 1951. Both authors published disappointing second novels: *The Beautiful and Damned* in 1922 for Fitzgerald and *Set This House on Fire* in 1960 for Styron. Both men were subject to negative criticism during their careers, Fitzgerald for wasting his talent on commercial short stories, and Styron for trespassing on the territory of racial and ethnic groups—African Americans in *The Confessions of Nat Turner* (1967) and the Jewish people in *Sophie's Choice* (1979).

The reputations of both writers were in limbo when they died. Fitzgerald was living in Hollywood where, after a stint on the payroll of Metro-Goldwyn-Mayer in 1937 and 1938, he was working as a script doctor and turning out short stories for *Esquire* magazine. He did have a new novel in progress, *The Last Tycoon*, which was published a year after his death in an edition prepared by his college friend Edmund Wilson. This unfinished narrative, which contains some brilliant writing, reawakened interest in Fitzgerald and was followed by a now-famous collection of autobiographical writings, also edited by Wilson, called *The Crack-Up*, published in 1945. These two books, plus a good biography of Fitzgerald by Arthur Mizener—*The Far Side of Paradise*, published in 1951—formed the foundation of his current reputation, which continues to grow today.

Styron published *Sophie's Choice* in 1979, then went through a period of severe depression in the mid-1980s from which he never fully recovered. He published a memoir of his breakdown called *Darkness Visible* in 1990 and produced a slim volume of three previously published short stories entitled *A Tidewater Morning* in 1992. After that he published no more fiction between hard covers, though he continued to produce opinion pieces, introductions, reviews, memoirs, and eulogies until 2002, when a recurrence of his depression, together with other ailments, silenced him. He too had a novel under way during his final period, a massive project called *The Way of the Warrior* which was to be a narrative of the Pacific War in its last stages. Excerpts from this novel were published over the years, but Styron was unable to pull his efforts together into a sustained narrative. Many hundreds of pages of holograph manuscript from *The Way of the Warrior* survive in his papers at Duke University. These drafts contain some excellent set pieces of writing but are finally formless and perhaps undeserving of publication—at least not for a long while.

No effort has been made so far to bring *The Way of the Warrior* into print. Instead Random House has published a collection of Styron's personal essays called *Havanas in Camelot* (2008) and a collection of his fictional narratives about the Marine Corps entitled *The Suicide Run* (2009). Both books contain writings that Styron put into print during his lifetime, together with previously unpublished items that were found among his papers after his death. I prepared the texts for both of these collections; I also edited an edition of the letters that Styron wrote to his father between 1943 and 1953. This collection, entitled *Letters to My Father*, was published by Louisiana State University Press in 2009. Styron's youngest daughter Alexandra has published a revealing memoir of him called *Reading My Father* (2011); and his widow, Rose Styron, has collaborated with a young scholar named Blake Gilpin to produce an edition of Styron's selected letters, published in December 2012. I have completed most of the work on a final volume of Styron's uncollected nonfiction to be called *My Generation*. I published my biography of Styron, called *William Styron: A Life*, in 1998—eight years before his death. This wasn't an authorized biography in the true sense, but I wrote it with Styron's cooperation and approval. Thus, at his death, there already existed a narrative of his life which subsequent editors, biographers, critics, and memoirists have been able to use for their own efforts.

For both of these authors, Fitzgerald and Styron, one sees an organized effort to collect Bourdieusian capital and put it into play by spending it, investing it, and selling it. Both authors left behind valuable assets—unpublished and uncollected writings, for example, and large collections of manuscripts and memorabilia. Both authors lived lives filled with events and controversies that make for good biography. Both authors left behind large archives of photographs and other images, saved in scrapbooks and boxes. In our visual age, these are essential to the posthumous fame of the author.

When Fitzgerald died unexpectedly at the age of forty-four, no thought (understandably) had been given to the posthumous publications. It took several years for biographers and editors to emerge and for critics to begin the work of assessing his oeuvre. I recently spent a lengthy period at Princeton University Library, where most of Fitzgerald's papers are kept, investigating this matter. I was not, however, working with *his* manuscripts and correspondence. Rather, I was examining the archives of his publisher, Charles Scribner's Sons, and the files of his literary agency, Harold Ober Associates, Inc. Neither the publisher nor the agent was prepared for what was to come. To judge from correspondence and other papers at Princeton, both Scribner's and Ober were caught flat-footed—not a surprise, given the fact that Fitzgerald's death at such an early age could not have been predicted. Neither the publisher nor the agent seems to have been certain that Fitzgerald would *have* a posthumous career, that he had written work that might endure, or that he had lived a life that might capture the interest of the literary public. Fitzgerald left only two heirs—his wife, Zelda Sayre, who was living alternately in her childhood home in Montgomery, Alabama, and in a mental institution in North Carolina; and his daughter, Frances, known as 'Scottie,' who was a teenager attending college. Neither was equipped to manage the cultural capital that Fitzgerald had left behind. Thus it fell to Fitzgerald's friends in the literary establishment, especially to Edmund Wilson and to the critic Malcolm Cowley, to encourage Scribner's and Ober to take action. Together with Maxwell Perkins and Harold Ober, Wilson and Cowley formed an initial 'precarious alliance' that would later grow to include many other players.

Wilson demonstrated Fitzgerald's appeal with *The Crack-Up*, which Scribner's had declined to publish, and which was brought out by the then-fledgling house of New Directions. When *The Crack-Up* sold well and was a great success with the reviewers, it became clear that Scribner's and Ober had miscalculated. Perhaps Fitzgerald's copyrights did have life and viability. Scribner's moved quickly to reprint his novels and short stories and, over the next thirty years, to bring out editions of letters, uncollected short fiction, and essays. This work continues today. For example, Scribner's published a well-received edition of Fitzgerald's personal essays called *A Short Autobiography* in 2011; the first printing of 12,000 copies sold out quickly, and Scribner's went back to press for a second impression. And Scribner's currently has in press a new edition of *The Beautiful and Damned*, with a new introduction and fresh historical notes and appendixes. Additional paperbacks are planned for future years.

An important category of cultural capital, not much remarked upon, is activity in the rare book and manuscript trade. Here we are talking about *objectified* capital, in Bourdieu's formulation. Collectors, dealers, and special collections departments at major libraries are often ahead of the game and anticipate which authors will be worth collecting. Activity by dealers and collectors will drive up the prices of these authors' manuscripts, personal papers, correspondence, first editions, and even fetish objects—a briefcase, for example, or a whiskey flask or a coin purse or an address book or a cane. This in turn adds to the aura surrounding a posthumous reputation. The presence of a significant collection at a major library often generates a large exhibition, an accompanying catalogue, a symposium, newspaper and internet publicity, and published proceedings. Dealers and curators understand that once an author has died, there will be no more holograph manuscripts, no more letters, and no more inscribed first editions. This is a simple enough insight, but it is not the sort of thing that literary scholars notice. The supply of such items of *objectified capital* is now closed; the market can begin to determine how much the manuscripts, letters, and artifacts are worth. This sounds cold-blooded but is in fact central to the development of the posthumous status of an author.

Some authors anticipate these developments and place their manuscripts and other papers on deposit at a particular library before they die. In the United States, an author can receive no tax deduction for such a donation if that author is living. This is a result of enormous tax deductions taken by politicians who gave their papers to libraries while they were still alive. Richard Nixon pulled the trick with his Vice Presidential papers in 1970 and 1971, angering some of his enemies in Congress and causing them to pass a law that closed the loophole, not only for politicians but for authors as well—indeed, for anyone who had been prominent in public life. American authors can therefore *sell* their papers to libraries while they are still living, but they must pay taxes on the money they receive. They can put their papers on deposit at a given library, and after they die their heirs can donate the papers permanently and reap the tax benefits. The heirs can also sell the papers outright (thereby incurring tax burdens) or can enter into what is known as a 'gift-purchase' agreement in which the papers are appraised and the library pays the estate roughly half of what they are worth. The heirs then donate the other half, take the tax write-off, and receive the money free of tax, often spread out over a period of years to lessen the spike in income. This has been a powerful method by which research libraries have built their archives of living or recently deceased authors. The collections thus formed are crucial in later years to biographers and literary critics, to scholars who want to edit collections of letters, and to editors who hope to discover previously unpublished work or who set out to establish the texts of the author's writings.

One of the most important factors in a posthumous career is the author's publisher. A publishing house deals with all three forms of Bourdieusian capital: *cultural, economic,* and *social*. Which publishing house holds the copyrights for the author's work? The ideal situation, of course, is for a single publisher—a strong one, with a long-term commitment to the author—to control everything. In these cases, the publisher can treat the work that has already appeared between hard covers as a body of property, a block of cultural capital that can be manipulated, marketed, added to, and managed over the long term. (In publishing circles this falls under the heading of 'milking the backlist.') A 'uniform edition' can be issued as a prelude to an eventual collected edition. The stronger titles will support the weaker ones; everything is kept in print and made available to readers, scholars, critics, and teachers. This simplifies immensely the tasks of the other members of the 'precarious alliance'—the surviving heirs, the acolytes, and the literary agency that handles the author's estate. All of these players can regard themselves as partners in the enterprise of building the author's reputation after death. Any publishing disagreements can be settled, quite literally, 'in-house.'

This situation came into play with Fitzgerald. He had only one book publisher during his lifetime, the highly regarded house of Charles Scribner's Sons. Fitzgerald's editor Maxwell Perkins was an influential person within the firm. Scribner's held the copyrights on Fitzgerald's four novels, on his four collections of short stories, and on a play called *The Vegetable* that had appeared in book form in 1923. Further, there was only one literary agency to deal with: Harold Ober Associates, Inc., still headed in 1940 by its founder, Harold Ober. Both Perkins and Ober were Fitzgerald's personal friends. Perkins had discovered him and shepherded him through his literary career; Ober had been his agent and had functioned as his banker, tax adviser, and bookkeeper. Ober had also been a substitute father to Fitzgerald's daughter, Scottie. These ties were extraordinarily tight, and they have endured. Scribner's remains Fitzgerald's publisher today (though Scribner's is now part of the publishing empire of Simon and Schuster), and Harold Ober Associates continues to function as Fitzgerald's agency. The literary rights are the property of descendants—at the moment, of three surviving grandchildren. This alliance of publisher, agent, and heirs has been extraordinarily successful in managing Fitzgerald's posthumous reputation, keeping his works in print, selling subsidiary rights (cinema, opera, television, translation, paperback, e-book, audiobook), and keeping Fitzgerald in the public eye.

Something similar is happening with Styron. As I have said, he published his first novel, *Lie Down in Darkness*, in 1951. The publisher was Bobbs-Merrill, a midwestern firm that was attempting to break into the trade fiction market, after being known for many years as a textbook and religious publisher. Styron moved to Random House from Bobbs-Merrill in 1955, following his editor and mentor Hiram Haydn. When Haydn left Random House for Atheneum a few years later, Styron stayed at Random House. His new editor there was his close friend Robert Loomis, with whom he had attended Duke University in the 1940s. In 1993, while Styron was alive and still writing, Random House made a savvy move: They purchased the rights to *Lie Down in Darkness* from Bobbs-Merrill, thus placing all of Styron's copyrights under a single roof. Bobbs-Merrill had failed to make a show in trade fiction; the house eventually went out of business, and the imprint no longer survives. *Lie Down in Darkness* was rescued before the ship went down, and the book is now the property of Random House. This has been a great advantage to Styron's heirs, who today (like Fitzgerald's heirs) deal with only one publisher—a strong and well-established one.

For Styron, the matter of the literary agency was more complicated. During his career he was represented by at least three different American agencies. His British and translation rights were managed from the late 1960s forward by another agency, the London firm of Hope Leresche and Steele, which changed its name several times but continued to market his work abroad until after his death. The last U.S. agent to handle Styron's writings was Don Congdon, but because Styron published so little during his final years, his contacts with this agent had lapsed. After Styron's death his heirs turned to the agent Michael Carlisle at InkWell Management. Carlisle's parents had been good friends of the Styrons, and Michael had been a childhood playmate of the Styron children. He could be trusted to manage the author's posthumous literary affairs in such a way as to generate emoluments but also to secure and lock down cultural capital. Today an alliance (not at all precarious) is in place for Styron. It consists of Random House, from which Robert Loomis has retired but at which he still functions as an influential advisor; Michael Carlisle, who is managing not only U.S. rights but also foreign rights; and a literary trust composed of the author's widow, his children, and their attorney. This alliance has set Styron's literary affairs in order and has begun the process of cementing his place in the cultural marketplace.

To see how important the issue of a single publisher, a single literary agency, and a well-organized group of heirs can be, one need only look at the posthumous careers of authors for whom these conditions did *not* apply. A good example among 20th-century American novelists is Dreiser. He did not trust publishers, enjoyed quarrelling with them, and switched from house to house during his most productive years. His novels and other clothbound books were published in succession by eight firms: Doubleday, Page and Co.; Harper and Brothers; The Century Company; John Lane Company; Boni and Liveright; Horace Liveright; Simon and Schuster; and back to Doubleday. When he died his copyrights were scattered amongst these firms, and it was impossible to develop a strategy which might bring the titles together to be managed as a body of cultural capital. Each publishing house continued to handle a few Dreiser titles; Dreiser's widow, Helen Dreiser, possessed the exclusive rights only to *Sister Carrie*, rights which her husband had purchased from Doubleday, Page, and Co. in 1907. Otherwise she received only a trickle of royalties from the reprints and, later, the paperbacks issued by other houses. Many of Dreiser's lesser works fell out of print.

Dreiser did not trust literary agents and nearly always negotiated on his own behalf. At his death there was no literary agency which was managing his career. No one, including Helen, was entirely sure what he had published, when or where it had appeared, and who owned what rights. Helen was the sole heir (Dreiser fathered no children), but she complicated matters at her death by appointing a young man whom she liked to manage Dreiser's literary estate. This man was not a publisher or agent; he had some knowledge of journalism but was primarily employed by the Jehovah's Witnesses, a religious group. He was not equipped to bring together the various publishers and copyrights and exploit them for maximum benefit to Dreiser. Perhaps as a consequence, Dreiser's reputation languished for many years after his death and even today has not solidified. Helen's friend passed away a few years ago. The copyrights are now under the control of the University of Pennsylvania, where Dreiser's papers are kept. Certainly this is a good development, but a university is not a literary agency.

These same problems arise in the posthumous careers of Edith Wharton, who switched publishers in mid-career, and of Willa Cather, who did the same. During his most productive years, Sherwood Anderson was not allied with strong publishers or literary agencies; this might help to explain why his reputation has faded. The same is true for Sinclair Lewis, who jumped from publisher to publisher toward the end of his life. An exception (and the only poet who comes to mind) is Robert Frost, who allied himself with Henry Holt early on and stayed there, to the great benefit of his posthumous reputation. Having a single publisher is particularly important for poets, since various editions of their work—selected editions, collected editions, editions of original groupings of the poems, editions of new groupings, gift editions, illustrated editions—can be published and republished so that the poems are recycled again and again for income and visibility, and are always available to teachers and readers.

Finally it is a great advantage, for the maintenance of a posthumous literary reputation, to have several disputes or disagreements in the air. These disagreements are a kind of *embodied* capital in the Bourdieusian taxonomy. The issues might concern the author's work, or perhaps his or her personality or artistic standards. Ideally the arguments for the two sides should be of about equal weight, so that the disagreements will never go away. I am put in mind of a passage in James Boswell's *Journal of a Tour to the Hebrides* (1785). Boswell reports a remark by Doctor Johnson as follows: "Fame is a shuttlecock. If it be struck only at one end of the room, it will soon fall to the ground." In the context of this discussion, I take these words from The Great Cham to mean that if everyone is agreed upon the importance of an author's work, and if everyone interprets that author's life in more or less the same way, then there will be little to talk, teach, write, debate, and publish about. It is much better to have disputes. For Fitzgerald, the abiding question is whether he was only a talented writer who wasted his gifts on commercial magazine fiction, a man who could not organize his personal life sufficiently well to get down on paper the seven or eight novels that he should have left us, instead of the 160-odd stories that he published, for a great deal of money (over three million dollars, in today's currency), in such venues as the *Saturday Evening Post, Redbook, Woman's Home Companion,* and *Liberty*—all high-paying 'slicks,' so-called because they were printed on glossy, coated paper. The opposite argument is that Fitzgerald was a serious artist who walked the tightrope between commercial success and literary respectability with considerable success. Litigants on this side, among whom I count myself, believe that Fitzgerald juggled art and commerce about as well as any author of his generation. My side has good arguments, but the other side does too, including perhaps a dozen execrable stories that Fitzgerald published only for money, and, perhaps as important, a great many mediocre stories, with stock characters and trick plots, which usually contain a few passages of brilliant description or clever dialogue but little else. The composition of these stories absorbed an inordinate amount of Fitzgerald's energy. Those of us in the Fitzgerald field (who are part of the current 'precarious alliance' that works on his behalf) do not want to resolve this matter. It touches on larger questions. Should one write, or create, only for a coterie; or should one aim for a large audience, artistic celebrity, and money? Is there a middle ground? Does one want to be a Hunger Artist, as in the Kafka story, if the onlookers will eventually become bored and drift away?

    For William Styron, the issues not subject to easy resolution have to do with artistic license and intellectual territory. In 1967, Styron published a controversial novel about a slave rebellion. Its title was *The Confessions of Nat Turner*. The novel was narrated in Nat's voice, as imagined by Styron. Was Styron justified, as a white Southerner, in merging his voice with that of a rebel slave who had led a bloody rebellion in Southampton County, Virginia, in 1831? In trying to blend his consciousness with Nat's on the printed page, did Styron appropriate an African American folk hero for his own purposes, emasculating him and making him ambivalent about his mission? Conversely, did Styron follow the road of high art in this novel, insisting upon the writer's duty to take and transform the past in order to comprehend the present? Was he not justified (and courageous) in blending his consciousness with Nat's? The same kinds of questions arise with *Sophie's Choice*, Styron's 1979 novel about a survivor of the death camps at Auschwitz. Sophie is Polish, not Jewish. By making her a gentile, did Styron universalize the Holocaust and deny that it was an evil aimed exclusively at the Jewish people? As an American with no experience of the death camps, was he even qualified to write about these events? Did he trespass on territory not his own, as with *Nat Turner*, or did he properly assert the writer's privilege of addressing the history of others? We will never settle these questions because the authors themselves could not settle them. Such questions are an important form of cultural capital.

What motivates the acolytes who do the work of consolidating the cultural capital of deceased authors? Some of their intentions are obvious. They want the author's work to endure and to compete successfully against the literary remains of other authors. Publishers and literary heirs want the work to be commercially viable; successful editions of letters, unfinished writings, and uncollected shorter works can stimulate anew the sales of old work. For the scholar, there is something different at stake—*institutional* capital. Bibliography, biography, and editing are not among the most glamorous fields in the academy, at least in the United States, but practitioners of these disciplines can acquire cultural cachet by being known as 'authorized biographers,' for example, or 'editors of the collected works.' They become players in the 'precarious alliances' of which we have been speaking, and they give intellectual respectability to the author's posthumous reputetion. Being part of such an alliance is helpful if one is dealing with academic administrators and with the multitudinous employees at every American college and university, who are charged with publicizing the institution and burnishing its image. It is the mission of these people to explain to the public, to the tuition-paying parents of students, and to wealthy donors just what it is that faculty members do when they are not in the classroom. Does their work translate into *prestige*—a most precious cultural commodity that all colleges and universities pursue avidly? If so, then will wealthy alumni give money to support such work? Recognition of this kind for faculty members, often coming through national print and broadcast media, or even in local press releases or articles in the alumni magazine, can translate into academic rewards such as high rank, released time from teaching, research assistants, and elevated salaries. These are prizes worth competing for; certainly they figure into the intentions of those who commit themselves to biographical and editorial labor for deceased authors. I have often thought that there must be easier ways to earn an endowed chair, but the work is satisfying and has a fair chance of enjoying a long shelf-life in the library, or an equally long life as an e-book.

I trust that these remarks on Bourdieusian capital, and on its consolidation and management by members of "precarious alliances," have demonstrated that an author's literary career never really ends. Strategies are adjusted as the publishing industry changes. Responsibility for the career shifts into new hands and comes under the control of people who have their own intentions. Some of these intentions they hold in common with one another. Other intentions are individual to the players. *Sic semper erat; sic semper erit.*

WORKS CITED

Bierce, Ambrose. *The Devil's Dictionary.* 1911. New York: Bloomsbury, 2009. Print.

Bourdieu, Pierre. "The Forms of Capital." *Handbook of Theory and Research for the Sociology of Education.* Ed. J. Richardson. New York: Greenwood, 1986. 241-58. Print.

Boswell, James. *The Journal of a Tour to the Hebrides with Samuel Johnson, LL.D.* 1785. New York: Konemann, 2000. Print.

Precarious Alliances:
The Case of Arno Schmidt

SABINE KYORA

Arno Schmidt is considered a misfit in the literary scene of the post-war Federal Republic of Germany. Already in 1961, Helmut Heißenbüttel described him as a "Solipsist in the heath" (cf. Heißenbüttel).[1] In the volume *Geschichte der deutschen Literatur von den Anfängen bis zur Gegenwart*, which is dedicated to post-war literature, Schmidt is canonized as "The Arno Schmidt Paradigm" (Barner 389) as if the name—and the name alone—was already sufficiently programmatic.[2]

Indeed, Arno Schmidt had made unfriendly comments on the literary scene and its players frequently enough to justify this reputation. At the same time, however, he needed access to the literary field in order to be noticed at all. His alliances with publishers, broadcasting crews, magazine producers, and feuilleton editors, as well as other authors were crucial in this respect. These alliances, however, were rather strategic in nature: As soon as he gained access, Schmidt broke off contact or behaved in a way that, virtually, forced participants in these alliances to terminate their relationship. An exception in this regard was his connection with Alfred Andersch which remained intact until his death. One of the objectives of the chapter in the above-mentioned literary history is to show Schmidt's pro-

---

1 "Solipsist in der Heide"; Heißenbüttel alludes to Bargfeld, a hamlet near Celle in Lower Saxony, where Schmidt lived from 1958 to his death.
2 This contribution, including those quotations for which no other translation is available, was translated from German by Katharina Bieloch.

grammatic self-positioning which he formulated in the realm of poetological prose and which aims towards a uniqueness in the literary field. In order to assert this position, however, Schmidt also needed alliances; alliances he tried to forge with Alfred Döblin, Andersch and Max Bense. It took him—and this itself is remarkable—roughly a decade to assert his position. By the time he moved to Bargfeld in 1958, this was merely the confirmation of his attained position as "Solipsist," who now lived in the heath.

In the following, I will investigate both forms of alliances that had developed by 1958: Alliances that aim rather at gaining access to the literary field, in the first part; in the second, those that serve the positioning of Schmidt in the literary field. The specific situation of this field, which was restructured in the aftermath of 1945 by the Allies and went on partly to restructure itself, needs to be taken into account, too. In this way, Schmidt also serves as an example for a particular situation of the literary field and for possibilities that resulted from these circumstances (cf. also Kyora).

MEDIA ALLIANCE

Firstly, I will focus on Schmidt's relationship with his publishers, with broadcasters, and literary critics—as far as they were able to provide and guarantee access to the literary field. Schmidt's first book *Leviathan* was published in 1949 by Rowohlt. Ernst Rowohlt and his son Heinrich Maria Ledig-Rowohlt had founded the Rowohlt publishing house after 1945 including different branches in Stuttgart, Hamburg, and Berlin. They displayed skills of entrepreneurship by obtaining translations and license of, for instance, Hemingway from the Allies. In this way, they could publish authors and texts that were new and sold well on the slowly restructuring market. Additionally, Rowohlt had a firm base of authors from the Weimar Republic and printed books by Erich Kästner, Kurt Tucholsky, and Joachim Ringelnatz anew. The first German novel that appeared in first edition was Ernst Kreuder's *Die Gesellschaft vom Dachboden* in 1946. German contemporary literature remained the exception rather than the rule to the publishers' catalogue at first though. In 1949, however, next to Schmidt's book, the prose anthology *Tausend Gramm* was published by Rowohlt editor Wolfgang Weyrauch. It features short stories by young German authors which are considered as an expression of the *Kahlschlag-* or *Trümmerlite-*

ratur of the immediate post-war years. The oeuvre of Wolfgang Borchert was published in the same year, too (cf. Gieselbusch et al.).

For his debut Schmidt then won over a markedly prestigious publishing house, which was also in the act of making a name in the area of contemporary literature. Schmidt did not have an agent, instead—and this has possibly to do with the situation on the book market in 1949—he sent his story *Leviathan* to the Rowohlt publishing house. Rowohlt required more material for a book and, finally, with *Gadir* and *Enthymesis* accepted two more stories (cf. Töteberg 4-11). Publishers, in general, were looking for 'young' authors, who were not burdened by any National Socialist connections and could therefore be printed without the veto of the Allies' board of censorship. There were not very many that had already appeared in publicly visible contexts, for instance in connection with the magazine *Der Ruf*. Hence even unknown authors had a chance of being published. Additionally, although this is purely speculative at this point, Schmidt's stories fitted in with Weyrauch's anthology and Borchert's texts: All three authors dealt with war issues and applied a soldier's perspective. Schmidt's and Borchert's texts also shared expressionist influences. The fact that the critic Walter M. Guggenheimer referred to Schmidt's book as a "Rowohlt catch" (qtd. in Bock 12) in *Frankfurter Hefte* might be viewed as establishing a relationship between Schmidt and those other new discoveries. This classification, however, also shows the publisher's kudos as discoverer of talented authors (cf. Töteberg 17). Another critic writes in a similar tone, "RO-WOHLT printed it, one thinks, and so there will be something to it and perhaps today a piece of literary history emerges and you may say you've been present"[3] (Percy Eckstein in *Der Standpunkt* 11.8.1950, qtd. in Bock 18). Another result of this prestigious imprint was presumably also that Schmidt's debut as well as his subsequent texts have been discussed by all major newspapers.[4]

---

3   "ROWOHLT hats gedruckt, denkt man, also wird schon etwas dran sein, und vielleicht hebt heute und hier ein Stück Literaturgeschichte an, und ihr könnt sagen, ihr seid dabeigewesen."

4   Reviews of *Leviathan* appeared, among others, in *Welt am Sonntag*, *Frankfurter Allgemeine Zeitung*, *Neue Zürcher Zeitung* and *Die Weltwoche*. And in addition to these, *Brand's Haide*, Schmidt's second volume of prose narratives, was reviewed in *Die Zeit* und *Der Spiegel* (cf. Bock 9-27).

Starting with his first novel, then, Schmidt became a Rowohlt author and continued so until 1953. In view of the echo to and success of his first volume of narrative prose to have been published by a well-known publisher it might be assumed that Schmidt's relationship with Rowohlt and Ledig-Rowohlt constituted an alliance between author and publisher. Contrary to this assumption, however, Schmidt's relationship, particularly with Ledig, was marked by distrust and accusations (cf. Töteberg 30-38). Schmidt accused Ledig of a lack of appreciation for his work and of delaying its publication, on which Schmidt depended to become known and have an income. The publisher, on the other hand, claimed time and again that it was all about placing Schmidt's text advantageously on the market and that publishing at a rapid pace was not beneficial to the work's reception. In 1954 the argument finally culminated in a letter to Schmidt by Ledig advising the author to find a different publisher:

> To be honest, we believe to have the prerogative to be upset as it has come to our attention that you submitted the MS [manuscript] not just to us but, at the same time, have offered and submitted to a different publishing house. That is a sort of communication between author a. pub. that, having guided your work for years, doesn't suit us. [...] In this respect, no relationship of trust can remain between us for future collaborations. Apart from such discordances, the reading of your current work has left an ambiguous impression. But since you don't value our critique, we refrain from further explanations and remarks.[5] (qtd. in Alice Schmidt, *Tagebuch 1954* 45)

Ledig demands "trust" between publisher and author as well as "loyalty" on the side of the author. He thus effectively calls for an alliance between publisher and author which goes beyond the contractual relationship: Schmidt

---

5   "Offengestanden glauben eher wir Grund zur Verstimmung zu haben, da wir hörten, daß Sie das MS nicht nur uns einreichten, sondern gleichzeitig einem anderen Verlg. angeboten u. vorgelegt hatten. Das ist eine Art Verkehr zw. Autor u. Verlg., die uns, nachdem wir nun schon jahrelang Ihr Werk betreut haben, nicht behagt. [...] In dieser Weise kann sich kein Vertrauensverhältnis zw. uns für die künft. Zus. Arbeit erhalten. Von solchen Dissonanzen ganz abgesehen hat uns die Lektüre Ihrer neuen Arbeit aber einen überaus zwiespältigen Eindruck hinterlassen. Da Sie aber unsere Kritik nicht schätzen, unterlassen wir nähere Begründungen u. Ausführungen."

only ever got an advance on the next book or the respective manuscript that was about to get published while the publisher retained the right to turn down his manuscripts or demand revision. As becomes evident in the quote, Schmidt reacted in a hostile manner towards revisions, considering them as illegitimate interferences in his texts. Additionally, Schmidt took offense at Wolfgang Weyrauch's negative editorial verdict on *Brand's Haide* and his rejection of the story *Die Umsiedler*. He told Alfred Andersch that he had not been valued or looked after either by the publishing house or by Ernst Rowohlt:

Possibly your impression of the "Big Rowohlt," the patron and discoverer, the understanding critic of spirited literary experiments is about to change a little bit: someone who continuously rejected me, and paid me as much for three books he has published as you did for one quantitatively much thinner: should I "trust" him or feel "looked after"?![6] (Schmidt, *Briefwechsel Andersch* 47)

From these differing assessments of their collaboration, it becomes evident that Ledig, indeed, envisioned a strategic alliance between author and publisher: With his publication policy, Ledig sought to ensure that the market did not become saturated so that Schmidt would not lose his readers. In exchange, he expected the author to trust his expertise in the literary field and its mechanisms and to remain loyal; that is to offer his manuscripts exclusively to 'his' publisher. Schmidt, on the other hand, demanded that Ledig publish all of his manuscripts instantly and without raising objections. Hence Schmidt looked for a type of alliance that only consisted in gaining him access to the market. Once this was achieved, the publisher ought to merely keep this door open. As far as Schmidt was concerned, the publisher had no say concerning content or programmatic questions. He also had to be content with low sales figures—*Leviathan* sold 400 copies in the first year—, he had to continue accepting the author's manuscripts, and preferably honor experimental aspirations with a generous fee. Schmidt took par-

---

6   "Wahrscheinlich ändert sich jetzt auch bei Ihnen die Vorstellung vom Großen Rowohlt, dem Förderer und Entdecker, dem verständnisvollen Beurteiler kühner literarischer Experimente etwas: wer mich ständig abgelehnt hat, und mir für 3 bei ihm erschienene Bücher so viel zahlte, wie Sie mir für eines, quantitativ viel dünneres, gaben: sollte ich zu dem 'Vertrauen' haben oder mich 'betreut' fühlen?!"

ticular offense at a meeting in Hamburg, when Rowohlt apparently waved Cerams non-fiction bestseller *Götter, Gräber und Gelehrte* (1949) in his face, demanding "Why don't you write something like that?"[7] (Schmidt, *Briefwechsel Andersch* 47) Schmidt's behavior reflects his concept of autonomy: The value of his literature is not determined by the economic profit, the publisher ought to assure the author's livelihood without necessarily being able to sell a corresponding amount of books on the market. After all, he has the 'privilege' to support innovative authors. In his alliance with the Rowohlt publishing house, Schmidt tries to put demands into practice which Bourdieu views as a typical *L'art pour l'art* positioning: Symbolic capital (prestige, innovation) and literary autonomy accompany a limited production of books that lead to pecuniary injury (which, in Schmidt's view, the publisher has to carry alone) (cf. Bourdieu 341-60).

The materials from the Rowohlt archive that Töteberg made accessible also show, however, that the positioning of Schmidt as a representative of autonomous art was supported by the publisher, that Rowohlt was even prepared to accept financial loss and that Schmidt erroneously imputed a reluctance to support his position to the publisher. Apparently, the publishing house had difficulties crediting Schmidt with being innovative and accused him of "self-copying" (Töteberg 37). While Schmidt's stories that followed *Leviathan* and *Brand's Haide* confirmed and supported his style, the editors of Rowohlt were looking for further credentials that would establish the author as an innovative representative of the avant-garde. On the one hand, this discrepancy shows different perspectives on Schmidt's positioning: The publisher, apparently, knew much better where Schmidt placed himself as regards the literary field than did the author himself. The "self-copying" which indeed applies to some of his stories of the 1950s may perhaps be read as the author's attempt to make his own voice recognizable to the reader and literary critic. On the other hand, there are also distinct elements of contradictory objectives: The publisher expected new and bigger narrative forms of Schmidt (cf. Weyrauch's opinion on *Kosmas* in Töteberg 37).

After the separation from Rowohlt, due to Schmidt's 'infidelity'—he had offered *Seelandschaft mit Pocahontas* to other publishers without waiting for Rowohlt's verdict—it is only thanks to Andersch's mediation that Schmidt found a new publisher, having spent a considerable time searching.

---

7 "Hier: so was müssen Se ma schreim!"

The Stahlberg publishing house (newly founded in 1946) did not match the reputation of Rowohlt, of course, but it was specialized on modern literature. As a small publishing house, it was not able to survive on the market and is taken over by the Holtzbrink publishing group in 1968. The collaboration between Ernst Krawehl (a co-owner) and Schmidt does not run entirely smoothly, but is decisively less problematic than with Rowohlt. In comparison to Ledig, Krawehl does not consider himself a literary connoisseur. Instead he presents himself as amateur, at least towards Schmidt: "Literature is his hobby"[8] (Alice Schmidt, *Tagebuch 1955* 206). Curiously, this is precisely why Schmidt allows him to interfere with his texts—doing exactly what he has denied Rowohlt. Krawehl 'defuses' *Das steinerne Herz*, the first text that appears with the Stahlberg group, because he fears that Schmidt might again be accused of blasphemy, pornography or the like, just as had been the case with *Seelandschaft mit Pocahontas* (cf. Reemtsma 34-72). With great reluctance Schmidt accepts most parts—he submits to the publisher's verdict, possibly because the access to the market is at stake in two ways, since he found this new publisher only after a lengthy search and he did not want to run the risk of having *Das steinerne Herz* banned or entering another lawsuit. More than that, Krawehl had initiated a kind of pay that (entirely contrary to Schmidt's concept of autonomous authorship) effectively made Schmidt an employee of the Stahlberg group: At the beginning of their collaboration, he lays down a fixed monthly salary as a kind of advancement that Schmidt would "work off" (Alice Schmidt, *Tagebuch 1955* 213) with his new text. So, on the one hand, the access to the market was a crucial aspect of the collaboration with the publisher to Schmidt. On the other hand, the bond with Krawehl was indeed one that created 'trust.' In parts, this is certainly tied to Schmidt's assumption that his publishers are foremost 'merchants,' whose currency is money and not 'loyalty'—he does not credit them with this form of symbolic capital.

Apart from Schmidt's relationship with the Rowohlt publishing house and Krawehl, commissioned work for broadcasting was another crucial possibility for his access to the literary market. Especially for the Süddeutscher Rundfunk (SDR), he wrote his night programs as well as shorter contributions, which were acquired and edited by Alfred Andersch, Martin Walser and Helmut Heißenbüttel. Since Schmidt did not view these con-

---

8   "Sein hobby sei nun die Literatur."

tributions as autonomous literature, he was willing to accept rejection of his ideas as well as requests for changes. Schmidt's correspondence with Andersch, Walser and Heißenbüttel shows him to be as strongly focused on securing access to the market for broadcasts, on which he depended for a significant proportion of his livelihood since 1955, as he had been in his dealings with the publishers of his printed works. Contrary to his behavior towards his publishers, he was willing to make compromises as concerning his target audience in order to secure his access to broadcasting. Still it becomes evident that Schmidt viewed his relationship with the editors as a programmatic alliance. He explained his idea of prose forms in great detail to Walser, for instance, because he views him as one of the few readers who truly understand his literature (cf. Schmidt, *Briefwechsel Kollegen* 225). Heißenbüttel's initially quoted description of Schmidt from 1961, as it were, confirms this assessment from a reverse angle. After all, in his correspondence, Andersch speaks of "us" and of Heißenbüttel as being "one of us" (Schmidt *Briefwechsel Andersch* 115). This form of alliance is going to be analysed below, in the second part.

In the 1950s and earlier 1960s Schmidt was not able to form alliances with literary critics although, as has already been mentioned, all major newspaper reviews were rather generous. Even damning reviews were generally appreciative of Schmidt's prose. Still, in the 50s Schmidt did not have critics who would regularly write about him and be generally sympathetic towards him. Since the mid-1960s, however, sympathetic critics such as Jörg Drews, Karl-Heinz Kramberg, Wolfram Schütte and Rolf Vollmann emerged, and even Heißenbüttel regularly wrote essays about him. The alliances with magazines and their editors evidently show Schmidt's specific place in the literary field: Next to Max Bense's magazine *Augenblick*, Alfred Andersch's *Texte und Zeichen*, published by Luchterhand, frequently printed texts of considerable length by Schmidt, which Schmidt did not view as part of 'breadwinning.' There is consensus with both editors as regards the pursued literary concept.

'Breadwinning,' however, includes translations, which Schmidt initially produced for the Rowohlt publishing house, as well as numerous short contributions and short stories, which appear in the arts section of newspapers. Schmidt sends several copies of those to various editors without maintaining close contact with either one of them. The idea was that through quantity, he would make enough money. In this scenario, he did not require a partner that would secure him access to the medium. In comparison to publishing houses and broadcasting, Schmidt did not rely on one particular agent, also because he did not care for what paper would ultimately print his text.

On the one hand, Schmidt's alliances focus on the access to a particular medium that is supposed to guarantee his economic safety. On the other hand, he demands independence as regards stylistic and content-related issues when it comes to a text that does not qualify as 'breadwinning,' i.e., a text of autonomous quality. All of Rowohlt's attempts to edit his texts get rejected. Only when Schmidt's novel *Das steinerne Herz* and the access to the book market as well as his very existence as author come under threat does he allow Krawehl to modify his text. As regards his idea of autonomy, this situation is highly paradox: He is possibly able to accept these modifications because they do not relate to the literary substance but to politically and erotically litigable statements. At the same time, however, these alterations can be viewed as a political invasion of the literary field as they harm the autonomous character of literature that he had vehemently defended against the Rowohlt publishing house. Schmidt's concept of autonomy appears to be one which he initially wants to enforce in the literary field as an expression of his autonomy as author with a distinct style. but once this autonomy is not questioned or restricted from outside, he seems to be willing to accept this kind of restriction of autonomy.

PROGRAMMATIC ALLIANCES

The context of 1945 is equally crucial for the issue of programmatic alliances. Possibly, we may conceive of a partial delegitimisation of the literary field through the involvement of publishers, critics, and authors in the Nazi regime that lead to a loss of autonomy. The "principles of [...] legitimacy" (Bourdieu 105) must, then, be newly formulated or reconstructed after 1945. Moreover a re-autonomization of the literary field sets in. The 'field of power' had, in the first instance, massively intervened in the literary field by way of censorship of the Nazi regime. Additionally, the book market had almost entirely come to a standstill due to the war economy. In the aftermath of 1945, the Allies controlled the literary field by banning Nazi affiliated literature and reorganizing the literary scene.

Against this backdrop, the authors of the western zone or the Federal Republic of Germany discussed whether the literature that emerged in Germany during the Nazi regime was legitimate in the literary field and whether the literary field must, in fact, be constituted anew. The different positions in this controversial discussion show particularly clearly in the case of Thomas Mann. Mann had made clear that to him any book written in Germany during that time was compromised because its status as a piece of art has no validity within a criminal regime and could thus under no circumstances be viewed as part of an autonomous literature. The representatives of the 'inner emigration,' however, refused Mann's theory because they viewed their literature as independent from the regime (cf. Mann/Thiess/Molo). Therefore, the question was under what circumstances literature could keep its autonomous character—implicitly, all opponents accepted that autonomy is a crucial feature of modern art and construed the literature of the Weimar Republic as having achieved this autonomy.

This confrontation between an exiled author and authors who remained in Germany repeated itself once more between the authors of the so-called 'young generation' and the elders, who had in many cases already published during the Weimar Republic. The young authors of the magazine *Der Ruf* accused the elders of 'calligraphy.' Calligraphy meant that the authors of the inner emigration—at least that was the interpretation—had written a particularly elaborate prose in order to escape censorship and to avoid compromising themselves politically (cf. Hocke). What appeared to be autonomous art due to its literary-aesthetic character was, in fact, none, according to this understanding, because this prose remained dependent on conditions of the Nazi regime and, thus, on the field of power. Subsequent to the collapse of the Nazi regime the new prose was now able to directly (that is, in sober, realistic style) formulate its concerns. This new form of Realism claimed to have 'true' literary autonomy.

Within this controversy, programmatic alliances emerge between authors, critics, and publishers who share a similar concept of literature and, oftentimes, similar political visions. Group 47 is certainly the most popular example in this regard. This group represented the concept of autonomous, realistic literature described above, in contrast to the 'calligraphy' of the elder authors. Group 47 did not just consist of authors and critics, but was also supported by publishers such as Rowohlt. The generation of critics that was associated with Group 47 achieved a status which allowed them to enforce their position not before the 60s. Conservative literary critics of the late 40s and 50s gave preference to classics of Modernity that were viewed as autonomous and exemplary to the modernization of Realism (cf. Pfohlmann 160-61). Critics such as Hans Egon Holthusen and Friedrich Sieburg repeatedly argued that German contemporary literature could not compete with the acclaimed autonomous art of the first half of the century because it was, apparently, too busy with circumstances of the time and the working up of innovations of the aesthetic Modernity that had not been received during National Socialism. For this reason, these critics view contemporary literature as unoriginal and not autonomous. Holthusen, for instance, conceives of Schmidt as an epigone of Joyce, but also lists other forms of epigonism in contemporary literature in his review of *Brand's Haide* (cf. Bock 19-20). In this situation a concept of autonomy formulated according to the literature of Classical Modernity serves as a model for comparing newer literature that, in turn, has not yet reached this level of autonomy.

The new formation of the literary field post-1945 also implies that positions of the avant-garde and experimental literature are initially not represented—banned as 'degenerate art' during the Nazi regime, it is not newly formulated in the years subsequent to 1945. The above mentioned circumstances certainly contributed to this situation. Moreover, Group 47 was not interested in experimental literature either, but focused, as already mentioned, on a modernized Realism. Literary reviews, on the other hand, filled this vacuum by recourse to those classics of Modernity that were still innovative. Schmidt's positioning takes place in precisely this area of experimental literature, however it does so in reference to Realism which made him appealing to Group 47.

In the late 1940s, Schmidt was looking for alliances with authors who were already successful during the Weimar Republic, namely Hermann Hesse und Alfred Döblin. Hesse was of particular interest to him because he was the author of *Steppenwolf*, Döblin because of his formal experiments in the field of prose. After Hesse's review of *Leviathan* which was appreciative but nevertheless critical at some instances, it became clear that Schmidt's appraisal of Hesse was built on a misunderstanding: He had compared the author with the figure Harry Haller and had expected an equally unconventional mindset which he thought he would satisfy with his prose.[9] Döblin, however, remained a pivotal reference point also during the 50s; with his death, Schmidt asks in his diary, "Who else is there?!"[10] (Schmidt, *Briefwechsel mit Kollegen* 45), since he had hoped to establish his literary conception with Döblin's help. Especially the correspondence with Döblin shows that Schmidt represents a similar concept of literature to Holthusen and Sieburg: By appropriating innovations of Classical Modernity, he tries to place his prose in this tradition and at the same time tries to go beyond it. The alliance with Döblin was supposed to warrant the public approval of this endeavor, especially since Döblin had assured him in a letter, "With pleasure, I have seen that you have read August Stramm; yes, we were at a different stage back then, but it is indeed quite something that you are approaching this and proving that you belong. Don't worry about those newspaper scribblings, their goal is merely to destroy"[11] (43). 'Being part' of the Döblinesque avante-garde tradition like the expressionist August Stramm was the kind of positioning that Schmidt had tried to assert with the help of other alliances. As a union of newer authors, Group 47 suggested itself, but was apparently not taken into consideration by Schmidt.

Schmidt received and accepted three invitations by Richter and Andersch to attend conferences hosted by Group 47. In 1953, Ledig also urged him to come to Mainz. Despite his indication that Schmidt had a good chance of receiving the group's prize, Schmidt refused on the grounds that he was no "literary mannequin."[12] One may very well understand this phrasing as an indication of Schmidt's dislike of the pressure of having to fashion himself, stage himself as author in the context of the reading. In 1953, it already shows that the Group's appeal went beyond the programmatic alliances with authors, raising publishers' and broadcasting's inter-

---

9   For Schmidt's particularly rude reply to Hesse's review of *Leviathan*, cf. Schmidt, *Briefwechsel mit Kollegen* 55ff.
10 "Wer bleibt nun noch?!"
11 "Ich habe mit Vergnügen gesehen, daß Sie August Stramm gelesen haben; ja wir waren damals weiter; aber es ist schon was, daß Sie darauf zustoßen und beweist, daß Sie dazugehören. Machen Sie sicht nichts aus den Zeitungsschmierern, deren Amt ist nur zu ruinieren."
12 From Alice Schmidt's diary entry, 28 March 1953; qtd. in Schmidt, *Briefwechsel mit Kollegen* 235; the Rowohlt-Ledig letter, which was a letter of invitation to Schmidt, as well as his reaction to this invitation, are also printed there.

est—Rowohlt donated 1,000 Deutschmarks for the prize; the SDR also paid 1,000 Marks—and, thus, had a good shot at setting up an influential opposition to the conservative establishment in the literary field. The group members clearly viewed Schmidt as a potential ally. Two reasons were probably crucial in this regard: First, Schmidt was an author of the 'young generation,' the first reviews in 1949/50 already classified him as such (after all, he had not published anything before 1945).[13] Second, his text critically addressed the war experience and the post-war situation, just as did texts by Ilse Aichinger, Alfred Andersch, Heinrich Böll, Günter Eich or Günther Grass. Schmidt's interest in new forms of prose had been understood as a variation of Realism, which constituted the programmatic consensus of the group, but not as experimental or avant-garde concept.

Schmidt promoted his positioning during the entire 1950s, chiefly through his connections to Ernst Kreuder and above all to Alfred Andersch. He met Kreuder at the Academy of Language and Poetry in Mainz whose prize he received in 1950 along with four fellow authors. Kreuder gave Schmidt advice on publication in newspapers and a list of contact persons (cf. Alice Schmidt, *Tagebuch 1955* 44, 46). However, Schmidt's negative review of Kreuder's book in 1959 caused a breakup in their relationship (cf. Schmidt, *Briefwechsel mit Kollegen* 111-12). But tensions had arisen before this because Schmidt was successful in selling his offers to newspapers and Kreuder increasingly came to view him as a rival. The case of Schmidt and Kreuder shows very clearly the 'precariousness' of alliances between authors. Kreuder's *Gesellschaft vom Dachboden* sold very well and made him famous. Additionally, he received the Büchner prize in 1953. Kreuder was, initially, the established and successful author who supported the newcomer Schmidt and opened up possibilities of 'breadwinning.' Kreuder also viewed Schmidt as an ally in respect of his Anti-Realist conception of literature, which he anticipated as an opposition to Group 47. Schmidt did not object to this and his distance to Group 47 was another reason why Kreuder assumed a consensus on this matter.

---

13 Rudolf Krämer-Badoni's collective review in the *Frankfurter Allgemeine Zeitung* (1950) was entitled "Der Ruf nach dem jungen Autor" (cf. Bock 11-12). Werner Weber also refers to Schmidt as one of the "junge deutsche Dichter" in his review in *Neue Züricher Zeitung* (1952) (cf. Bock 13-16).

At the end of the 50s, this balance of power changed: Kreuder could not continue his success, while Schmidt was taking root (with Kreuder's help). Thus Kreuder's publisher approached Schmidt asking for the favor of crafting some words of praise for the blurb of Kreuder's new book; that is, the publisher expected positive effects from Schmidt's complimentary text. Schmidt wrote a review and published it. But he also sent it to the publisher, so he could use some of the praise for his purposes. In its overall assessment, though, the review was not all too friendly. In this way, it became clear that Schmidt did not support Kreuder's conception of literature. Schmidt suspected Kreuder of becoming a "priest" (112), that is, of searching for religious values or trying to convey them in his literature. By doing so, Kreuder was impinging on Schmidt's idea of autonomy. Kreuder broke off their correspondence—he had also passed criticism on Schmidt[14]—but he now realized the changed power positions which he, apparently, found hard to accept. As the literary field continued to develop during the 50s, the status of both authors changed as well. Their alliance, however, was tied to their individual positions in the early 50s and transformed into a rivalry when Kreuder started feeling a loss of influence and power.

The alliance between Andersch and Schmidt, on the other hand, remained strong until Schmidt's death. Their correspondence began as early as 1952 and Andersch is the only colleague whom Schmidt addresses informally. Andersch secures Schmidt's access to radio broadcasting, but is, by all means, replaceable in this position. By the time he leaves the SDR in 1959, Heißenbüttel takes his place, but Schmidt's connections are well established and he cultivates extensive contacts with other broadcasting stations. In comparison to the relationship with Kreuder, both Andersch and Schmidt share the same concept of autonomy, which differs from others because independence from all religious belief is equally important to both. In the mid-50s, both Kreuder and Andersch are important to Schmidt, but an unqualified programmatic alliance only exists with Andersch. Thus Schmidt's negative reply to Wilhelm Michels, who tries to persuade him to join in on a trip to Yugoslavia, reads:

---

14 Kreuder writes in reference to *Seelandschaft mit Pocahontas*, for instance, that it is "somewhat too tame, too ordinary, too un-existential." He concludes, "Well, the two of us are allowed to criticize each other" (Schmidt, *Briefwechsel mit Kollegen* 82).

I can't let Andersch, who has virulently fought for me, go to prison cold-heartedly without standing by his side! And I also can't decline Ernst Kreuder's invitation for July again who, even though belonging to 'the other side,' has caringly looked after me.[15] (Schmidt, *Briefwechsel Michels* 21)

The context here is the *Seelandschaft mit Pocahontas*-litigation against Schmidt and Andersch as editor and publisher of *Text und Zeichen* where one of the charges against them was blasphemy. Referring to Kreuder as representative of 'the other side' can in this particular context only mean that Schmidt views Kreuder as a religious person and as a writer who represents religion in his literature, respectively. Andersch, on the other hand, is on the right side because he is committed both to an irreligious position and to a reconception of Realism. Andersch also has prejudices against Kreuder because "for years [he] fought a spiteful battle against realists or what he assumes to be Realism. Even in his short, praising reference [...] he greets you as anti-realist—a grotesque misunderstanding"[16] (Schmidt, *Briefwechsel Andersch* 45). Schmidt assures Andersch that he too finds this part of Kreuder's poetics questionable.

Andersch's and Schmidt's alliance is grounded on the rejection of religious influence on the conception of literature, and on a common concepttion of Realism, but also on a community against conservative literary criticism. Andersch refers to Friedrich Sieburg as the "biggest and smelliest rat in what is today called 'German literature'"[17] (194), and when Schmidt receives an adverse review Andersch likes to console him with the thought that the critic who wrote a bad review is a former Nazi (cf. 85, 105). Although Schmidt's and Andersch's reform of Realism is similar to positions

---

15 "Ich kann Andersch, der seit meinem ersten Bändchen berserkerhaft für mich gekämpft hat, nicht kalt lächelnd ins Kittchen ziehen lassen, ohne an seiner Seite gestanden zu haben! Ebenso kann ich Ernst Kreuder, der sich, obwohl der ‚anderen Seite' angehörend, rührend um mich kümmerte, nicht noch einmal seine Einladung für Ende Juli absagen."
16 "[Er hat] jahrelang einen gehässigen Kampf gegen die Realisten geführt, oder das, was er für Realismus hält. [...] Auch in seinem kurzen, begeisterten Hinweis auf Sie [...] begrüßt er Sie als Anti-Realisten—ein groteskes Mißverständnis."
17 "größte und stinkendste Kanalratte in dem, was sich heute 'deutsche Literatur' nennt"

of Group 47, their rejection of religion as a subject that gives meaning to the text and as their assessment criteria is apparently a special aspect of their alliance. But there is an additional, important facet: Both occupied a particularly strong position against politically conservative Catholicism. Schmidt's snide remarks against the catholic Rhineland at the beginning of *Seelandschaft mit Pocahontas* are as obvious in this respect as Andersch's statements in their correspondence:

Please consider the radical change of regime in the 'Süddeutscher Rundfunk!' A young, sharp, and tactically smart conservative Catholic is in charge now. [...] Since you don't delude yourself as regards the character of our 'democracy,' I hope you'll understand that Heißenbüttel and I are going tactically 'underground.'[18] (Schmidt, *Briefwechsel Andersch* 203)

The autonomy of literature, which should not be subordinated to religion, is one concern in Andersch's letter. It deals, however, predominantly with crucial factors that can obstruct authors such as Schmidt (or Andersch) if they are controlled by the 'antagonistic' party.

At the same time, Andersch is also the driving force behind the promotion of Schmidt as an autonomous, avant-garde author (despite the literary conception that he pursues in his own texts). Time and again he writes letters in order to highlight Schmidt's importance in terms of a "reformation of the German language"[19] (Andersch to Eduard Reifferscheid, qtd. in Schmidt, *Briefwechsel Andersch* 38), to promote his position as an author who "daringly" transgresses (to Schmidt's later publisher Ernst Krawehl, qtd. 63) societal norms, and to present him as the "strongest language force among the young authors"[20] (to Adorno, qtd. 85). This support may possibly be best explained by the lack of correspondence between Schmidt's experimental direction and Andersch's position in the literary field: Schmidt

---

18 "Bedenke bitte den radikalen Regime-Wechsel im Süddeutschen Rundfunk! Dort herrscht jetzt ein junger, scharfer, dabei taktisch gerissener Rechts-Katholik. [...] Da Du selbst Dir ja über den Charakter unserer 'Demokratie' keine Illusionen machst, bitte ich Dich um Dein Verständnis dafür, daß H.[eißenbüttel] und ich unsererseits taktisch 'underground' gehen."

19 "Erneuerung der deutschen Sprache"

20 "stärkste Sprachkraft unter den Jüngeren"

was no danger to Andersch's position. Although Kreuder and Schmidt did not belong to the same segment, Kreuder still perceived Schmidt as a rival. Ultimately, there seems to be a 'personal vestige' that is not solvable even in programmatic alliances.

Schmidt's positioning as avant-gardist is so solid by the end of the 1950s that his publisher advertises his new novel with sentences like, "The Darmstadt jury has awarded *Die Gelehrtenrepublik* by Arno Schmidt the book of the month in February 1958. A German author who is equally admired and scorned as literary avant-gardist was honored and this courage is deserving of thanks"[21] (Dunker 78). The cover page and lengthy review in the magazine *Der Spiegel* no. 20 from 1959 that portrays Schmidt as loner and experimental author is proof of his importance—although the writer of the contribution is not entirely sure whether the experimental character should be viewed as avant-garde or epigonic in the Holthusenesque sense. But the article's length and Schmidt's photograph on the cover page alone indicate that he has finally arrived in the literary field; he no longer needs to rely on alliances to gain access. And so he limits himself to cultivating his programmatic alliance with Andersch, and his position as the avant-gardist in the heath.

WORKS CITED

Barner, Wilfried, ed. *Geschichte der deutschen Literatur von 1945 bis zur Gegenwart*. Vol. XII. München: Beck, 1994. Print.
Bock, Hans-Michael, ed. *Über Arno Schmidt: Rezensionen vom "Leviathan" bis zur "Julia."* Zürich: Haffmans, 1984. Print.
Bourdieu, Pierre. *Die Regeln der Kunst*. Frankfurt/Main: Suhrkamp, 2001.
Dunker, Axel. *Arno Schmidt (1914-1979). Katalog zu Leben und Werk.* München: edition text + kritik, 1990. Print.

---

21 "Die Darmstädter Jury hat unser Verlagswerk *Die Gelehrtenrepublik* von Arno Schmidt im Februar 1958 zum Buch des Monats gewählt. Mit dankenswertem Mut wurde ein deutscher Schriftsteller ausgezeichnet, der als literarischer Avantgardist ebenso bewundert wie gescholten wird."

Gieselbusch, Hermann, Dirk Moldenhauer, Uwe Naumann, and Michael Töteberg. *100 Jahre Rowohlt: Eine illustrierte Chronik*. Reinbek bei Hamburg: Rowohlt, 2008. Print.

Heißenbüttel, Helmut. "Der Solipsist in der Heide." *Deutsche Zeitung Köln* 21./22. June 1961; Rpt. *Der Solipsist in der Heide: Materialien zum Werk Arno Schmidts*. Ed. Jörg Drews and Hans-Michael Bock. München: edition text + kritik, 1974. 47-51. Print.

Hocke, Gustav René. "Deutsche Kalligraphie oder Glanz und Elend der modernen Literatur (Nov. 1946)." *Der Ruf: Eine deutsche Nachkriegszeitschrift*. Ed. Hans Schwab-Felisch. München: dtv, 1962. 203-8. Print.

Mann, Thomas, Frank Thiess, and Walter Molo. *Ein Streitgespräch über die äußere und innere Emigration*. Dortmund: Druckschriften-Vertriebsdienst, 1946. Print.

Kyora, Sabine. "Lost Generation: Arno Schmidt und die Nachkriegsliteratur." *Bargfelder Bote* 303-4 (2007): 3-12. Print.

Pfohlmann, Oliver. "Literaturkritik in der Bundesrepublik." *Literaturkritik. Geschichte – Theorie – Praxis*. Ed. Thomas Anz and Rainer Baasner. München: Beck, 2004. 160-91. Print.

Reemtsma, Jan Philipp. "Politik und Pornographie: Zur Publikationsgeschichte des Steinernen Herzens." *Über Arno Schmidt. Vermessungen eines poetischen Terrains*. Ed. Jan Philipp Reemtsma. Frankfurt/Main: Suhrkamp, 2006, 34-72. Print.

Schmidt, Alice. *Tagebuch aus dem Jahr 1954*. Ed. Susanne Fischer. Frankfurt/Main: Suhrkamp, 2004. Print.

Schmidt, Alice. *Tagebuch aus dem Jahr 1955*. Ed. Susanne Fischer. Frankfurt/Main: Suhrkamp, 2008. Print.

Schmidt, Arno. *Der Briefwechsel mit Wilhelm Michels*. Ed. Bernd Rauschenbach. Bargfeld: Haffmans, 1987. Print.

---. *Der Briefwechsel mit Alfred Andersch*. Ed. Bernd Rauschenbach. Zürich: Haffmans, 1985. Print.

---. *Briefwechsel mit Kollegen*. Ed. Gregor Strick. Frankfurt/Main: Suhrkamp, 2007. Print.

---. *Berechnungen I und II*. Bargfelder Ausgabe III/3. Bargfeld: Haffmanns, 1995. Print.

Töteberg, Michael. "Das ist ein genialischer Mann mit tausend Unarten. Ein Blick in Verlagsinterna: Gutachten, Aktennotizen und Briefdurchschläge im Rowohlt-Archiv." *Bargfelder Bote* 354-6 (2012): 3-41. Print.

Touched by an Author:
Books and 'Intensive' Reading
in the Late Eighteenth Century

GEOFFREY TURNOVSKY

Rolf Engelsing famously characterized the late 18th century as a transformative moment for the history of reading, the context of which, in the German-speaking world, was a massive rise in the numbers of books published after 1760 (946-1002). Assessing this notion of a "Reading Revolution," (302) Reinhard Wittman points to increases manifest in the catalogues of the Leipzig book fair, which advertised 1,384 titles for 1765; 2,713 for 1785; and 3,906 for 1800, making for an almost threefold expansion in the short span of 35 years. These figures may not match the post-Gutenberg textual tidal wave of 1450-1500 for unprecedented explosiveness,[1] but they certainly showed a marked enough escalation of the presence of the printed word in day-to-day life to catch the eye of many contemporaries who described the shift, often in terms of anxieties about a 'reading mania.' Such a

---

1 The first 'printing revolution' started, of course, from a lower baseline. Yet, with appropriate skepticism about the exactness of the numbers (especially in reference to manuscripts copied, which has certainly been enormously underestimated), Elisabeth Eisenstein highlights Michael Clapham's evocative observation: "[a] man born in 1453, the year of the fall of Constantinople, could look back from his fiftieth year on a lifetime in which about eight million books had been printed, more perhaps than all the scribes of Europe had produced since Constantine founded his city in A.D. 330" (1:45).

diagnosis sought to account not just for the surge, but also for the new behaviors it seemed to elicit among new readerships accessing new kinds materials. "[C]lasses who otherwise did little or no reading," in the words of one commentator cited by Wittmann, dropped their old devotional manuals in order to devour novels and periodicals (whose numbers increased at a higher rate than did books as a whole),[2] which they lapped up for news about the world, useful information, gossip, and above all for entertainment (300).

'Extensive' was the term Engelsing applied to the reading practices adapted to this rapidly expanding print culture, in which an individual chose from a plethora of texts and consumed many of them, scanning each one just once to absorb its message before throwing it away and moving on to the next item. Engelsing contrasts this pattern with an older, traditional mode—'intensive' reading—, which was shaped by scarcity rather than abundance, and by the sway of powerful institutions—the Church, universities—that oriented reading in a conservative, stabilizing manner. To read intensively was to focus on a small set of works, *rereading* each one over and over, not for original ideas, new information, or surprising amusements, but as part of a ritualistic re-affirmation of faith, understanding, or inclusion in a recognized community. If skimming a daily newspaper for the latest current events and chatter emblematizes modern reading as it was transformed after 1750, the liturgical recitation of biblical passages under the watchful guidance of a priest symbolizes that from which this new form departed. In this respect, the move from intensive to extensive reading also reflected secularization, along with the triumph of the individual over the collective.

Engelsing's *Leserevolution* has been influential in articulating the significance of the late 18th-century moment for the development of reading in Europe. Yet it has attracted its share of critics who question the overly reductive opposition on which the periodization rests. In particular, the explosive arrival on scene of the novel in this same period has stood out for many as a reflection not of the sudden prevalence of casual speed-reading but the evolution of a deeply-focused reading that appeared to reflect the continuity of traditionally religious textual practices in the modern era

---

2   According to Blanning, the numbers of new periodicals appearing in the German states rose from 64 in 1701-1710 to 260 in 1741-1750 to 1,225 in 1781-1790 (5-14).

rather than a sharp break from them. In his "Éloge de Richardson," written on the occasion of the English novelist's death in 1762, Denis Diderot describes an absorptive, emotionally charged experience that was a far cry from the distracted, overloaded, indiscriminate approach that, in Engelsing's account, characterized 'extensive' reading. Readers of Richardson, Rousseau, Goethe, and other 18th-century novelists cherished their copies of *Clarissa*, *La Nouvelle Héloïse* and *Werther*; they pored over the texts obsessively, perusing them many times, attaching themselves to the fates of their characters. Wittmann sees in this new literary fashion a "'revolution' in reverse" (296). Similarly, examining the fan mail that these novelists famously received from their impassioned readers, Jean Goulemot and Didier Masseau describe an "intimist [intimiste]" style that calls for a "major nuancing" of the reading revolution thesis (39).[3]

Part one of this essay considers 'neo-intensive' reading in contrast not with extensive reading, but rather in the context of a broader evolution in reading practices characterized by dematerialization. The latter represents a long-term tendency, over the course of centuries, to conceptualize reading as a purely intellectual or spiritual process, the material aspects of which—represented, for instance, by books and their physical manipulation—are seen as extraneous to the reading experience, and as such, to be downplayed and ideally forgotten. In this framework, neo-intensive reading is not a throwback to older reverential styles but an articulation of the textual modernity represented by dematerialization.[4] Part two returns to the notion of an 'intimist' reading through a reflection on the motif of 'touching.' Readers had frequent recourse to this trope as they endeavored to put into words experiences of the text that were built on an intensely personal author/reader relationship. At first glance, such a bond seems anything but precarious; but we will see that the framework of dematerialization reveals this intimacy to be a more intricate and delicate construction than we might realize.

---

3   In his study of Rousseau's readers, Robert Darnton writes about one of his primary case-studies, Jean Ranson, a Protestant merchant from La Rochelle obsessed with the author and who "devoured everything he could find" by him, "[o]ne could hardly find a more intensive reader [...], and his reading became more intense as he did more of it. If anything, it illustrates a 'reading revolution' in reverse" (228, 250).

4   I will therefore use the term 'neo-intensive' rather than 'intensive.'

It does seem important to distinguish absorptive, neo-intensive novel reading from the hurried, distracted scanning of periodicals. There are, though, some commonalities between the two modes that might help us to better define a broader concept of the evolution of reading post-1750, without having to over-rely on Engelsing's polarity. In particular, in both extensive and neo-intensive versions, reading is increasingly viewed to be, in its essence, a purely mental or psychological experience. That is, reading is pointedly not conceived, in either case, as a physical or mechanistic activity; indeed, it does not appear to have any kind of concrete sensory valence at all, or more precisely not one that is not exclusively metaphorical. This idea needs to be quickly clarified given that neo-intensive reading is often associated with powerful physical effects: swooning, hyperventilating, "violent flailing" (Chartier, *Inscriptions* 111), and especially, with crying.[5] Yet it is important to emphasize that these effects are almost always distinct from actual reading; and inasmuch as they grow stronger, far from being continuous with the reading process, they tend to interrupt and impede it, as suggested by the report of one prominent reader of *Clarissa*, Lady Bradshaigh. Reacting to Clarissa's death, she writes: "Would you have me weep incessantly?... I long to read it—and yet I dare not—in Agonies would I lay down the Book, take it up again, walk about the Room, let fall a Flood of Tears, wipe my Eyes, read again... throw away the Book crying out... I cannot go on" (qtd. in Pearson 28).[6]

---

5   Roger Chartier highlights this "*somatisation*" of reading, citing a passage from Diderot's "Éloge" (46) where Diderot describes the reader's physical response on reading the passage from *Pamela* in which the protagonist's old father, having walked all night, arrives at the chateau in which his daughter's virtue was to be comprised, in order to save her: "[W]e cannot hear him presenting himself to the valets of the house without experiencing the most violent flailing."

6   Jacques Pernetti writes to Rousseau on behalf of Jean-Vincent Capperonnier de Gauffecourt, to thank him for the gift of his book, relating that, "the movements of his [i.e., Gauffecourt's] heart were so strong on the reading of your novel that he was obliged to interrupt this reading, and to read only a few lines at a time" ("Pernetti to Rousseau, 26 February 1761." Letter #1328. *Electronic Enlightenment*, ed. Robert McNamee et al., University of Oxford. www.e-enlightenment.com). Examples of this type could be multiplied. Throughout this

Compare this with the physicality described in the 11th century by St. Anselm in his *Meditation on Human Redemption*, which offers a guide to monastic reading: "Taste the goodness of your redeemer... chew the honeycomb of his words, suck their flavour which is sweeter than honey, swallow the loving and rejoicing" (Clanchy 42). Here, the bodily exercise of reading and the reader's internalization of the meaning that the text conveys are not opposed but consistent, as they are, similarly, in medieval and early modern conceptions of reading that underscore the aural experience of hearing the words pronounced aloud. Michael Clanchy cites a reference in the 12th-century *Estoire de Waldef* to Wace's versed history of Britain, *Brut*: "If anyone wants to know this history / Let him read the Brut, he will hear it there" (42). Clanchy notes that a modern reader would expect either to *find* this history in Waltheof's story—thereby substituting an experience of abstract intellectual discovery for one of sense perception—or alternatively, to *see* it there.

The shift from oral to visual reading marks, of course, a hugely significant moment in the history of literacy, one that has been extensively analyzed. That such a shift has taken place has proven less contestable than when and how it occurred. Paul Saenger points to 7th- and 8th-century Irish monastic culture in which scribes introduced word-spacing into their copying, thus liberating the reader from having to voice the syllables in order to recognize the words and sentence structures. Others highlight the persistence of voiced, out-loud reading not only in the late Middle Ages, but well into the modern era.[7] A detailed investigation of this issue is obviously well outside our purview; yet we might stress a few points. First, however we might want to nuance Engelsing's concept of extensive reading, the post-1750 reading revolution was in any case an evident triumph of visual

---

essay, I refer readers to this extremely useful database, abbreviated as *EE*, both for all letters addressed to Rousseau and a number addressed to Bernardin de Saint-Pierre. The texts of Rousseau's letters are based on the definitive edition of his correspondence, edited and annotated by Ralph A. Leigh: *Correspondance complète de Jean-Jacques Rousseau*, ed. R.A. Leigh, 52 vols (Geneva: Institut et Musée Voltaire, 1965-1998). Within each parenthetical reference, I will include the correspondents, date, and the reference number assigned by Leigh's edition. Translations of all the letters are mine.

7 See, for instance, Petrucci 275-82; Chartier "Loisir" 127-47.

modes; and in this respect, the neo-intensive styles characterized by Goulemot, Darnton, and others were ultimately quite distinct from the medieval *lectio divino* described by St. Anselm. As ritualistic and deeply focused as novel reading became in the 18th century, it was almost always silent, solitary, and undertaken only with the eyes. This is the case despite powerful images of the time celebrating—nostalgically, I would suggest—reading *en famille* or in the salon. Relative even to the 17th century, let alone the Middle Ages, far fewer individuals would have accessed the work of prose fiction by *hearing* it enunciated aloud. In fact, it seems likely that the characteristic absorptive effects of such reading hinged on the mute, internalized nature of the process. For the intensity of the novel reader's experience lay in an ability to be drawn into the scenes that the words conjured, whether fictional scenes populated by characters—as she reads Walter Scott, Emma Rouault, future Mme Bovary, "dream[s]" of "old manor[s]," "guardrooms," and "troubadours" (Flaubert 32)—or the authorial scene in which the reader visualized the writer in the act of expressing—often in his own voice—his genius. The purely optical nature of 18th-century reading thereby opened up an *imaginary* auditory (and visual) experience, through which the reader felt close to the author: "I believe sometimes that I see and hear you exhorting me to wisdom and encouraging me to virtue," writes one appreciative reader in a letter to Bernardin de Saint-Pierre, referencing the pivotal dialogue from *Paul et Virginie* in which the old man who narrates the story consoles Paul after his beloved Virginie has left Île de France (today's Mauritius), where they had grown up together in the innocence of the tropical island's luscious nature, for decadent, civilized Europe (Degars to Bernardin de Saint-Pierre, 1 April 1791, *EE*).[8]

Either scenario implies transport from an actual reading scene, and both seem a far cry from the rumination of the medieval monk "chew[ing]," in the sacred space of the cloister or abbey, the words of the Gospel. Indeed, the shift to visual reading rests on a stark disjuncture between the physical

---

8   Under the direction of Malcolm Cook, Bernardin de Saint-Pierre's correspondence is being edited for inclusion in the *EE* database. Not all the letters are as yet accessible. For those I cite that are not for now included in *EE*, I will refer to the relevant dossier in the municipal library of Le Havre, Bibliothèque Armand Salacrou, where the manuscript letters I discuss—those especially that Bernardin de Saint-Pierre received from his readers—are archived.

act of reading and the intellectual experience of it, reflected, for one thing, in an optical vocabulary now used solely as metaphor. As applied to reading, the verb 'seeing' almost never referred to the literal perception of printed letters on the page, but pointedly to what the reader could only see in his or her mind's eye: an image, a truth, a sentiment, an individual (including the author) that the text more often 'painted' than it 'de-scribed.' Another Bernardin de Saint-Pierre fan named Gavoty admired the "marvelous and simple art that you possess to paint nature" (Gavoty to Bernardin de Saint-Pierre, 15 January 1788, *EE*). In turn, this disconnect took root within a new material culture which integrated reading into the comforts and habits of 18th-century social and domestic life. The bare, often backless wooden stools and large parchment tomes of the Middle Ages, maneuverable only with two hands, combined with the conventions of oralization, made it difficult to forget that reading was, at a basic level, a physical activity as much as a purely cognitive one, requiring an exertion of the body as well as a good amount of bodily coordination as preconditions for accessing the text.

Upholstered reading chairs countered such an effect. Mimi Hellman analyzes a 1783 engraving by François Dequevaullier showing an elegantly appointed Enlightenment-era French salon, with groups of individuals engaged in card games and conversation; on the left of the panel, a women—the only solitary figure in the tableau—sits apart by a large window, nestled in a chair with legs crossed, absorbed in the silent reading of a book (her mouth is closed) that, like so many painted female readers from this era, she effortlessly holds up in one hand (421).[9] To be sure, smaller format books, especially the highly portable duodecimos of the age, further allowed for the seamless incorporation of reading into the normal rhythms of the

---

9   Images of novel reading from the 18th century often depict young women sitting in comfortable chairs or sofas, mouths closed (i.e., reading silently), holding a small book in just one hand. The most famous is perhaps Fragonard's "La Liseuse" from about 1770, in which a young girl in a bright yellow dress leans back against a plush cushion. An etching from the 1790 issue of the *Taschenbuch zum Nutzen und Vergnügen* portrays a melancholy-looking woman leading back on a sofa, with a small dog sleeping next to her. Again, she easily holds in her left hand a small book, while her right arm leans against a cushion and props up her head. A caption underneath reads: "Da sitzt sie schon, die arme Frau, / Und liest in Werthers Leiden" (Hanebutt-Benz 121).

everyday, where its particular exertions were easily disregarded. When, following standard book-gifting protocols, Bernardin de Saint-Pierre proposed to have a copy of his *Etudes de la nature* elegantly bound [*relié*, probably in leather] for one of his correspondents, Mme de Boisguilbert, the latter refused the offer, asking him instead to send her the volumes simply sewn [*broché*, with just a paper cover]; a heavy leather binding, she explained, is too hard to keep open, requiring "two hands [...] to hold the book which always wants to close." Moreover, binding is good for "a library book and yours, Monsieur, is not yet destined for that; it must first roam the woods with me, see the banks of my pretty river, go into a small valley to search for the source of a spring; for wherever I stop on my walks, reading must help me spend my hours agreeably" (Mme de Boisguilbert to Bernardin de Saint-Pierre, 21 March 1786, *EE*).

There's a hint of irony in the notion that a reading so rooted in a stark disconnect between the material and intellectual experience of the book, and in the eclipse of the former in favor of the latter, would at the same time collapse the boundary between life and text in the way Mme de Boisguilbert suggests, with reading viewed as a seamless add-on to daily activity rather than as a discrete exercise in and of itself. Wittmann begins with a quote from a German observer in Paris, noting that, "[e]veryone, but women in particular, is carrying a book around in their pocket. People read while riding in carriages or taking walks; they read at the theatre during the interval, in cafés, even when bathing" (285). In this perspective, reading appears more as a mindset or attitude than any particular action; in the formulation that Rousseau employs when he reflects on reading in *Rousseau Juge de Jean-Jacques*, it is a "way of seeing," one, of course, that had nothing to do with the ocular perception of alphabetic symbols on a page, as we have noted.[10] Needless to say, not all saw the intellectualized effects of vi-

---

10 The *Dialogues: Rousseau Juge de Jean-Jacques* stages a conversation between Rousseau and a Frenchman over the morality of Jean-Jacques, about whom the Frenchmen had heard terrible things. Rousseau convinces him to read the author's works rather than believe the scurrilous rumors being spread. The Frenchman finally heeds Rousseau's advice; he reads the texts and reports back: "I found in them ways of feeling and seeing that distinguish him easily from all the other writers of his time" (Rousseau, *Collected Writings*, 1:212; *Oeuvres complètes*, 1:933-944).

sual reading in a positive light. Chartier, for instance, considers *Don Quixote* to be a satirical take on the spread of silent reading in the 17th century, expressed through Cervantes' central comic motif of the reader who can no longer distinguish fiction from reality (cf. Chartier, "Loisir" 146). The anxieties through which a 'reading revolution' was perceived almost two centuries later stressed a lot of the same themes.

Many readers, however, stressed the beneficial effects of a life/text conflation that silent, visual reading seemed to facilitate. Individuals were not, in this view, led to neglect reality for the more exciting, exotic worlds celebrated in texts. Rather, their experiences of the 'real world'—of, say, nature, in the case of Mme de Boisguilbert—were enhanced through an intensification of feeling and sensibility that reading enabled. Above all, reading imposed moral clarity and direction on everyday life. In the "Éloge de Richardson," Diderot relates the example of a married acquaintance who had been involved in a flirtatious correspondence with another man. On reading *Clarissa*, "horrified at Clarrisa's fate," she immediately broke off the compromising exchange (42). The letters to Rousseau and Bernardin de Saint-Pierre offer numerous analogous cases of readers reporting how they were able to adapt the lucid moral viewpoints they found in the works to the circumstances of their own lives: "Your book is a true treasure of wisdom. I have never seen virtue so pure or so brilliant," writes one reader to Rousseau (Louis-François to Rousseau, 24 March 1761 [#1379], *EE*). Another, Jean Louis Le Cointe, tells the same author that reading *La Nouvelle Héloïse* with his young wife helped both spouses understand their relationship in a new and profound way: "what had seemed to us as a simple attachment by habit [...] was the most tender Love" (Jean Louis Le Cointe, seigneur de Marcillac to Rousseau, 5 April 1761 [#1387], *EE*).

Readers had recourse to quite a number of expressions and tropes in order to articulate the benefits of a reading that, by collapsing life and text, helped them find meaning and value in their circumstances. One, though, stands out for us in this context, namely the trope of 'being touched.' Diderot opens his "Éloge de Richardson" by suggesting we find a term other than the discredited *roman* for moralistic prose narratives such as *Clarissa* that "touch spirits and inspire throughout a love of goodness" (29). While capturing the characteristic emotional experience of neo-intensive reading, 'being touched' is also a motif that conjures the paradoxes of dematerialization we have been considering. Much like the visual metaphors discussed earlier, and in contrast with medieval images of rumination, 'to be touched,' as an effect of reading a text, specifically does not imply any physical contact with the book considered as an object, but on the contrary, mobilizes a vocabulary of sense perception in order to define an experience with no concrete sensory dimension at all, at least not insofar as the senses were activated by reading itself (sitting in a chair, holding a book, optically scanning printed symbols on a page). Thus, a brief analysis of the commonplace can help us better understand how the context of dematerialization shaped neo-intensive reading. It will, in particular, call attention to the intricate mix of spiritualized sentiment, personal desire, commercial interest, and material constraint that set the framework for the spread of this type of reading.

Examples from correspondence and other sources are rife and can be cited at length, with the term used to describe either a scene, image, or discourse—Rousselot writes Rousseau to thank him for the "touching portraits of virtue" he discovered in *La Nouvelle Héloïse* (Rousselot to Rousseau, 15 March 1761 [#1361], *EE*)—or their effects on the reader. Referring to the tragic deaths of Paul and Virginie, Louis Debreuil confides in Bernardin de Saint-Pierre that "their deplorable end touched me more than any circumstance in their lives" (Debreuil to Bernardin de Saint-Pierre, 8 July 1796 [dated 20 messidor, year 4 in letter] Bibliothèque Salacrou, MS134, f.33v). The motif posits the reading experience to lie in a pure emotional or spiritual sentiment that the text generates: "your touching book," writes L. de Vigneras to Bernardin de Saint-Pierre referring again to his best-known work, "will leave in my soul an enduring impression" (L. de Vigneras to Bernardin de Saint-Pierre, 5 April 1788, *EE*). This sensation results from an intuittion of moral clarity that a 'touching' image triggers in the reader who beholds the struggles of virtue against the forces of vice. The latter may be externalized in the form of venal merchants or cruel fathers tormenting innocent children, lovers, or artists; or alternatively, they consist in the carnal desires of the individual who heroically resists them within him or herself. The abbé Cahagne effuses to Rousseau how "touched" he was by the "peril of the promenade on water," invoking the scene in *La Nouvelle Héloïse* in which Julie and Saint-Preux, former lovers resolved to live innocently as friends (Julie is married and dedicated to her duties as wife and mother), suddenly find themselves alone in a boat that was blown off-course in a storm. With their old feelings welling up, they reaffirm their commitment to their chaste attachment, and to the virtue that it embodies (Abbé Cahagne to Rousseau, 27 February 1761 [#1331], *EE*). "There, my friend," writes Saint-Preux as he relates the event to his English confidant, Milord Edouard, "you have the detail of the day of my life in which without exception I have experienced the most powerful emotions. [...] I will tell you that this adventure has convinced me more than all the arguments, of the freedom of man and the merit of virtue" (Rousseau, *Collected Writings*, 6:428 and *Oeuvres complètes*, 2:521-22).

To be touched meant, for the reader, to identify with Saint-Preux's self-elevating emotions as he reflects back on the adventure. The peril that moved Cahagne was represented by the lovers' surging desire not by bad weather, meaning that the reader did not identify with the adventure *per se*, but with Saint-Preux's lucidity as he internalizes the lessons of the incident after the fact and 'sees' the necessity of their virtuous choice. Nicholas Paige shows that the sentimental identification considered so typical of Rousseau's readers, and often defined in terms of a naïve desire to believe in the authenticity of the letters and characters, must be understood as an experience of spectatorship rather than participation. That is, the fans who wrote to Rousseau, even as they inquired whether or not Julie was a real person, did not do so because they were, like Don Quixote, so completely lost in the novel that the scenes it depicted appeared more real to them than their own lives. To be sure, bemused contemporaries worried that novel readers would abandon their 'real world' responsibilities in order to adopt the more appealing lifestyles of romance heroes. Such anxieties were misplaced, however, at least as far as those readers who conveyed their admiration for *La Nouvelle Héloïse* were concerned. None betrays any desire to live Saint Preux's life in place of his or her own; their pleasure was not that of escapism. Their interest in Saint-Preux was based exclusively on the ability of the character to mirror a clear vision of their own lives back to them. It was this observer's clarity that they sought, along with the personal elevation associated with such a privileged, knowing perspective. They were, as a result, prone to identify with attendant characters, friends and confidants who empathized with the protagonists, rather than with the suffering figures themselves. Paige cites a representative letter from the Marquise de Polignac who writes after reading volume six in which Julie dies:

"[T]his dying Julie was not an unknown being; I thought I was her sister, her friend, her Claire" (140).[11]

Of course, the very existence of fan mail addressed directly to Rousseau or Bernardin de Saint-Pierre suggests, in the end, that it was to the person of the author that readers looked for the source of the vision that 'touched' them. Diderot's portrait in the "Éloge de Richardson" of the "femme de goût" obsessed with Richardson's *Grandisson* who asked one of her friends travelling to London to "visit on my behalf Miss Émilie, M. Belford, and above all, Miss Howe, if she is still living" (42), may support a view of 18th-century sentimental reading as an exercise in naïve immersion. But an examination of relevant letters reveals that whatever benefits readers drew from the novels, they quite deliberately ascribed them to their authors; and their interest in the novels' characters was rooted in a conviction less of the characters' 'real-life' existence, than of their reliability as prisms for the author's insights and ethical clarity and as faithful models that readers could then apply to their own lives. In other words, as Paige argues, the authenticity they craved lay not in the historical veracity of the letters or their fictional writers, but in a belief that the moral vision and exalting sentiments that these letters articulated, and that the characters embodied, were the sincere expression of a *living* author's vision and experience: "rare and happy man," writes Le Cointe to Rousseau (5 April 1761), "you, who have all the sentiments that you describe, and who must therefore be the happiest mortal that the Heavens have seen born."

The reader's appreciation and more saliently, his or her self-affirming appropriation of these authorial perspectives, was then reflected in the intimacy which the reader came to believe he or she shared with the writer. Neo-intensive reading certainly rested, as Goulemot and Masseau showed, on a firm belief that the text offered the means for such a close, personal bond with its writer, expressed in the epistolary sharing of private details, in a propensity to assume, in those letters, the role of friend or family—L. Debreuil begins his letter to Bernardin de Saint-Pierre by addressing him as "my father (for what more tender name should I call you, you who have filled my heart with joy and hope [...])" (f.33r)—and in assertions of a pri-

---

11 Paige cites the letter from Marie Louise de La Garde, marquise de Polignac to Marie Madeleine de Brémond d'Ars, marquise de Verdelin, 3 Febuary 1761 (#1258), *EE*.

vileged intellectual connection with the writer: "How virtue would be obliged to you, Sir, if all your readers paid both to you and your unequalled work the same justice as I do!" writes one reader to Rousseau (Unknown to Rousseau, 5 February 1761 [#1263], *EE*). All this in spite of the fact that reader and writer had, in many if not all cases, never met personally. Robert Darnton's description of "Rousseauistic" reading as a "communication between two lonely beings, the writer and the reader" suggests an affectionate familiarity that, despite being cultivated exclusively through the circulation of the printed word—or maybe because of this fact—seems a long way from a precarious alliance (249, 231).

We should, however, consider a number of key points. For one thing, this reader/author intimacy existed primarily—if not to say exclusively—in the mind of the reader, and was not reliably shared by the writer. In the example cited above, the reader's assertion of his privileged connection with Rousseau needs to be relativized by the fact that he remains to this day 'unknown,' his identity a mystery not only to us two centuries later but to Rousseau as well. Moreover, it was not from a modest desire to remain anonymous that this person's identity remained hidden to Rousseau—some readers did, in fact, withhold their names intentionally, for a variety of reasons[12]—but simply because Rousseau could not decipher the handwriting.[13] Such a mundane technicality of early modern epistolary exchange places this 'intimate' relationship in a far more uncertain light than that anticipated by the reader, whose belief in the bond was fundamental to his or her ideal experience of the text. And let us recall that the letters from delighted fans were not just unsolicited by Rousseau, but actively unwanted by him. A

---

12 For instance, a soldier, confiding to Rousseau that the Julie of *La Nouvelle Héloïse* recalls his own "Julie," whom he had to leave behind, tells the author, "I must hide my name from you, and it is another sacrifice I make to my Julie" (Unknown to Rousseau, 6 April 1761 (#1389), *EE*).

13 See Unknown to Rousseau, 5 February 1761 (#1263), editorial note 1. Rousseau mentions his inability to decipher the correspondent's name in a letter to his friend François Coindet, dated February 13, 1761. He is able to identify this reader as a "fermier général"—i.e., a private tax collector—and sends a response to this correspondent to Coindet, asking Coindet to fill in the name and address if he is able to determine what they are. See Rousseau's letters to Coindet (letter #1286) and to Unknown (letter #1287), both dated 13 February 1761, *EE*.

February 1762 letter to his publisher, Marc-Michel Rey, complains that "[a]ll the idle of France and Europe write me through the mail, and what is worse, expect replies" (Rousseau to Rey, 4 February 1762 [#1664], *EE*). In the April 1762 issue of the *Mercure de France*, he placed an announcement asking "Messieurs les Beaux-Esprits" to stop sending him "letters of compliment [...], not being in a state [...] to answer so many [of them]."[14]

Moreover, while the image of a "communication between two lonely beings" conjures a relationship that would seem to be established outside of any structure or social order—one that might have its true place in, say, nature, a small provincial village, or in a realm of celestial beings—in fact, the deep connection between reader and author was a highly structured, hierarchical one. The transitivity of 'toucher' conveys the seemingly unidirectional nature of the exchange, with the author as an active subject, the reader invariably a passive object, and their interaction one that was decidedly *not* between equals. The author stood as a fount of wisdom, truth, moral clarity; the reader's role was to subordinate him or herself before this transcendent figure in the hopes of partaking of his knowledge. The author was a spiritual guide, a teacher, or a kind of lay priest, according to the influential account of Paul Bénichou (1996). The reader was a disciple or student, and to read meant to be opened up to this position of subservience, as Debreuil had done when he assumed the role of Bernardin de Saint-Pierre's son, submitting to the authority of the father.

That said, if the grammar of 'toucher' implied the reader's passivity, it did so by hiding a context of remarkable and multi-layered assertiveness on his or her part, which not only stood in strong contrast with the submissive role ostensibly assigned to the reader by the conventions of neo-intensive reading, but which, I would suggest, established the very conditions of possibility for this new textual practice. In fact, more than any particular reading style, it is this assertiveness that lies at the heart of the 18th-century

---

14 *Mercure de France*, April 1762, 209. In both the letter to Rey and in this announcement, Rousseau complained about authors who sent him "brochures" and "beaux-esprits" who sent him letters. In addition to the time and effort required to respond, he also objected to the expense this unasked-for correspondence imposed on him, given the Old Regime postal conventions that generally required the recipient to pay for the service. Rousseau estimated that such mail cost him 500 livres a year.

reading revolution. Michel de Certeau's famous chapter, "Reading as Poaching," is often cited by historians arguing for the active role of readers in the production of a text's meaning, against a tradition of literary historical research that has predominantly focused on the figure of the author, and in so doing has assumed the reader to be no more than clay to be molded: "What has to be put into question," de Certeau writes, "is [...] the assimilation of reading to passivity" (ch. XII).[15] Of course, oriented by its authorial obsessions, neo-intensive reading might seem to call for just such a characterization, and certainly many important studies of it have tended to play up the 'power' of a particular author to elicit the relevant experiences in readers, which presumably they would otherwise not have known. In Darnton's study, it was Rousseau "who broke the barriers separating writer from the reader." He goes on to describe his famous case-study, the Protestant merchant from La Rochelle, Jean Ranson, as reading "exactly as Rousseau intended," "[a]bsorbing the texts as Rousseau taught him" (234, 241, 252).

It is not hard to see why Darnton and others would frame Rousseauist reading largely in terms of authorial agency. *La Nouvelle Héloïse* was published with two prefaces by Rousseau, the second of which staged Rousseau himself in dialogue with an interlocutor. Both reflected at length on how the letters between the two Swiss lovers should and would be appreciated. Numerous readers referred directly to these paratexts in their letters: "Your book has had more or less the effect on me that you predicted in your preface," writes one (Unknown to Rousseau, 15 March 1761 [#1365], *EE*). Others appeared to emulate the models they offered, even if they did not specifically mention the texts. Le Cointe's account of reading with his "young wife," cited above, appears to be derived from a scene in the second preface:

I like to picture a husband and a wife reading this collection [i.e., of letters] together, finding in it a source of renewed courage to bear their common labors, and perhaps new perspectives to make them useful. How could they behold this tableau of a happy couple without wanting to imitate such an attractive model?" (*Collected Writings* 6:16 and *Oeuvres* 2:23)

---

15 Chartier ("Laborers" 49-50) opens with a passage from this essay.

Yet to stop the analysis too abruptly at this dynamic defined by the author's singular power to shape his readers is to miss a number of important complexities. For one thing, we should not ignore the fact that Le Cointe, whether or not he is consciously imitating the model of marital perusal supplied in the preface, seems in any case to misinterpret its lesson, which entailed that the married couple realize, through their shared appreciation of *La Nouvelle Héloïse*, not their *love*—in the novel, Julie and her husband do not, in fact, love each other; and in the preface, Rousseau goes on to note that the reading couple he envisions can learn to be happy with "the charm of conjugal union, even in the absence of love's charm"—but their duties and responsibilities (*Collected Writings* 6:16 and *Oeuvres* 2:23).

As it turns out, Le Cointe took from the text less the message that Rousseau sought to inculcate in him, than the one he wanted to hear, one that affirmed his domestic content in terms that made sense to him. In this respect, a more dynamic role for readers should be discerned, in which they were able, decisively, to inflect the lessons they learned and determine the conditions of their reception. Indeed, if the neo-intensive reading of the late 18th century stands out as a noteworthy stage in the history of literacy[16], it is due not just to the striking nature of the tears and moralistic emoting that typified it, but to the initiative that readers were able to take in order to have these experiences and to give expression to them. Of course, they did so most emblematically by seeking to communicate their transport directly to authors, a gesture whose daring they often underscored in letters which, despite their presumptuous claims to intimacy with the novelist, were nonetheless full of embarrassed self-consciousness about their assertiveness: "Although I don't have the good fortune of knowing you," writes Bruner in one example to Bernardin de Saint-Pierre, "I know—and who doesn't—your sublime works"; he continues, seeking the author's views on whether or not society has a right to kill an individual (pertinent, of course, in the

---

16 A number of recent collections devoted to the history of reading include chapters on the "reading revolution" of the late 18th century, with attention paid to the advent of what I am calling neo-intensive reading. See chapter 9 of Martyn Lyons' useful *A History of Reading in the West* entitled "The Reading Fever, 1750-1830" and Reinhard Wittmann's essay "Was There a Reading Revolution at the End of the Eighteenth Century," in the equally useful *A History of Reading in the West* (Cavallo/Chartier 284-312).

latter months of 1792, when Bruner wrote), "[i]t will seem surprising to you, Monsieur, that a young man of 18 years would ask you a question" (Bruner to Bernardin de Saint-Pierre, 1 December 1792, Bibliothèque Salacrou, MS132, f.109r-109v).

It is no doubt true that only a tiny subset of total readers reached out in this fashion; in the case of Rousseau, about sixty letters are normally identified as belonging to the archive of his fan mail, a number that needs to be appraised in light of the tens of thousands of copies of the novel that circulated in the decades after its first publication in 1761.[17] Moreover, many of these correspondents were not obscure individuals taking the unprecedented step of contacting a distant celebrity. Rather, if they were not already directly acquainted with the author, they were, more often than usually acknowledged, integrated into contiguous personal networks at just one or two degrees of remove from Rousseau.[18] But let us assume anyway that the gesture of writing the author, if not typical in and of itself, might nonetheless stand in for a broader array of dynamic behaviors that were, in fact, coming to define reading in the 18th century. As such, neo-intensive reading was not just the quiet absorption of a text's moral lessons. It was also an effort, through these behaviors, of assertively defining for oneself and plac-

---

17   McEachern (205) identifies 70 true editions of the *Nouvelle Héloïse* published before 1800, plus some 35 additional issues of an edition.

18   To take one example, in "Readers Respond to Rousseau," Darnton cites the letters of about 24 readers who contacted Rousseau. It is possible to ascertain that at least 10 of these had some kind of prior personal connection with the author; they knew him directly, had previously been in correspondence with him, had received the Nouvelle Héloïse as a gift from him (sometimes via an intermediary), and/or had another kind of affiliation with Rousseau that might have made the gesture of writing a letter seem somewhat less presumptuous than it might otherwise be. For instance, Daniel Roguin (mentioned by Darnton on p. 243), writes on February 27, 1761 to thank Rousseau for, among other things, not forgetting his family. Either his father or his uncle, army officers in the service of the King of Sardinia, was actually mentioned in a postscript to one of Saint-Preux's letters to Julie (letter 34 in part I), in which he tells her that he has been offered the command of a troop in the Regiment that "M. Roguin" is raising (Rousseau, *Collected Writings* 6:88 and *Oeuvres* 2:108). See R.A. Leigh's editorial note 1 to Roguin's letter (letter #1329) in *EE*.

ing oneself in the positions that made the appropriation of these lessons, along with the personal improvement and affirmation that this entailed, possible. That is to say, as a reading experience, being touched was not a passive disposition, despite the grammatical inflection. It was the articulation of concerted, purposeful activity on the part of an individual who resolutely sought, and knew how to bring about a desired outcome.

And it bears emphasizing that, in this light, the individual's purposeful reading started long before his or her eyes scanned page one. It began with his or her decision to become a reader in the first place and to turn to books for a particular type of emotional or ethical uplift. It continued with the search for the right books, which took the reader not into nature or a small alpine village, but into the hustle of the book trade. We should not forget that, before anything else, neo-intensive reading was a phenomenon with roots deeply planted in commercial print and that it developed, as a distinct style, from as commercialized a relationship to books as there had ever been in the history of reading. In the *Tableau de Paris*, Louis-Sébastien Mercier describes a young girl who was told by her mother that she didn't want her to read. This has the predictable effect:

The desire to read builds in her; [...] she goes out furtively, enters the store of a bookseller, asks him for *La Nouvelle Héloïse*, of which she's heard people speak; the man smiles; she pays and holes up in her room. What is the result of this clandestine pleasure? I owe my heart to my lover; and when I'm married, I will be everything to my husband. (1:1047)

The scene shows the absurdity of reading prohibitions and echoes the neo-intensive authorial claim that reading brings moral direction and purpose to the reader. It also, of course, highlights all the requisite efforts that called the experience into being, including the girl's determination to overcome whatever obstacles were put in her path.

Above all, though, it is her easy willingness and ability to navigate the book trade that allows us to reframe the question of neo-intensive reading and to understand it in a new light. Mercier's image raises questions about how uni-directional the textual exchange conceptualized in the fan mail, and in the studies based on this correspondence, really was. For the girl's sentimental education rested not simply on Rousseau's ability to speak to her and open her eyes to virtue. It rested no less on the girl's *a priori* longing for a certain type of affective experience, on her assumption that a particular kind of book was the place to look for it. It relied on her access to this book and on her understanding, once she had acquired it, of how to use it (reading alone in her room...). Essential to the realization of this experience was, then, a developed market that comprehended her desire and was reliably able to channel and satisfy it. I find the bookseller's smile significant in this respect, because he has anticipated her demand and is rewarded for his acumen. The girl, in turn, shells out what the book, and the experience she gleans from it, are worth to her. At root, we have a commercial transaction that, I believe, is just as defining of neo-intensive reading than the penning of a letter to an author. In fact, we might surmise that it is precisely the context of the impersonal market that makes the 'intimist' connection between reader and writer so meaningful. In this respect, neo-intensive readers were not just lonely beings absorbing in quiet solitude the wisdom of an author; they were, in essence, book trade customers—we know of Jean Ranson's feelings about Rousseau from his ongoing correspondence with a friend from schooldays in Neuchâtel who had gone into the bookselling business and served now as one of his suppliers—and their venturing into the market was as much part of what defined them as readers as the tears they privately shed, or at least confessed to shedding in the letters that recounted these emotional reading experiences.

The reader/author relationship that defined neo-intensive reading was, as such, more precarious and less direct than its articulations imply, for it was mediated by the reader's presence in the commercial sphere of the book trade, and was dependent on a series of other relationships—with booksellers and go-betweens—that provided the necessary framework for an 'intimist' reading premised on the denial of any mediation of the experience of the text as pure communion with its author. Most precarious of all perhaps was the complex relationship that then prevailed between two seemingly distinct personae of this modern reader him or herself, that is, the obedient disciple who submitted to the author's moral vision and the paying customer whose demand for the validating experience of partaking in such a vision and whose initiative in seeking it out mobilized a publishing business to produce the desired books, marketing them as what the reader wanted: not an object that the reader would care to touch, but the pure sincere expressions of a transcendent authorial figure, by whom, of course, the reader would *be touched*. The feasibility of this 'communion' of two selves was a key manifestation of the dematerialization of reading; for it was only by forgetting that one held in one's hands a commodity produced for the mass-market by a profit-seeking dealer that one could be 'touched' by the text and more saliently, by the author's vision that this text conveyed.

WORKS CITED

Bénichou, Paul. *Le Sacre de l'écrivain 1750-1850, essai sur l'avènement d'un pouvoir spirituel laïque dans la France moderne*. 1973. Paris: Éditions Gallimard, 1996. Print.

Blanning, T.C.W. *The Culture of Power and the Power of Culture: Old Regime Europe, 1660-1789*. Oxford: Oxford UP, 2002. Print.

Chartier, Roger. *Inscription and Erasure. Literature and Written Culture from the Eleventh to the Eighteenth Century*. Trans. Arthur Goldhammer. Philadelphia, PA: U of Pennsylvania P, 2007. Print.

---. "Laborers and Voyagers: From the Text to the Reader." Trans. J.T. González. *Diacritics* 22.2 (Summer 1992): 49-61. Print.

---. "Loisir et sociabilité: lire à haute voix dans l'Europe moderne." *Littératures classiques* 12 (1990): 127-47. Print.

Clanchy, Michael. "Literate and Illiterate; Hearing and Seeing: England 1066-1307." *Literacy and Social Development in the West: A Reader*. Ed. Harvey Graff. Cambridge: Cambridge UP, 1981. 14-45. Print.

Darnton, Robert. "Readers Respond to Rousseau: The Fabrication of Romantic Sensitivity." *The Great Cat Massacre and other Episodes in French Cultural History*. New York: Vintage Books, 1985. 215-56. Print.

De Certeau, Michel. "Reading as Poaching." *The Practice of Everyday Life*. Berkeley, CA: U of California P, 1988. Print.

Diderot, Denis. "Éloge de Richardson." *Oeuvres esthétiques*. Ed. Paul Vernière. Paris: Garnier frères, 1968. 21-48. Print.

Eisenstein, Elisabeth. *The Printing Press as an Agent of Change: Communications and Cultural Transformations in Early Modern Europe*. 2 vols. Cambridge: Cambridge UP, 1979. Print.

Electronic Enlightenment. Dir. Robert McNamee. Vers. 2.4. University of Oxford, 2013. Web.

Engelsing, Rolf. "Die Perioden der Lesergeschichte in der Neuzeit." *Archiv für Geschichte des Buchwesens* 10 (1970): 946-1002. Print.

Flaubert, Gustave. *Madame Bovary: Provincial Ways*. Trans. and ed. Lydia Davis. New York: Viking, 2010. Print.

Goulemot, Jean, and Didier Masseau. "Lettres au Grand Homme ou Quand les lecteurs écrivent." *La lettre à la croisée de l'individuel et du social*. Ed. Mireille Bossis. Paris: Éditions Kimé, 1994. 39-48. Print.

Hanebutt-Benz, Eva-Maria. *Die Kunst des Lesens. Lesemöbel und Leserverhalten vom Mittelalter bis zur Gegenwart*. Frankfurt/Main: Museum für Kunsthandwerk, 1985. Print.

Hellman, Mimi. "Furniture, Sociability, and the Work of Leisure in Eighteenth-Century France." *Eighteenth-Century Studies* 32.4 (Summer 1999): 415-45. Print.

Lyons, Martyn. *A History of Reading and Writing in the Western World*. New York: Palgrave Macmillan, 2010. Print.

McEachern, Jo-Anne. "*La Nouvelle Héloïse*: Some Bibliographical Problems." *Eighteenth-Century Fiction* 1.4 (July 1989): 305-18. Print.

Mercier, Louis-Sébastien. *Tableau de Paris*. Ed. Jean-Claude Bonnet. 2 vols. Paris: Mercure de France, 1994. Print.

Paige, Nicholas. "Rousseau's Readers Revisited: The Aesthetics of *La Nouvelle Héloïse*." *Eighteenth-Century Studies* 42.1 (Fall 2008): 131-54. Print.

Pearson, Jacqueline. *Women's Reading in Britain 1750-1835: A Dangerous Recreation*. Cambridge: Cambridge UP, 1999. Print.

Petrucci, Armando. "Reading in the Middle Ages." *The History of Reading: A Reader*. Ed. Shafquat Twoheed, Rosalind Crone, and Katie Halsey. London: Routledge, 2010. 275-82. Print.

Rousseau, Jean Jacques. *Collected Writings of Rousseau*. Ed. Christopher Kelly, Roger D. Masters, and Peter G. Stillman. 13 vols. Hanover, NH: UP of New England, 1990-2010. Print.

---. *Correspondance complète de Jean-Jacques Rousseau*. Ed. R. A. Leigh. 52 vols. Geneva: Institut et Musée Voltaire, 1965-1998. Print.

---. *Oeuvres completes*. Ed. Bernard Gagnebin. 5 vols. Paris: Gallimard, 1959-1995. Print.

Saenger, Paul. *Space Between Words: The Origin of Silent Reading*. Stanford: Stanford UP, 1997. Print.

Wittmann, Reinhard. "Was There a Reading Revolution at the End of the Eighteenth Century?" *A History of Reading in the West*. Ed. Guglielmo Cavallo and Roger Chartier. Amherst, MA: U of Massachusetts P, 1999. 284-312. Print.

Authorship, Participation, and Media Change: Perspectives from Medieval Studies

ALBRECHT HAUSMANN

Participation has so far played a minor role for the description of medieval societies and their predominant forms of social interaction.[1] This could be owing to the term's normative-ideological connotations which nearly inextricably bind it to political and social concepts of the modern period. Discussing participation usually presupposes a modern society that is based on the division of labour—a society that is characterised by a conception of justice in which each individual's sharing in the entire system's resources and decision-making processes is a desirable norm. Participation, in this sense, is at the core of all western democracies and especially of the democratic welfare state of European design (cf. von Ungern-Sternberg/Reinau 1-2, Riescher/Rosenzweig). Medieval society, however, being organized according to feudalism and strict hierarchies, allocated a clearly defined place to each individual. Participating in other spheres than those assigned was uncalled for and punished as transgressive. This also applies to what is at the heart of this contribution—vernacular court culture. It exists within a small, exclusive area that is accessible only to members of the courtly aristocracy.

---

1   Some recent studies, for instance, deal with the political participation of members of the aristocracy (Dendorfer) or participatory concepts during the early modern period (Auge/Büsing; Mertens).

Conceptions of participation did exist in the Middle Ages. The individual participated in the redemptive deed of Christ and the mercy of God (cf. Meinhardt; Hedwig); members of a dynasty or group could share in their leader's or ancestor's social prestige. Usually, however, these forms of 'participation' were not organised along or modelled against a modern understanding of the concept of participation. They were rather based on the idea of giving (and possibly receiving rewards in return), all within the framework of personal relationships (cf. Oswald 13-56). Participation was hence understood as the result of another person's generosity. The master bestowed a gift upon an inferior and rewarded a service, God bestowed mercy. These actions expressed a sense of justice that could not be attained by participation but understood as a personal virtue on the part of someone who commands resources. It appears that medieval production of literature follows the same logic: Secular and clerical patrons commissioned authors to produce certain texts. The return for resources provided by the patron was the completed literary product.

The following article does not focus on the alliance between patron and author. This has already been explored (cf. Bumke *Mäzene*; Bumke *Höfische Kultur* 595-784). I am more interested in the medieval production of (literary) texts, in which a functional differentiation is significantly less developed than in similar structures in the modern age. My immediate interest is the indistinct role of the author and his relation with the audience. Throughout the long history of research into medieval concepts of authorship (cf. Minnis; Partridge/Kwakkel), medieval studies has shown time and again that authorship in pre-modern times is completely different from authorship today. The notion of the author that emphasizes the creation of a new work attributed solely to his self as a great achievement did not become manifest in the domain of vernacular medieval literature—despite the importance of authorship as an important concept of order and estimation in certain genres and certain texts (collections of lyrics according to the author principle, attribution of anonymous texts or of 'forgeries' to names of authors, in order to valorize those texts).

Texts that had been reworked multiple times varied to a high degree, which has led medieval studies to conclude that the authorial text was less significant (cf. Cerquiglini 105-16; cf. Bußmann et al.). In fact, reproducers (editors, scribes) were considered to have participated in the process of reworking in an author-like manner. In the manner supported by Joachim

Bumke (*Vier Fassungen* 42-53), this claim may be considered problematic for several reasons (Hausmann, "Mittelalterliche Überlieferung" 76-80) but it nevertheless opens up a broad field of 'alliances' and processes of participation (Hausmann, "Überlieferungsvarianz und Medienwechsel"). Notwithstanding, in comparison to other actors involved in the processes of creating and reworking texts, the author's position appears to have been less strongly differentiated. Ways of participation and practices of forming alliances, however, can indeed be discerned at this point and show parallels with the development of the 21st century's Web 2.0 culture (Hausmann, "Zukunft der Gutenberg-Galaxis" 37-39).

The lack of mechanical possibilities of mass reproduction was crucial for this: Prior to the age of letterpress printing, texts were on the one hand received in oral presentations and on the other hand reproduced manually by ways of medieval manuscript culture. In these two sectors—and this is my initial hypothesis—producer and recipient were more closely connected than is the case in the sector of printed books, where the recipient has no opportunity of participation that reflects back to the text directly and without mediation and thus cannot participate.[2] The individual cannot change the text but merely document his reception of the same via markings and marginalia.

Below, I aim to test whether this proximity between production and reception in oral presentations and hand-written processes of distribution indeed enabled historically specific formations of alliances as well as possibilities of participation and in what shapes these are documented. In the context of the invention and dissemination of the printing press, the question of whether these possibilities of participation changed at all, in what ways these changes occurred and what kinds of new alliances can be identified around 1500 is raised. This article argues that the medieval culture of performance and manuscripts did offer ways of participation. At first sight, these appear to have faded to the background in the age of the printing press but have actually continued to exist on the margins of cultural production and could be relevant to our perception of the changing Web 2.0. After all, observations regarding the fluidity and processuality of texts online— think ever-changing Wikipedia articles—and regarding the dissolution be-

---

2   Reader-response criticism would consider the receivers' reading of the text an achievement itself. The following contribution's focus, however, lies elsewhere.

tween author and recipient in the realm of fan fiction can obviously be compared with phenomena from pre-Gutenberg times.

PERFORMATIVE AUTHORSHIP AND PARTICIPATION

According to all that we know, the vernacular literature at high medieval courts was presented orally to a larger or smaller audience (cf. Green 105-12; 208-10); it was not made for an individual reading in private but for a group of listeners in a primary situation of reception where it was probably the author himself who recited his own work. This performative act took place in court, which was a site of exclusively aristocratic conviviality and soon enough copied by the urban elites.

During the in-situ oral presentation of literature, authors and recipients were close to one another physically: They were in the same spot at the same time. The number of listeners, however, did not matter. What mattered was the rank and prestige of those present, not the overall turnout. Unlike is the case with the printed book (or, for that matter, modern theatre where you pay to participate), the success of orally-recited vernacular literature in the Middle Ages is measured against the high-ranking recipients' approval or disapproval and not against the number of recipients (and consequently buyers). Out of these conditions arose possibilities of participation for recipients, which only marginally, if at all, exist for the printed book.

Even if these possibilities are hard to reconstruct owing to their being bound to oral representation, some can at least be distinguished roughly:

(1) The roles of author and recipient in more concise literary forms like lyric poetry or shorter narratives were interchangeable among attendees. Whenever those present recited songs or stories to one another, literature became part of the social life and convivial gatherings at court which rendered participation possible for potentially all members of court in a playful fashion. This phenomenon, considered from the point of view of social life and sociability as well as in connection with the term 'conversation,' has been a focus in research over the past few years.

In a broad study of literary depictions of "Geselligkeit" (or social life, to which this text also refers to as sociability or conviviality) in texts, Caroline Emmelius has shown that the tension between the hierarchic social order and a socially levelling conviviality, both characteristics of premodern societies, is presented and discussed in literature itself (cf. 1-27). The most prominent example of this type of literary presentation is the frame narrative in Giovanni Boccaccio's *Decameron*. At the signs of social disintegration, ten young adults—seven women und three men—flee to a country house outside the city of Florence and for ten days form a community within which a literary game is played. Presided over by an elected 'King' or 'Queen of the Day,' each member of this alliance tells one story per day, producing a total of one hundred stories. This practice of 'novellare,' which denotes the telling of stories to one another, is seldom found in the German-speaking region. Only the beginning of the *Nonnenturnier* (*nuns' tournament*) indicates that telling stories to one another also contributed to social life at court:

Ir herschaft, ir solt gedagen,
so wil ich euch sagen.
ir sollent stille sweigen
beide tanzen und g[e]igen.
des sollen wir beginnen
und ein ander kurzweile bringen
(on manigerlei seitenspil)
das gelt uns freuden vil,
das uns dest minner möge betragen:
wir sollen nu abenteur sagen. (*Nonnenturnier* v. 1-10)

(Kind people, settle down now, so I can tell you something. Quit all of that dancing and fiddling. Let us begin instead and take up a different pastime (without all that music), which will give us much pleasure, so that we are even less bored: We shall tell stories.)

Yet, the *nuns' tournament*, an extremely gory story about a severed but nonetheless very lively penis that has gone into hiding in a convent and is turned into an object of desire for the sadistic and libidinous nuns, is not a representative text. Similarly, the *Decameron* stages a literary utopia rather than reflecting social realities.

Minnesang, which is a highly artificial love poetry that is presented/ delivered as a song and dates from the time between 1160 and 1350, reveals that participation in the context of social life at court did exist after all. Those minnesongs that were passed on suggest that authors and recipients were not strictly separated at the beginning of this development and within certain circles even into the 13th century. Furthermore, male members of the higher nobility as amateurs created small works themselves and thus participated in a representative art form that was claimed to be highly aristocratic. The aristocratic society used it to discuss and sing about their elaborate and cultivated concepts of erotic love (cf. Lembke 13-48).

However, it transpires that professional or semi-professional singers became increasingly active, which limited the recipients' possibilities of participation to the intellectually active reception of the songs presented. Within this context, *Minnesang* has been characterised as a 'para-ritual' (Müller; cf. Strohschneider), in which participation means taking part without actually producing a literary text.

(2) Even when longer texts were presented orally by one and the same speaker/author, participants could intervene in the process of presentation by means of applauding, objecting, suggesting improvements, and so on. Considering that extracts of longer works were being presented whilst still being created and prior to the completion of the entire work, it can be supposed that experiences during recitals as well as feed-back did impact the texts. These types of situations can be found in middle high German works as worked into the texts themselves and integrated as fictions and fictional apostrophes by the audience. *Erec* by Hartmann of Aue (c. 1180) is a well-known example for this: Upon the narrator's description of the elaborately decorated saddle that the female protagonist Enite's horse is endowed with, he is interrupted by a listener:

"nû swîc, lieber Hartmann:
ob ich ez errâte?"
ich tuon: nu sprechet drâte.
"ich muoz gedenken ê dar nâch."
nu vil drâte, mir ist gâch. (*Erec* 7493-97)

("Quiet now, dear Hartmann, might I be able to guess it?" —Agreed: Now speak at last. "I have to think about it first."—Make haste, I'm in a hurry.)

The ensuing dialogue between narrator and interjector continues for nearly 40 lines and ends with the narrator's remark: "ir sult mich'z iu sagen lân" (7525—Leave the report to me). This certainly is a literary stylisation in which the interfering listener is characterised as a fool who has not grasped the principle of staging literature (cf. *Erec*, Commentary 911-16).

On the one hand, the passage reveals that this type of interference was marked as a break of convention among Hartmann's contemporaries. On the other hand, it does indicate that direct interaction with the audience was not unheard of. The passage bears in mind the oral situation of presentation: For the recital/performance of the text to work, there needs to be a silent alliance between the author and the larger part of the audience, an alliance in which tasks are clearly divided. Only if no one disputes the author's claim to the text's design, can the audience appreciate the recital.

(3) A further possibility of forming an alliance is closely connected with the oral practice of presentation and the texts' performative design: Because the recipients are also physically a community of attendees, it is all the easier for the author to establish a spiritual community of recipients. This spiritual community is addressed and even reaffirmed in the narrative texts' prologues but also in the poetry itself. This creation at times works by means of a negative process in which a rejecting attitude towards reception is addressed, one that is not to be found in the real performative situation. The actual audience is affirmed as understanding as well as gifted with a good attitude towards reception by means of this seeming "performative antagonism" (cf. *Kaiserchronik*, prologue). The antagonism itself is only stated and it is actually establishing a performative alliance.

Gottfried of Strassburg's *Tristan* novel is probably the most significant example of the formation of an alliance between author and audience (in fact: narrator and audience as evoked by the text). This highly problematic story about the 'necessity' of adultery is presented to the recipients as 'innelîchen guot'—good from the inside—as early as in the prologue (*Tristan* v. 173). According to the narrator, you could only grasp this if you belonged to the *edlen herzen* (noble hearts), meaning an exclusive group of people who have experienced love themselves and hence possess a special sensitivity and a special understanding for narrating love. Gottfried may create exclusivity by this, at the same time he affirms his true audience: It is during the act of reception, which in this case means accepting the story at hand and which is made visible through the audience's presence and their listening, that the exact same people are shown to be of "noble hearts." Although this process works when reading in private, the community established by the text is of a spiritual kind. In contrast, the alliance is forged during a presentation at court is one that integrates and stabilises courtly society beyond a purely literary context.

I have so far described phenomena that can be reconstructed for the praxis of orally presenting vernacular literature and that emerge as specifically 'medieval' when juxtaposed with the developed culture of the printed book in modern times. In those times, it could be assumed that the strict division between production and reception impedes a similar achievement of social integration. From a producer's perspective, the act of reception is virtualized: Nobody can know for sure where the printed book is headed and who will receive it where and how. Courtly society, to which the act of reception can add stability but which already exist prior to this (people may know each other from other contexts), is replaced by a largely anonymous 'public' in the case of the printed book.

This clearly discernible contrast may lead to simplifications. Oral ways of presentation have by no means disappeared along with the development of the printing press—they have been marginalised. Similar forms of participative literary social life have for a long time survived in the modern era and still exist today. The young poets of the *Sturm & Drang* period recited their poems to each other, as do participants of the recently popularised poetry slams. Still, practices like these usually appear as preforms or deficit-ridden substitutes for the printed publications of a work. Since letterpress printing has been firmly established, being a 'proper' author requires finding a publishing house that publishes the work in print. Printing has pushed direct literary conviviality to the margins of the literary field and replaced it with virtualised forms of reception that have an elevated author figure at their core.

RE-TELLING AND THE ALLIANCE WITH THE AUTHOR'S SOURCE MATERIAL/ORIGINAL

Despite having mainly been presented and received orally, vernacular literature of the 12th and 13th centuries is not oral poetry (cf. Zumthor; Schäfer; Green). The authors conceived of and recorded their works in writing and orally presented them afterwards. It is presumed that these written texts are the origin of the records preserved until today, which only in rare cases consist of autographs and usually consist of more recent transcripts. Literary texts are hence part of a script-based process of production and distribution, one that is typical for medieval manuscript culture and in which the author of the text was only one of several actors. In the case of German narrative texts dating from ca. 1200, this process started out with a master copy in Old French;[3] that a pre-texts exists even for this, is neglected at this point.

The German author, who in all likelihood acted on the orders of a patron or a group of interested people and not of his own accord, translated this original into German (cf. Bumke, *Mäzene* 13-21). This was not a translation in any 'modern' sense but a relatively free reworking that interferes—sometimes to an astoundingly high degree—with the depictions and the content of the original text (cf. Worstbrock, "Übersetzen und Wiedererzählen"; Bumke, "Retextualisierung" 13-43; Bußmann et al.). Being bound to the original in the (narrative-)literary production around the year 1200, the medieval status of authorship was affected in an entirely different manner than has been the case since the 18th century under the influence of modern aesthetics of genius and innovation and the resulting claim to autonomy by the author. In the Middle Ages, the author understood himself as a reproducer, not as an inventor (cf. Worstbrock, "Dilatatio materiae").

Poetics at the time provided authors, whose tasks were by no means limited to the transmission/transfer of one language to another but also included intralingual reworkings, with a refined and scholarly set of instruments aided by which an author could treat his original (cf. ibid.). The term 're-telling' has been introduced for this in German medieval studies. This re-telling might also be a way of participating in a process of text creation

---

3 Cf. the debate on the so-called "Adaptation courtoise" (as prompted by Huby in 1968). Having been influenced by national undertones, the discussion was firmly and historically accurately located by Worstbrock (cf. "Dilatatio materiae").

and reception over several steps. Within this framework of participation, the German-speaking author enters a sort of alliance with the author of the original, albeit a highly problematic alliance. These types of reworkings are not translations but very free adaptations that sometimes even run counter to the original author's intentions, which the following example illustrates.

In Chrétien de Troyes first Artus novel *Erec et Enide* (originating ca. 1160-1170 in France), a coincidence that is astounding, yet vital to the plot's progress, happens after Erec, who has recovered from a state of suspended animation, frees his wife Enide from the hands of the Duke of Limor: Erec and Enide enter the castle's yard in urgent need of a horse for their escape. Help is conveniently on its way when a knave happens to be passing the yard with his horse, which is even bridled and saddled:

Erec corut son escu prandre;
Par le guige a son col le pant,
Et Enide la lance prant;
Si s'an vienent parmi la cort.
N'i a si hardi, qui la tort;
Car ne cuidoient pas, que fust
Hon, qui si chacier les deüst,
Mes deables ou anemis,
Qui dedanz le cors se fust mis.
Tuit s'an fuient, Erec les chace,
Et trueve fors anmi la place
Un garcon, qui voloit mener
Son destrier a l'eve abevrer,
Atorné de frain et de sele. (Chrétien, *Erec* v. 4886-99)

(Erec ran to get his shield. He straps it around his neck and Enide takes the lance. They proceed to the middle of the yard. No one dares offer resistance since no one not believes that a human being could be chasing them off but that it is the devil or a demon that has/had entered the corpse. All escape and Erec is chasing them when outside in the middle of the yard encountering a knave, who had wanted to lead his saddled and bridled horse to water.)

Chrétien laconically comments the coincidence he himself created: "Ceste avanture li fu bele" (v. 4900—He was fortunate).

Upon creating a Middle High German version of the novel's Old-French original, Hartmann's of Aue interferences with the original copy emerge in his reworking of the passage at hand. In his version, the escape is not a coincidence but a direct consequence of God's mercy and thus an illustration of Erec's *saelikeit* (beatitude). By directly calling on God, the narrator had ceded power over the events before the actual escape:

nû müeze got gesenden
disen ellenden,
Êrecke und Ênîten,
ros dâ si ûfe rîten. (Hartmann, *Erec* v. 6698-6701)

(Now may God send a horse to Erec and Enide, the strays, so they can ride away.)

For the recipient, the potency of divine decree is confirmed once by the granting of the appeal in the plot and once more explicitly by the narrator, who dispels all doubts: "ez vuocte eht gotes wille" (v. 6726—and it fell into place by God's will).

This emphatic sentence (*eht!*) can be read as a revision of what the narrator in Chrétien commented: It is not by chance that is merely because an author wants it, that something happens. For Hartmann, the randomness of the escape and the authorisation of the plot as staged as a coincidence by the author, were not enough. It transpires that God's special mercy has come to rest on Erec. As re-teller of Chrétien's novel, Hartmann does not claim sovereignty over the proceedings but presents himself (more precisely: his narrator) as an interpreter of events guided by God and reported by him. He claims to be a type of secondary author who merely claims to repeat what the actual author—God and by no means Chrétien as the author of the original narrative—has let happen.

The following point may only be touched upon briefly. By using this or other means, Hartmann critically engages with the original and focuses on an aspect that scholars time and again understood as a major innovation by Chrétien. Medieval studies described the clear direction of plot arrangement, in which a worldly author is at the helm instead of God, as an innovation and at times as the true "invention of fictionality" in the Middle Ages (cf. Haug 91-107; Utti 36). Hartmann distances himself from exactly this aspect.

This example exposes the licences of the 're-teller': Although he does not change the narrative's actual course of events, their evaluation changes significantly. These interferences are not only located on the *discours* level but also concern *histoire*, considering that the questions of whether and how God intervenes are not purely evaluative for the medieval author but are also understood as part of the narrated story. Hartmann of Aue's approach differs extremely from what is expected from an interpreter today: His approach neither aims to accurately reproduce the original (defying the criterion of equivalence), nor to 'understand' the original in the spirit of the original author (Chrétien de Troyes) nor to pass on this understanding (hermeneutic approach)—Hartmann develops the original further and endows it with a different and distinct direction.

It becomes clear at this point that medieval processes of transmission bear a special potential for participation: Because the postulate for equivalence, which is regarded as essential to modern translating, obviously does not apply in the same way here as it does in modern times, reproducers could keep reworking their originals in a process that is never quite terminated. Whether re-tellers had developed awareness of their actually altering the original cannot always be accounted for. It appears that in a few cases their behaviour merely exhibits a different type of 'hermeneutics': They rendered absolute their own efforts of reception, turned those into texts and remained in good faith of exactly expressing what had been included in the original. In other cases, the reproducers seem to have known what they did. This is where a certain form of autonomy held by the medieval re-teller emerges. It is exactly because he had received the outside order of reworking a certain original that he could develop a critical stance towards the original text and interfere with it.

As has been done for the area of orality, research in medieval studies has tried to identify the special specifics of medieval vernacular narrative literature in connection with the term 're-telling.' 'Re-telling,' the assumption goes, may reveal a specifically medieval way of handling literary originals whereby elements of interpreting (in a narrower, hermeneutic sense) and elements of free invention mix without differentiation. This argument should be treated with caution. Phenomena of the modern age, which may be regarded as very meaningful and characteristic for the modern era by traditional literary scholars and philologists and are part of their privileged objects of investigation are employed as points of comparison by this hypothesis. Yet, they do not stand in isolation.

Examples for 're-tellings' in the medieval sense have existed in the modern age and up until today: The integrity of the original is of minor importance when adapting a novel for the screen; adaptations of narratives ('for a young audience' or for learners of a foreign language) alter the original; works newly adapt and stage classical texts over and over again. The medieval practice of re-telling is by no means a historically specific and unique way of participating in the further development of a work. Similar processes are taking place today but have not been at the center of tradtional medieval literary studies aligned with originality for a long time. Medieval studies has so far also only taken a marginal interest in researching adaptations. It can be argued that forms of re-telling still exist, despite their being less connected with the translation from one language into another and move alongside changes in the mediascape or addressees ('for a young audience,' 'for learners'). Owing to the cultures of the 20th and 21st centuries being medially heterogeneous, the term 'text' needs to be modified, it either needs to be specified more closely or to be widened to include different media-related phenomena.

The status of authorship within a culture of re-telling also calls for a differentiated inspection. The medieval re-teller is certainly nor as emphatically an author in the sense of a modern author subject to an aesthetics of genius and conceptions of autonomy. Still, this limited notion of the author although it is not alien to the modern age, although it is not at the centre of literary scholarship either: The script writer of a novel's screen adaptation is thus more closely related to the medieval re-teller than to the genius-laden author whom literary studies have been primarily concerned with since the 19th century.

REWORKING AS A PRODUCTIVE FORM OF PARTICIPATION

Medieval texts from around 1200 nearly always came to us as copies that are often considerably younger than the texts themselves. There are frequently decades and sometimes even centuries between the likely date of the work's inception and the oldest manuscript in which the work has been preserved. The process of copying between these points can only be reconstructed based on scripts that have been conserved. Among these, the form of the text frequently differs, there are frequent variations on various levels (such as scope or extent of the text, or wording), which is why it can be assumed that processes of copying were not mainly concerned with staying true to their original. Medieval scribes appear to have commonly interfered in originals and to an extent clearly adapted the texts to their own needs.

As one of the most striking phenomena when examining textuality in medieval manuscript culture, the variance of copies has triggered discussions about how this aspect can be made perceptible in the texts' editions. Scholars have once more suggested interpreting the phenomenon as a historical characteristic of the Middle Ages. Medieval reworking is claimed to have been shaped by the scribes' licence to alter and early writers especially could be understood as editors of versions and thus similar to authors (cf. Bumke, *Vier Fassungen* 30-60; Hausmann, "Mittelalterliche Überlieferung" 76-80). Effectively, this licence can be understood as a possibility of participation for the group of recipients to whom the scribes also belong: They may cause the distribution of the texts but nevertheless interfere with them, which means that the author's original texts can sometimes no longer be identified. The process of re-telling continues into the reworking and it could be argued that medieval texts should not be regarded as solid texts but as processes that can only be grasped by their processuality.

Nevertheless, there is a danger of overestimating this historical phenomenon when choosing an ill-fitted modern reference. When taking the printed book as a starting point, differences between several versions of one and the same text will be striking. In the age of the letterprinting press, after all, the copies of one edition are not only usually identical, but the printed version of a work is also treated in a privileged manner and will sooner enter the literary canon than a manuscript. The 'text' of a work then comprises the first edition and the respective autographs. Everything else, be it a reader's excerpt or side notes in a printed book, are no longer part of the work's tradition but belong to the area of private reception. This does not apply in manuscript culture where the records of the process of reception as written down by the scribe are perceived as part of the work's tradition.

When taken to extremes, a text clearly intended as an excerpt of the original may serve as material for tradition—and from a philologist's point of view will provide a 'bad' text. To put it differently, recipients of literary works had access to a large site of participation in medieval manuscript culture because certain recipients—that is to say the scribes—could directly inject their impressions of reception in the process of reworking the text. In the case of a printed book, the text does not change by the different readers' different receptions;[4] who understood what and how is simply not considered. In medieval manuscript culture, at least a few readers directly participated in the text's design, which was the case whenever they copied the text. Whereas in manuscript culture (re)production and reception amalgamated, they are separated strictly in the culture of printed books. Once it is printed, a book cannot be altered.

SUMMARY

When compared to the modern period, conception of authorship was less distinguished in the medieval centuries owing to the oral situation of reception, the dominating practice of re-telling and the amalgamation of reproduction and reception within manuscript culture. The audience's and the re-producers' participation in literary (re)productions was hence possible to a palpable extent and was being tolerated. Authors saw themselves as reproducers participating in the process of re-telling, they formed an alliance with the originals' authors without leaving the latters' products untouched. Only since the establishment of letterpress printing have reception and reproduction become more clearly distinguished. The printed text defies control by recipients and is admitted to the canon. Even though many more people consumed literature in the times of letterpress printing than in medieval times, this initially also entailed a limitation of people's possibilities of participation. In return, however, the author could sharpen his profile and obtain authority/sovereignty over his text, a process that is ambivalent.

Authorship on the one hand develops into a core concept of modern textuality and literariness/poeticity and on the other hand the talk of 'autonomous authorship' conceals the actual involvement of authors in an openly

---

4 Of course, this only applies to copies of the same edition. Printers and publishers are able to alter texts from one edition to their next; their creative leeway was similar to a medieval scribe's. Still, opportunities to intervene were only open to a very small number of reproducers in the age of letterpress printing.

and latently constrained literary business. As described by Barthes, the notion of an emphatic conception of authorship in the modern era appears to be an ideological correlative to a development in which the author is increasingly forced to enter precarious alliances with publishers, professional editors and literary critics. Becoming a literary author in modern times requires his or her book(s) to be printed. Authorship is consequently linked more and more to an economic process: Those who want to pass off as authors must find a financier willing to pre-finance the costly procedure of mechanical reproduction based on expected profits. The alliance between author and publisher thus characterises the entire modern period.

Although perceived as marginal and are commonly disregarded in traditional literary studies, the medieval ways of participation as listed here (literary conviviality, re-telling, reproduction by hand) continue to exist. In modern times, the phenomenon of 're-telling' is attached to changes in media (dramatization of narratives, adaptation of films). Re-telling hence exists in areas that are free from the printed book's conception of textuality and thereby escapes the notion of an author-text set in stone. Only within these areas is it regarded as legitimate.

Against the backdrop of these medieval circumstances, current developments on the Internet and in social media are of particular interest since certain Web 2.0 practices imitate ways of medieval social life. Users in literary online forums are not either readers or authors but fulfil both roles by 'alternately' uploading their products. Financiers to bankroll the costly operation of reproduction are no longer needed when publishing online and homepages are easily affordable. The new capital on the Internet is the recipients' attention, which has turned into a scarce and sought after good. In order to attract attention, oral forms of communication are being imitated more and more. At the same time, face-to-face communications in real life (readings, concerts etc.) is vital if authors want to increase their online presence. The development of the Internet may give the impression that literary practices were marginalised or even oppressed in the era of the printing press—practices that were well-known in medieval centuries and that are now slowly re-emerging opposed by a well-established copyright industry that also includes literary publishers. Putting this current development into a historical perspective is a new task for medieval studies.

Works Cited

Auge, Oliver, and Burkhard Büsing, eds. *Der Vertrag von Ripen 1460 und die Anfänge der politischen Partizipation in Schleswig-Holstein, im Reich und in Nordeuropa*. Ostfildern: Thorbecke, 2012. Print.

Bumke, Joachim. *Mäzene im Mittelalter. Die Gönner und Auftraggeber der höfischen Literatur in Deutschland 1150-1300*. München: Beck, 1979. Print.

---. *Höfische Kultur. Literatur und Gesellschaft im hohen Mittelalter*. 2 vol. München: Deutscher Taschenbuch-Verlag, 1986. Print.

---. *Die vier Fassungen der 'Nibelungenklage': Untersuchungen zur Überlieferungsgeschichte und Textkritik der höfischen Epik im 13. Jahrhundert*. Berlin: De Gruyter, 1996. Print.

---. "Retextualisierung in der mittelalterlichen Literatur, besonders in der höfischen Epik. Ein Überblick." *ZfdPh-Sonderheft 124: Retextualisierung in der mittelalterlichen Literatur*. Ed. Joachim Bumke and Ursula Peters. Berlin: Schmidt, 2005. 6-46. Print.

Bußmann, Britta, Albrecht Hausmann, Annelie Kreft, and Cornelia Logemann, eds. *Übertragungen: Formen und Konzepte von Reproduktion in Mittelalter und Früher Neuzeit*. Berlin: De Gruyter. 2005. Print.

Cerquiglini, Bernard. *Éloge de la variante: Histoire critique de la philologie*. Paris: Éditions du Seuil, 1989. Print.

Chrétien de Troyes. *Erec et Enide. Erec und Enide*. Ed. Ingrid Kasten. München: Fink, 1979. Print.

Dendorfer, Jürgen. "Autorität auf Gegenseitigkeit: Fürstliche Partizipation im Reich des 13. Jahrhunderts." *Autorität und Akzeptanz: Das Reich im Europa des 13. Jahrhunderts*. Ed. Hubertus Seibert, Werner Bomm, and Verena Türck. Ostfildern: Thorbecke, 2013. 27-42. Print.

Die Kaiserchronik eines Regensburger Geistlichen. Ed. Edward Schröder. Hannover: Hahn. 1892. Monumenta Germaniae Historica: Deutsche Chroniken und andere Geschichtsbücher des Mittelalters 1,1. Web.

Emmelius, Caroline. *Gesellige Ordnung: Literarische Konzeptionen von geselliger Kommunikation in Mittelalter und Früher Neuzeit*. Berlin: De Gruyter, 2010. Print.

Gottfried von Straßburg. *Tristan und Isold*. Ed. Walter Haug and Manfred Günther Scholz. 2 vols. Berlin: Deutscher Klassiker-Verlag, 2011. Print.

Green, Denis H. *Medieval Listening and Reading: The Primary Reception of German Literature 800-1300*. Cambridge: UP, 1994. Print.

Haug, Walter. *Literaturtheorie im deutschen Mittelalter. Von den Anfängen bis zum Ende des 13. Jahrhunderts.* Darmstadt: Wissenschaftliche Buchgesellschaft, 1985. Print.

Hartmann von Aue. *Erec.* Ed. Manfred Günter Scholz. Trans. Susanne Held. Frankfurt/Main: Deutscher Klassiker Verlag, 2007. Print.

Hausmann, Albrecht. "Mittelalterliche Überlieferung als Interpretationsaufgabe: 'Laudines Kniefall' und das Problem des 'ganzen Textes'." *Text und Kultur: Mittelalterliche Literatur 1150-1450.* Ed. Ursula Peters. Stuttgart: Metzler, 2001. 72-95. Print.

---. "Überlieferungsvarianz und Medienwechsel: Die deutschen Artes dictandi des 15. Jahrhunderts zwischen Manuskript und Buchdruck." *Revue Belge de Philologie et d'Histoire* 83 (2005): 744-68. Print.

---. "Zukunft der Gutenberg-Galaxis." *Aus Politik und Zeitgeschichte* 42/43 (2009): 32-39. Print.

Hedwig, Klaus. "Partizipation. I. Philosophisch." *Lexikon für Theologie und Kirche* 7 (2009): 1398-99. Print.

Huby, Michel. *L'adaptation des romans courtois en Allemagne au XIIe et au XIIIe siècle.* Paris: Klincksieck, 1968. Print.

Lembke, Valeska. *Minnekommunikation: Sprechen über Minne und Sprechen über Dichtung in Epik und Minnesang um 1200.* Heidelberg: Winter, 2013. Print.

Meinhardt, Helmut. "Teilhabe." *Lexikon des Mittelalters* 8 (1999): 527-29. Print.

Mertens, Dieter. "Auf dem Weg zur politischen Partizipation? Die Anfänge der Landstände in Württemberg." *Auf dem Weg zur politischen Partizipation? Landstände und Herrschaft im deutschen Südwesten.* Veröffentlichungen der Kommission für Geschichtliche Landeskunde in Baden-Württemberg: Reihe B Forschungen 182. Ed. Sönke Lorenz and Peter Rückert. Stuttgart: Kohlhammer, 2010. 91-102. Print.

Minnis, Alastair. *Medieval Theory of Authorship: Scholastic Literary Attitudes in the Later Middle Age.* 2nd ed. Philadelphia: Penn P, 2009. Print.

Müller, Jan-Dirk. "Ritual, Sprecherfiktion und Erzählung: Literarisierungstendenzen im späten Minnesang." *Wechselspiele: Kommunikationsformen und Gattungsinterferenzen mittelhochdeutscher Lyrik.* Ed. Michael Schilling and Peter Strohschneider. Heidelberg: Winter, 1996. 43-76. Print.

"Nonnenturnier." *Novellistik des Mittelalters: Märendichtung.* Ed. Klaus Grubmüller. Frankfurt/Main: Deutscher Klassiker Verlag, 1996. 944-77. Print.

Oswald, Marion. *Gabe und Gewalt: Studien zur Logik und Poetik der Gabe in der frühhöfischen Erzählliteratur.* Göttingen: Vandenhoeck & Ruprecht, 2004. Print.

Partridge, Stephen, and Erik Kwakkel, eds. *Author, Reader, Book: Medieval Authorship in Theory and Practice.* Toronto: U of Toronto P, 2011. Print.

Riescher, Gisela, and Beate Rosenzweig. "Partizipation und Staatlichkeit: Ideengeschichte und aktuelle Theoriediskurse." *Partizipation und Staatlichkeit: Ideengeschichtliche und aktuelle Theoriediskurse.* Ed. Riescher and Rosenzweig. Stuttgart: Steiner, 2012. 13-17. Print.

Rückert, Peter, ed. *Landschaft, Land und Leute: Politische Partizipation in Württemberg 1457-2007. Begleitbuch und Katalog zur Ausstellung des Landesarchivs Baden-Württemberg, Hauptstaatsarchiv Stuttgart und des Landtags von Baden-Württemberg.* Stuttgart: Hauptstaatsarchiv Stuttgart, 2007. Print.

Schäfer, Ursula. "Zum Problem der Mündlichkeit." *Modernes Mittelalter: Neue Bilder einer populären Epoche.* Ed. Joachim Heinzle. Frankfurt/Main: Insel-Verlag, 1994. 357-75. Print.

Strohschneider, Peter. "Aufführungssituation: Zur Kritik eines Zentralbegriffs kommunikationsanalytischer Minnesangforschung." *Methodenkonkurrenz in der germanistischen Praxis.* Ed. Johannes Janota. Tübingen: Niemeyer, 1993. 56-71. Print.

Uitti, Karl D., and Michelle A. Freeman. *Chrétien de Troyes Revisited.* New York: Twayne, 1995. Print.

von Ungern-Sternberg, Jürgen, and Hansjörg Reinau. "Einleitung." *Politische Partizipation: Idee und Wirklichkeit von der Antike bis in die Gegenwart.* Ed. von Ungern-Sternberg and Reinau. Berlin: De Gruyter, 2013. 1-2. Print.

Worstbrock, Franz Josef. "Dilatatio materiae: Zur Poetik des 'Erec' Hartmanns von Aue." *Frühmittelalterliche Studien* 19 (1985): 1-30. Print.

---. "Wiedererzählen und Übersetzen." *Mittelalter und frühe Neuzeit: Übergänge, Umbrüche und Neuansätze.* Ed. Walter Haug. Tübingen: Niemeyer, 1999. 128-42. Print.

Zumthor, Paul. *La Lettre et la voix: De la littérature médiévale.* Paris: Éditions du Seuil, 1987. Print.

Politics, Institutions, Movements

Literature happens in the public sphere. This familiar observation has been fundamental to the several angles of inquiry pursued in the previous two sections. The market-related explorations in Section One have placed the focus on the production and circulation of literary and other cultural products which is open for 'general' observation—in which the participants interact with each other on public platforms and using public media. Similarly, as Section Two has demonstrated once more, the establishment of an author is an entirely public affair. Whether we encounter it in its general form, as the exalted discursive status of the concept of authorship, or in the form of the distinctive and characteristic position awarded to an individual author, the status of author is beyond the power of an individual writer to achieve. It is, indeed, beyond the power of any individual agent to confer. Instead, it is the result of the collaborative agency of a whole array of different actors, among whose prominent 'interfaces' is the ensemble of media and mediated phenomena which we generally describe as the 'public sphere.' In the same way the types of multi-agent activities that lead to the production and circulation of literary and cultural artifacts are frequently connected to intentional and concerted action, but appear to result just as much from non-subjective connections between diverse practices and effects.

All of these phenomena—the effects of manifold open or covert market considerations and motivations, and the multi-agent efforts whose point of crystallization is the figure of the author—are made possible by the fact that they happen in a public setting, i.e., in a setting where agents may not be necessarily personally known to each other, and need not even be conscious of each other, yet can become contributing agents to chains of effects which produce the phenomena of market success or authorship. It is these—more or less spontaneous or prearranged—connections of effects, based on—

more or less spontaneous or institutionalized—relationships between actors which our volume seeks to capture under the designation of *precarious alliances*: effects which appear to result from concerted action between actors who are not necessarily in any stable and formalised connection to each other, and whose connection, however stable or temporary the constellations which sustain them may be, is precarious in the sense that they will never achieve permanence.

A complementary consideration is required in relation to the constitutive publicity of the phenomena which we have been analyzing. After all, literature is by no means the only thing that happens in the public sphere. The final section of this volume turns its attention to the fact that, as a consequence, literature often stands in connection to the other phenomena which are prominent in the public sphere. It recognises that neither market considerations nor aesthetic considerations are exclusively responsible for the public presence of literary phenomena—and more specifically that there may be strong interferences between the public discussion of literature and the social structures and the political confrontations, the set of forces which make up what Bourdieu has described as the field of power.

Modern societies also use (or perhaps it is more precise to say: they negotiate) the public sphere both in order to stabilise themselves and to revise the particular forms in which they exist, and the relationships and constellations which exist between their different members. This leads to interferences between the literary and the political which may work in both ways, as the contributions to this section demonstrate for a range of different historical and political settings. Different as the situations and conditions analysed in these contributions may be, they are all set in modern, post-revolutionary societies which all have in common, as a basic structural feature, that their shape and their development can be understood as resulting from the interplay—the confrontation, the negotiation—between diverse and divergent forces and positions.

Two different approaches to the confrontation between these forces may be distinguished, which might be designate respectively as an 'economy of attention' as opposed to an 'economy of directives.' This distinction makes it possible to abstract two partly opposing and partly complementary strategies on the part of those who seek to take control: One strategy, linked to an 'economy of directives,' seeks to dominate and to directly determine the structure of what is publicly sayable by others, through moves of limitation and control—moves to which in the various settings individual measures of subversion or circumvention are developed. The other strategy, linked to an 'economy of attention,' can be seen to work by developing means of achieving a dominant public presence which will overwhelm the opponents through sheer amount or attractiveness of content.

Clearly these two strategies are linked: The public sphere is necessarily correlated to an economy of attention, while the goal of different participants consists in directing this attention, by whatever means they find available or useful. Nevertheless, the contributions to this section show how these respective strategies come into play in different settings, employed by different actors and with varying effects.

Wil Verhoeven's examination of "Print Capitalism and the Birth of Political Modernity" sheds light on a crucial moment in the emergence of this. By analyzing, among other items, what might be described as the reactionary artefacts and cultural products circulated by anti-revolutionary anti-radical propaganda in Britain in the aftermath of the French revolution, Verhoeven turns the spotlight on a point in history when an essentially directive political ambition discovers the efficacy of channelling public attention by means of creating attractions of one's own, rather than (exclusively) by means of seeking to suppress those oppositional positions which might otherwise gain public attention.

The contributions of Gun-Britt Kohler and Arvi Sepp, by contrast, elucidate 20th-century situations in which an 'economy of direction' prevails. Drawing on a field-theoretical approach as proposed by Pierre Bourdieu, both examine the establishment of literary groups and circles in societies which are in the process of being reorganised according to a state-run socialist model, and both trace the options which existed in these settings for literary groups who wished to establish their poetological positions in the public eye. Alternative literary positions, it turns out, are neither completely impossible nor completely absent in these settings, but they are clearly and especially precarious. Their precariousness stems not least from the fact that they require skill and caution to establish, that they involve considerable risks on the part of those who seek to establish these positions or contribute to maintaining them, and that the shifts in the underlying political constellations may produce quiet sudden, throughgoing and decisive shifts in the constellations of the literary field.

In a contribution which also draws on Bourdieu's field theory, Ralf Grüttemeier highlights the fact that patterns of direction have been employed in various pluralistic and democratic countries as well. Analyzing the handling of literary censorship in Australia, and using the case of the Netherlands for the purpose of comparison, Grüttemeier's contribution throws into relief the history of a culture of literary censorship in which the field of power seeks to maintain a directive option through the paradoxical measure of delegating it to literary experts who are placed in the positions of censors. However precarious it still might be, this move itself is read here as a growing recognition of the autonomy of literature at a point when the degree of institutional autonomy in the Australian literary field is relatively low—the establishment of a form of censorship which helped to pave the way for the stronger and more pluralistic literary field emerging in Australia since the 1960s.

In the final contribution to this volume, Anton Kirchhofer analyzes the concept of 'movement' as a special form of precarious alliance, involving—potentially—those who may see themselves as members of a movement, as well as—necessarily—those who identify others as members of movements. Reviewing both the thematic spread of the concept and the divergent and discontinuous state of conceptualizations of the phenomenon across a range of disciplinary contexts, Kirchhofer sketches a view of the emergence of the discourse on movements. In the context of this section, this this historical and functional conceptualisation of 'movements'—as a phenomenon which has, after all, been central in the literary history as well as in political debate of the past two centuries—may be placed in the context of the interplay between strategies belonging to the economies of directive and of attention. The concept of 'the movement,' the literary movement as well as the political or social movement, may then be understood as a bid for directing public attention, as well as a bid for giving a direction to the developments in literature, politics, or any particular field—while leaving it to the outcome of a process of negotiation, which unfolds in the various participant media, what precise direction that the development will take. The rise of a discourse on 'movements,' and the more or less precarious (discursive) alliances which sustain each a 'movement,' could then be seen as the consequence of a permanently precarious alliance among those who stand to gain a mode for potentially guiding perceptions in a pluralistic public sphere, in which an 'economy of directives' is no longer possible except in the context and the form of an 'economy of attention.'

(Anton Kirchhofer)

The War of Systems: Print Capitalism and the Birth of Political Modernity in Britain, 1789-1802

WIL VERHOEVEN

It is impossible to overemphasize the importance of the 1790s to the study of the dawning of political liberty and social equality in modern British society. That is to say, any historical account of the period between the fall of the Bastille and the Peace of Amiens must in some way negotiate with the British response to the French Revolution. Although the precise nature of that response is still a matter of debate, there is little disagreement among historians that the coming of the French Revolution provoked "perhaps the most crucial ideological debate ever carried on in English" (Copeland 148). Ideology essentially involving an encounter between power and signification, the French Revolution debate was, at heart, about the desirability, or otherwise, of the full democratic participation in the production and reproduction of real life, and, hence, of the collaborative making of culture as a network of shared meanings and activities. Never before in British history had the issue of the plurality of the nation's cultural experience been debated in such a common, participatory form. As Gregory Claeys has put it, the 1790s "produced one of the most voluminous and theoretically significant bodies of political literature, indeed the most important debate about democratic principles, in British history" (Copeland xviii). So complex and compelling were the issues at stake, that the 1790s' debate on the French Revolution has been described as "perhaps the last real discussion of the fundamentals of politics" in Britain (Cobban 31).

And yet, although the 1790s saw widespread mob rioting, mass public rallies, vigilante thuggery, police harassment, random political arrests, show trials, and *even* a mob attack on the King's carriage—Britain did not in the end come even close to a violent popular uprising of the kind witnessed across the Channel in France. Nor did the so-called 'Revolutionary decade' produce any new pieces of legislation aimed at overhauling Britain's antiquated constitutional arrangement and democratizing its outmoded system of Parliamentary representation. What was then so revolutionary about the French Revolution debate in Britain? This much is certain: The epochal sociopolitical changes ripping through French society at the time broke the mold of traditional thought patterns in Britain. This 'epistemological rupture,' I want to argue, released into the social imagination the possibility of alternative histories and experimental sociopolitical orders. It was as a *symbolic* incarnation of Britain's possible future society that the French Revolution—as well as residual perceptions about the American Revolution—came to be implicated in the Revolutionary debate of the 1790s.

The French Revolution debate ushered in the birth of the modern British subject and, with it, the birth of modern political discourse. This decisive transformation in the evolution of participatory politics in Britain arose from a bitter and systemic clash between, on the one hand, a cluster of entrenched ideas and assumptions one might loosely describe as 'conservative'; and on the other hand, a broad rainbow coalition of emerging political ideas and assumptions one might label as 'liberal.' Although both sides disagreed over the merits and demerits of the French and American Revolutions, they both rooted their responses to these events in a shared British tradition of liberal political thought. The Glorious Revolution had given Britain a Constitution and even a Bill of Rights: Yet, unlike the Revolutions in America and France, it had stopped short of constructing an autonomous and participating individual political subject. It was precisely this aspect of Britain's liberal constitutional arrangement that lay at the heart of the French Revolution debate of the 1790s. Whereas for reformers, individual political subjectivity was the capstone in the constitutional edifice of Britain, for the Tories political subjectivity was precisely what would cause the structure of the state to come crashing down.

If the 1790s saw the birth of the plebeian radical and loyalist subject in Britain, this historic transition toward political modernity was crucially premised on the emergence of what could be called an 'alliance culture.'

Partisan politics were clearly not new to Britain, but never before had so many individuals from across the entire social spectrum either actively or passively been involved in a public debate about the future shape of British society. As so often in the history of mankind, technology was the prime mover in this momentous push for societal change. It was technology of print that facilitated the emergence during the 1790s of an extended "communication circuit"—to borrow Robert Darnton's phrase. Individuals and groups of individuals began to assert autonomy and citizenship by virtue of their reading and publishing. Habermas, of course, famously described a similar development in his treatise on the rise of a new public sphere political discourse from the late 17th century onward. However, by comparison, the print market in late-18th-century Britain was much more heavily capitalized, which had led to a vast increase in the dissemination of print. This explosion of printing and printed media in turn gave rise to the creation of expansive networks of what one might call 'sympathetic readers' and 'partisan audiences.' Gravitating toward circulating libraries and reading clubs, corresponding societies and coffee houses, spouting clubs and printing shops, these diverse constituencies would at various times overcome their mutual rivalry and establish strategic affiliations and expedient alliances. In short, it is my contention that the French Revolution debate in Britain can fruitfully be analyzed as the late-18th-century's version of what we would now describe as a system of 'networked cultures' and 'participatory media.'

SYSTEMIC RIVALRY

It is a widely held view these days, then, that, in the words of one commentator, "[t]he blasts and counter-blasts, charges and counter-charges of the French Revolution debate were not mere literary exercises, but serious assertions of political principles which were intended to affect the course of events" (Claeys liii). Yet, ultimately, the Revolutionary debate of the 1790s involved much more than a clash between two mutually exclusive sets of political principles. In the final analysis the Revolutionary debate in Britain was symptomatic of a systemic rivalry between two different cultures; or, rather, between two different approaches to the idea of 'culture.' On the one hand, there was the Burkean tradition of culture-as-civility; on the other, there was the early Romantic idea of culture-as-identity. Jacobin culture-as-identity was dominated by particularism, or an awareness of the centrality of the accidental particulars of existence, such as gender, ethnicity, nationality, social origin, sexual tendency. Hence Jacobins would put the individual over society, and individual rights and identity over national cultural values and the duty of individuals to the whole of society. By contrast, Burkean culture-as-civility emphasized man's common humanity, or those human values and habits of feeling that define us as a species and that bind us, largely unconsciously, to a traditional way of life. The Jacobins believed in individual subjectivity; the conservatives in collective, human subjectivity. For the conservatives, culture was crucially rooted in tradition, and was hence a matter of ritualistic behavior and observance, rather than of reason and consciousness. For the Jacobins, culture was not so much a ritual of unconscious and voluntary conformism as the product of rational thought, which was timeless and universal—and which for that reason was dubbed as 'system' or 'new philosophy' by their opponents. The Jacobins believed that culture was essentially about signs, meaning, values, identity, solidarity and self-expression. All of these converged in the emancipatory ambitions of marginalized groups in society, giving rise to the contemporary socio-political phenomena of feminism, abolitionism, regionalism as well as the campaigns for parliamentary representation and sovereignty of the people. In the eyes of the conservatives, culture was a way of life, or *habitus*, in Bourdieu's term, which was dominated by community, kinship, manners, affection, instinct, reverence, custom, tradition, history.

POLITICS FOR THE PEOPLE

Like the political agenda of the reform movement, British conservative political thought arose in response to the overthrow of the *ancien régime* in France. Prior to 1792, the absence of a sustained conservative political doctrine reflected a more fundamental lack in political interest among the people at large. "The stability of the régime," J.D. Western observed, "did not primarily depend on the active support of public opinion mobilized by propaganda and political mass movements. It was based more on the apathy and indifference of a nation which confined its political activity to incoherent protests at moments of crisis" (603). As a result, in the decades before the Revolution in France, conservative arguments aimed at rebutting calls for social and Parliamentary reform did not constitute a coherent body of thought, let alone form the basis of a political theory (Christie 158).

With the British political establishment having adopted a conservative interpretation of the Glorious Revolution, the Tories were generally quite contented that, within the framework of the constitution and English common law, a system of government had emerged that protected the civil liberties of the masses by providing pragmatic solutions to specific social problems. Much of the stability of this constitutional settlement rested on the shared conviction among the élite and the people, that public liberty had to be protected from despotism and corruption of whatever source—be it the monarchy or the mob. Modifications of the political system would from time to time be expedient, but these should not be aimed at extending people's political rights but at promoting the pursuit of prosperity and social happiness. Real social grievances could be redressed by concrete political settlements.

Yet at the start of the Revolutionary decade, this arrangement was no longer politic, nor effective. Abstract political thought—notably the doctrine of universal human rights—was inciting a growing dissatisfaction among the disenfranchised part of the population. The efforts by the Jacobins to destroy the existing social order by means of an ideologically inspired attack on the Constitution required a response from the conservatives that was at once practical and theoretical. Accordingly, they resorted to the use of political force, and to something that has been described as "a conservative ideology of considerable appeal, endurance and intellectual power" (Dickinson, *Liberty* 272). Even if we grant, as historians have suggested, that conservative ideology in the latter part of the 18th century was less rational and less systematic than radical theory, it is equally clear that it had far greater social impact than radical 'system,' mainly because it was more populist and *völkisch* (cf. 291). In fact, what ultimately undermined the Jacobin cause perhaps more than anything else was that they *had* an explicit system of thought (albeit a somewhat loosely organized one). By contrast, conservative ideology was—in Marxist cultural critical terms—both 'lived' and 'hegemonic,' and, for that reason, ultimately both effective and dominant.

Exactly how deep the roots of anti-reformism were among the popular masses in Britain is hard to ascertain. In his "First Letter on a Regicide Peace" (from 1796), Burke computed that there were about 400,000 men in England and Scotland who were in some degree or other aware of the political issues of the day. Of these 400,000 "political citizens," whom he famously identified as "the people" and "the British Publick," he estimated about one fifth "to be pure Jacobins," the rest to be "perfectly sound" (Burke 223-25). But if it was true that the great majority of the pamphlet- and newspaper-reading public was conservative, was the same true for the laboring poor, who made up two-thirds of the population? The indications are that until the early part of the 1790s, the popular mood in Britain was predominantly loyalist, and that, outside of a few radical hot spots such as Sheffield and Norwich, reformists were conscious of being only a beleaguered minority in a population that was either hostile or indifferent (cf. Dinwiddy 47-48). Yet, as E.P. Thompson has shown, in the period between 1795 and 1802, a major shift took place in "the inarticulate, 'sub-political' attitudes of the masses" (78). Claiming few other rights than the right to be left alone, the inarticulate 'free-born Englishman' was traditionally less democratic than anti-absolutist. However, those among the populace—and they formed a majority—who were more *au fait* with the political climate of the day, knew full well that the new rhetoric of 'liberty' covered much more than freedom from absolutism. Liberty to them was

> freedom from arbitrary arrest, trial by jury, equality before the law, the freedom of the home from arbitrary entrance and search, some limited liberty of thought, of speech, and of conscience, the vicarious participation in liberty (or in its semblance) afforded by the right of parliamentary opposition and by elections and election tumults, . . . as well as freedom to travel, trade, and sell one's own labour. (86)

Although in daily social practice they may not have added up to all that much, these freedoms constituted the common Englishman's 'birth-right.' Taken together, they represented a fundamental red line in the 18th-century ideological and constitutional landscape, which the political authorities were careful not to cross and which John Bull was willing to defend at all times—if necessary using what he felt was his post-1688 'constitutional' right to riot. It was because of this implicit understanding between the plebeian mob and the ruling élite that, prior to the 1790s, the conservative established order had always valued consensus more than majority rule.

As a result, when in the wake of the French Revolution, radical activists increasingly began to organize themselves into extra-parliamentary political platforms—such as debating clubs and correspondence societies—and began to disseminate the rights-of-man doctrine among the 'free-born' Britons, the established order feared that the old entente between the mob and the state would soon be undermined. It saw itself faced with a difficult and unprecedented challenge. Whilst it was vehemently opposed to any form of democratization, at the same time it needed the support of the popular masses to counter the radicals' attack on the social and political status quo. The delicate position the established order found itself in was further compromised by the fact that the laboring poor had been on the receiving end of increasing political repression and economic distress. Few of Pitt's repressive measures were hated as much as the press-gang, which was aimed at strengthening Britain's military capacity in the face of an anticipated French invasion. At the same time, Pitt's laissez-faire economic system had produced serious food shortages and had caused a steep rise in the price of provisions. The former had led to mob attacks on military recruiting facilities in August 1794; the latter to extensive food riots, peaking in 1795-96, when Britain was on the brink of a famine (Thompson 70, 88). The conservatives knew only too well that in a situation like this, the brooding dissatisfaction of the populace might be successfully targeted by the new, Jacobin reformist doctrine. The emergence of a self-conscious radical coalition could cause a potentially disastrous shift of allegiance, and hence of the balance of power.

EXPEDIENT (MIS-)ALLIANCES

If it is hard to demarcate the conservative ideological order within British society in the 1790s, it is even harder to establish what radicalism exactly stood for. "Reformism or radicalism in the 1790s is protean stuff," as Mark Philp has observed: "It resists a simple definitive classification of its nature and objectives, and it demands a more complex understanding of its ideology and political objectives than is often offered" ("Ideology" 56). Philp primarily tends to hold modern commentators responsible for misrepresenting reformism as "a single, consistent, continuous programme" (ibid.) that somehow remained static and uniform throughout the decade. However, other historians have located the indeterminacy surrounding radicalism within the movement's own agenda. According to Royle and Walvin, for instance, "[r]adicalism was more a state of mind or loose collection of ideas than a plan of action. Indeed, some groups of radicals were diametrically opposed to others" (9). Dickinson went even further and claimed that the reform movement was "hopelessly divided on what changes ought to be made" and that reformers "failed to devise any effective means of implementing their policies" (*Liberty* 271). Dickinson had a point in claiming that the British radicals never developed a coherent manifesto for social change, let alone a political platform for implementing such a manifesto. However, it has to be stated in their defense that for many in the reform movement, the possibility of radical societal change was first and foremost a *utopian thought process*. Reformism was essentially a radical conversation among like-minded utopians, rather than a political doctrine or a roadmap to a better society. Appropriately, in the Seditious Meetings Acts of 1795, the Pitt administration would identify radicalism as "treasonable correspondence."

Thus, being at heart both discursive and heterogeneous, the ideology of reform went through a process of evolution and revision during the 1790s. Even prominent radical thinkers like Paine and Godwin were constantly responding to events, texts and debates as they emerged. As a result, almost inescapably the French Revolution in Britain was perceived through the prism of domestic British concerns and domestic traditions of political controversy. Three groups in particular tried to adapt the French Revolution for domestic political consumption: the Society for Constitutional Information (who promoted parliamentary reform); the Protestant Dissenters (whose attempts to repeal the Test and Corporation Acts had failed); and, finally, the opposition Whigs (who after the collapse of the Rockingham administration needed to regain some of the power they had lost to the Tories). During the early years of the French Revolution, these three radical factions formed *ad hoc*, and generally short-lived alliances aimed at the wholesale remaking of British society—albeit for very different reasons and with different aims in mind.

The conservative reaction, too, rode on the tide of events in France as seen through the prism of the political situation at home. Thus, Edmund Burke's *Reflections on the Revolution in France* was specifically aimed at exposing the easy application of French political solutions to perceived British political problems. Burke thus pitted British common sense and experience against French political fanaticism; and British tradition, inheritance and hierarchical order against French ideological zeal and abstract universalism. Burke's *Reflections* have come to be regarded as a compendium of British conservatism, yet this was far from evident at the time. Burke's conservative intellectualism, for instance, had little in common with the jingoistic ravings of the High Tories, or the bitter personal vendettas launched by some of the anti-Jacobin hack-writers later in the decade. In the final analysis, "we come closer to the realities of the 1790s," to cite Mark Philp again, "if we think of people as responding to events, debating issues and affirming or changing commitments within this frame, rather than as subscribing to a particular set of radical principles or particular ideology." We ought to take much greater account, Philp goes on to remind us, of

> the extent to which reformist and loyalist movements shaped and conditioned each others' objectives and tactics, the way that government and judicial action against reformers helped focus and narrow the range of strategies open to them, and the manner in which events in France fed into each group's understanding of the dangers of and potential for reform in Britain. ("Ideology" 66, 56)

POPULAR POLITICS AND THE MEDIATION OF PRINT

The political and intellectual debate over the meaning of the French Revolution and its significance for British society generated a truly unprecedented variety of printed materials—pamphlets, treatises, histories, memoirs, correspondence, periodical publications, chapbooks, broadsides, sermons, songs, poems, satirical prints, as well as political novels. This generic exuberance was matched by some staggering circulation figures.[1] For instance, while it has been estimated that Burke's *Reflections* sold around 30,000 copies in the first two years after its publication, it attracted over one hundred hostile replies, as well as over two hundred publications in support of its arguments. On a conservative estimate, the era's most important answer to Burke, Paine's *Rights of Man*, sold between 100,000 and 200,000 copies

---

1   Prior to the French Revolution debate, the English Civil War gave rise to a similar sharp upsurge in print publications. Printed and disseminated in London from 1640 to 1661, the Thomason collection of Civil War tracts contains over 22,000 items, representing around 80 per cent of publications released in England during this period. However, the collection pales in comparison to the proliferation of printed material during the 1790s in terms of the generic diversity and the print runs of many individual publications.

in the first three years after publication (Philp, "Introduction" 5). It was precisely because it was so intensely 'mediated' that the 'mighty debate' of the early 1790s distinguished itself from earlier episodes of political commotion, when political debates had remained confined to small coteries of the politically savvy and powerful. Claims about the general public's participation in the Revolutionary debate have in the past been exaggerated by some commentators; and yet, it is evident that many contemporaries, not in the least the loyalists, were well aware that this particular debate had spread too far to be easily contained. In fact, the 1790s can be credited with having launched a new, popular style of partisan political discourse.

The impact of the French Revolution on British society and politics in the 1790s generated a specific set of historical conditions that facilitated a network of spontaneous, impromptu alliances between the literary field and the political field, as well as between a wide range of individual agents within those fields. Evidently, no radical knew how to read the rapidly changing spirit of the age better than William Godwin. He rightly sensed that the initial euphoria over the Revolution in France had rendered British liberals particularly receptive to arguments in favor of radical change and that it was therefore a propitious moment in history "for the publication of a valuable book [that might] give birth to the most auspicious reforms" (Godwin 1:280). The publication of William Godwin's *Enquiry Concerning Political Justice* had such an immediate and profound impact on Britain's social and political landscape that it brought the nation to the brink of civil war. "No work in our time gave such a blow to the philosophical mind of the country as the celebrated *Enquiry Concerning Political Justice*," William Hazlitt observed retrospectively in 1825 (18). To lend further firepower to what he regarded as the all-decisive "artillery of opinion," Godwin was quick to follow up on his radical manifesto with his Jacobin novel *Things As They Are; or, The Adventures of Caleb Williams* (1794), perhaps the most versatile, and certainly one of the most popular voices of the movement for sociopolitical change in Britain during the 1790s (1:259).

At first sight it may seem odd that 'the Philosopher'—as he was known at the time—would abruptly abandon the rational discourse of philosophical enquiry (his "child of the French Revolution") and embark on a fictional tale of pursuit and adventure (Godwin, "Thoughts" 2:163). His long-time friend and secretary James Marshall, for one, rejected the manuscript outright as being an utter failure and unworthy of the great mind that wrote it.

Yet, it is important to realize that, although a zealous advocate of rational anarchy, Godwin at no point in his career believed in the efficacy of sudden and violent revolutions, or, as he referred to them, "wild schemes of uproar and confusion" (*Enquiry* 1:250). Like Paine, Godwin was well aware that *real* social and political changes are effected only in the minds of the people, and that the only successful revolutions are those won "by compromise and patient expostulation," by nourishing and promoting "reason" and "the right passions" (1:271). Godwin later confessed that his decision to try his hand at the "slight composition" of a popular novel was motivated primarily by "mercantile considerations" ("Analysis" 1:55). Yet, it is at the same time evident that the radical activist in Godwin was never far behind the hack-writer when he chose the novel as a tool to conquer the people's imagination. Despite his unprecedented shift in generic modes from moral philosophy to sensationalist fiction, neither Godwin's deep-held principles nor his political ambition had undergone any change during the shift— something that did not escape the attention of the Tory press.

Indeed, to the alarm and frustration of their anti-Jacobin opponents, generic promiscuity soon became a conscious discursive strategy among many radical authors. Genre-crossing allowed Jacobin novelists to break up conventional molds and modes of thinking, while at the same time it rendered their ideas less susceptible to conservative satire and diatribe. The result of this literary experimentation was a 'diabolical' Jacobin fabrication that the anti-Jacobins dismissively referred to as a 'political novel': an oxymoronic novelty they believed was aesthetically disgusting, morally revolting, and ideologically suspect. Champions of the radical cause, however, hailed the generic and ideological changeability of the 'political romance' as a significant literary innovation that could radicalize political discourse.

The political and media volatility that was at the heart of the French Revolution debate catapulted many an unlikely and unassuming figure to meteoric notoriety. One such figure was the Dissenting minister, William Winterbotham. A revolutionary malgré lui, Winterbotham was unwittingly drawn into the thick plot of post-Bastille British history by merely expressing in public what many people at the time were thinking in private. Having run foul of Pitt's repressive machine of state power, Winterbotham ended up in Newgate Prison, after receiving one of the harshest sentences handed down by the regime's corrupt judiciary: four years of imprisonment and fines totaling more than £1,400. During his lengthy incarceration, he became radicalized by his interaction with some of Britain's most seasoned reformers, with whom he shared his prison lodgings, and by his exposure to the republican literature of the age, to which he had easy access. It would be the beginning of one of the most extraordinary ad hoc print alliances of the Revolutionary decade.

In Newgate, Winterbotham was able to enjoy a private room in a suite of apartments; a personal servant (one of the female prisoners); the society of several well-educated individuals all, like himself, confined for political offences; and the courtesy visits of friends at all reasonable hours. Apparently, anything short of liberty could be purchased at Newgate for the right amount of money. Nor was Winterbotham deprived of contact with the outside world. A fee to the turnkey never failed to open the door to visitors in Newgate Prison. The arbitrariness and severity of his sentence had turned Winterbotham's trial into a *cause célèbre*; consequently, many radicals were eager to come and pay their respect to one of the martyrs of their cause. Before long, Winterbotham's 'stateside' suite had become something of radical *salon* where prominent London Jacobins could socialize with their incarcerated brethren inside. With so many like-minded spirits cooped up within its walls, Newgate generated a radical synergy that defeated the authorities' very purpose of putting them there in the first place.

Among the other occupants of Winterbotham's prison suite was the cream of the crop of London's radical printers and booksellers. Most of these had been confined in Newgate on indictments for seditious libel in the course of 1793. The group included James Ridgway, Daniel Holt, Henry Symonds, Daniel Isaac Eaton, Thomas Spence, George Westley and William Holland. It soon emerged that prison conditions and a common enemy facilitated the suspension of commercial rivalry between Newgate inmates and encouraged the formation of ad hoc business partnerships. James Ridgway, for instance, had been a radical but little-known bookseller-publisher who had mostly worked alone. As soon as he was confined in Newgate, however, he joined forces with Henry Symonds, who had been sentenced on the same day as Ridgway for publishing a pirated edition of Paine's *Rights of Man*. Symonds and another radical printer, Daniel Isaac Eaton, had been printing competing editions of Paine's *Age of Reason, Part II*, but once they found themselves "State Side of Newgate," they pooled their wits, contacts and recourses and carried on their publishing business as usual (Winterbotham 1:viii). All the while, Joseph Johnson, Martha Gurney and other booksellers who were sympathetic to the radical cause but who had not been detained by the authorities were taking care of the actual printing and marketing of the writings produced by the Newgate radicals.

Spending most of his time reading and writing when he was not entertaining guests, Winterbotham soon entered into a curious literary partnership with his room-mates Ridgeway, Symonds, Holt and Eaton. With his publishing friends supplying him with the books and other materials he needed for his research, Winterbotham began to produce a steady flow of copy, which his comrades would arrange to get printed and disseminated under their own imprints. In this way Winterbotham managed to launch a career as a best-selling radical author, even whilst being immured in Newgate.

The precarious alliances formed between the reformist writers, printers, and booksellers in Newgate, and between them and their literary and political allies outside prison, gave a significant boost to the grassroots movement of oppositional activists, who developed new ways to draw a non-elitist audience into public debates about national issues, notably the war with France and food shortages. By spreading the doctrine of change to as many people as possible, Thomas Paine, Daniel Isaac Eaton, John Thelwall, Thomas Spence and other radical campaigners managed to draw artisans and sections of the working-class into the extra-parliamentary reform movement—"Politics for the People," after the title of one of Eaton's publications. Central to their activities were the corresponding societies. It was through them that local activists were reached and organized, and through them that pamphlets and other radical documents were published and circulated. Without a doubt the most influential of these societies was the London Corresponding Society, but there were dozens of provincial reformist societies as well. Whereas earlier societies had catered almost exclusively to minor gentry and the professional classes, the London Corresponding Society, founded in January 1792 by the shoemaker Thomas Hardy, specifically canvassed support for the reform agenda amongst the working classes.

But if the 1790s saw the emergence of the plebeian *radical* reader, it also witnessed the appearance of the plebeian *loyalist* reader. Prior to the 1790s the stability of the regime had not depended on the active support of the people and public displays of its loyalty. Instead, it had relied on the passive compliance of an indifferent nation. But from the early 1790s onwards, when the reformers began to enlist popular opinion to further their political aims, at least some within the loyalist élite realized that they had to actively win the support of the populace. Given that it had always governed on a popular mandate of inert acquiescence, the loyalist élite did not take to the challenge naturally. The loyalists had always intuitively avoided engaging with the people through any sort of intellectual discourse, fearing that, quite literally, it might 'give them ideas.' It is mainly for that reason that instead of arguing the counter-revolutionary case on the basis of intellectual arguments, they instead adopted the dual strategy of, on the one hand, ridiculing radical discourse and discrediting the reputation of individual reformers, and, on the other hand, activating latent feelings of patriotism, nationalism, popular loyalism, anti-intellectualism, anti-modernity, nostalgia, and traditionalism.

The loyalist bid for the public's support was organized along similar lines as the reformists had developed. In November 1792 John Reeves founded the "Association for the Preservation of Liberty and Property against Republicans and Levellers." It has been estimated that by early 1793 as many as two thousand such loyalist organizations had sprung up all over Britain (Philp "Introduction" 8). Mainly run by men of property, these associations would organize demonstrations, bonfires, burnings of effigies of Paine, as well as harass known reformists and disrupt their meetings. Backed up by the physical force provided by the loyalist Volunteer movement, the loyalist societies unleashed a fierce propaganda offensive against the Paineite press, publishing or overseeing the publication of a great number of loyalist pamphlets, books, broadsides and songs.

Gayle Pendleton has calculated that the conservatives produced and sold considerably more publications than their reformist rivals. At the same time, however, Pendleton shows that well over half of the attributable publications with substantial political content were written by place-holders or place-hunters. Similarly, the majority of the pamphlets—especially the more popular ones—were written by individuals belonging to the patronage network, who were either in the pay of the government, or clergymen of the Church of England (cf. Thomas 459ff.). Since these publications were produced in bulk for free distribution among the populace, their wide dissemination was probably less a measure of their popularity among the people than of the loyalist élite's anxiety over a Jacobin uprising (Pendelton 56-57, 185-86). Even so, the sheer bulk of loyalist propaganda that flooded the pamphlet market in the course of the second half of the 1790s effectively drowned out the reformist voice.

It is sometimes suggested that the orchestrated attack of the anti-Jacobin press on the reform movement did more to *stir up* a frenzy of reactionary jingoism among the British people than that it reflected any real anxiety concerning radical societal change (cf. Grenby 5-6; Butler 105). Godwin, for one, was somewhat perplexed by "the flood of ribaldry, invective and intolerance" that was unleashed against his person and his writings in the course of 1797-1798—by which time the reformists had all but given up their campaign and virtually no-one in Britain called themselves a Jacobin anymore. "What has happened since the spring of 1797 to justify [the anti-Jacobin] revolt?," Godwin wondered; "Has any new system of disorganization been adopted in France? Have the French embrued their hands in further massacres? Has another Robespierre risen, to fright the world with systematical, cool-blooded, never-satiated murder?" ("Thoughts" 2:168). However, even though none of conservative Britain's apocalyptic nightmares had come true by that watershed year of 1797, there were sufficient reasons for the established order to feel threatened by the specter of radicalism.

Thus, although by 1796 the London Corresponding Society had suffered a sharp drop in membership numbers and was as a result in grave financial problems, an upsurge in LCS activities in the course of 1797-98 had the authorities considerably worried. In July 1797 the Riot Act was read to disperse a large outdoor LCS meeting. In the same year a breakaway group of LCS members formed a new society called the United Englishmen. Modeled on Theobald Wolfe Tone's United Irishmen, the United Englishmen explicitly aimed to incite radical political action. Some of its members were even intent on arming for revolution. In April 1798, when the government was encouraging volunteers to arm against a possible invasion by the French, meetings of LCS divisions and a general committee were interrupted by Bow Street officers, who arrested several dozen members. Despite these arrests, some groups within the LCS continued to meet throughout 1798, and in early 1799. Then, in July 1799, the authorities officially banned the Society by name—thereby acknowledging the significance of its threat—or its perceived threat (cf. Thale xviii). All the while, fear of a foreign invasion was kept alive by French attempts to land troops in Wales and Ireland in 1796, 1797 and 1798. On the continent, Bonaparte had already overrun the Italian republics and confiscated the Austrian Netherlands when he invaded Switzerland in 1797 and turned it into a vassal state. In 1798 the "Commissary General for the Southern District of England," Havilland Le

Mesurier, warned in a pamphlet that "[t]he menace of a French Invasion, which formerly afforded a subject for ridicule, cannot now be treated in so light a manner" (1). The 1797 naval mutinies at Spithead and the Nore, in which the LCS allegedly had a hand, were according to Ian Christie "the most dangerous manifestations of th[e] revolutionary element" in Britain in the 1790s (52). Although quickly contained, the Irish Rebellion of 1798, which was supposed to have coincided with a French invasion, made many loyalists fear that English towns and villages would soon be scenes of *sansculotte* style carnage and confusion.

Following in the footsteps of George Canning's short-lived but ferociously conservative *Anti-Jacobin* weekly newspaper, the *Anti-Jacobin Review and Magazine* was launched with the specific purpose to 'counteract' the radical periodicals. Referring to the collective body of their publications as a "dangerous system," John Gifford defiantly sounded the battle cry in the *Anti-Jacobin Review*'s "Prospectus": "we shall frequently *review* the *Monthly*, *criticise* the *Critical*, and *analyse* the *Analytical Reviews*" (*Anti-Jacobin Review* 1, 1798: 3). In the Prefatory Address to the first collected volume (1799), the editors of the *Anti-Jacobin Review* duly congratulated themselves on having dealt a death-blow to the *Analytical Review*, which had suspended publication in December 1798. In the preface to the third volume (1799) the editors vaunted the "dissolution" of another of their "political and religious opponents," the *New Analytical Review*: "Thanks to the meliorated spirit of the times […] this democratic viper […] expired" (*Anti-Jacobin Review* 1, 1799: v; *Anti-Jacobin Review* 3, 1799: vi). It is this sharp increase in anti-reform activism from 1797 onwards, when the conservative press began to churn out periodical and novel publications specifically designed to wipe out the reform movement, that can most meaningfully be described as the 'anti-Jacobin' phase within the wider late-18th-century conservative ideology of order. While it never represented the broad conservative consensus in its entirety, anti-Jacobinism almost certainly constituted the hegemonic mode in conservative thought in the decade straddling the 18th and 19th centuries.

In a move similar to that used by the Federalist press in America in order to silence the Jeffersonian Republicans, the anti-Jacobin writers tried to eradicate their opponents under the pretext of their 'patriotic duty' to safeguard the liberty of the press against abuse. Accusing the radical reviewers of having corrupted "the channels of criticism" and having sunk "the critic in the partisan," the *Anti-Jacobin* adopted the moral high-ground as a defender of the British Constitution and liberties. Like the Whig Constitution, a 'free press' was for the anti-Jacobins the mark and guarantee of a free people. But a free press, in their sense of the term, was by no means an unbiased press. On the contrary, analogous to Burke's concept of liberty, what the anti-Jacobins proposed in effect amounted to guaranteeing the liberty of the press by curbing it. A free press—anti-Jacobin style—was a press that was off-limits to reformist propaganda in terms of content, and off-limits to all but the élite in terms of authorship and readership. William Atkinson spoke for many anti-Jacobins when he expressed his alarm at the rapid dissemination of radical ideas among the lower orders of society through the circulation of print:

It is a well-known fact, that Hawkers and Pedlars of every description, have throughout Europe been employed to disseminate cheap Editions of Sedition; 20,000 of Paine's Rights of Men, were circulated in this way through the North of Ireland; and one society ordered 12,000 copies of Paine's Letter to Dundas to be printed and distributed throughout Great-Britain: a Gentleman in the road from Leeds to Liverpool was observed distributing doses of republican poison, from under the seat of his carriage, to poor children without stockings; and the celebrated Mr. H—— not far from Huntingdon, put not a few Ladies and Gentlemen in bodily fear by gallantly galloping up to their carriages, and popping a blue roll of sedition through the window. (4 n.)

Although its role and impact have sometimes been overstated, the dissemination of printed material in the late-18th-century was a significant factor in the democratization of knowledge. Logistically and socially, this process was facilitated by the sharp rise in the number of circulating libraries and reading societies, which by the end of the century had sprung up in all but the most remote corners of Britain. Regarding the mobility of ideas as the chief threat to the hierarchical order of society, the anti-Jacobins had a deep distrust of the rapid proliferation of circulating libraries, as well as debating societies and spouting clubs. Thus, the *Anti-Jacobin* was convinced that

the arts employed, and the industry exerted, by the disaffected to render Book Clubs, particularly those in the country, [were] instrumental to their own base designs of overturning our constitution, by the infusion of bad principles into the minds of the middle and lower classes of people. (*Anti-Jacobin Review* 1, 1798: 476)

The *Anti-Jacobin Review* applauded the prospectus of a plan for a proposed book society in Maidstone, but only because this particular society was to be established by local Church of England ministers "for the purchase and circulation of cheap tracts among the lower classes of the community, calculated to promote their happiness, and to meliorate their minds"—that is, "for the preservation of religion, loyalty, and patriotism" (473, 474). Inspired by the examples of the ministers of Maidstone, the author of the article calls for an immediate revision of the rules and regulations governing the conduct of all book societies, stressing the need to "purify" their membership:

After purifying those Book Clubs whose members chiefly consist of the upper part of the middle classes of society; it will behove the clergy and gentry to exercise a peculiar degree of vigilance in attending to the publications that are circulated, by means of a subscription, among the lower class of people; tradesmen, labourers, and artisans. (477)

If the anti-Jacobins were concerned about the spread of radical political pamphlets among the middling and lower orders of society, they were decidedly panic-struck by what they feared would be the disastrous impact of the proliferation of prose fiction on the moral fiber of the nation. Like America, late-18th-century Britain had succumbed to a heavy bout of novel-mania. The exponential increase in the production and consumption of fictional prose in the late 18th century triggered an equally extraordinary, indeed hysterical barrage of censure. "Our market for novels has lately become so much overstocked," a reviewer of the *New London Review* complained in 1799, "that the commodity is now actually reduced to a drug. The vendors and factors in this article are, of course, excited to take all the advantage they can of every incident that occurs; or which, in any shape, can afford the least entertainment" (407). Obtuse critics claimed that novels were merely lies; the pious contended that they inflamed the passions, adorned vice, and corrupted the heart; the utilitarian, that they spoiled the reader's taste for useful books; the patriotic, that they poisoned the British mind with pernicious foreign—particularly French and German—ideas and unrealistic schemes.

Novels were considered to be much more treacherous than the old romances. Romances were so clearly out of touch with the reality of everyday life that they would only appeal to the most foolish of readers. However, because it engaged the reader's social imagination, the contemporary novel—and particularly the 'Jacobin' novel—was able to penetrate the networks of symbolic representation. By thus bringing about profound sociological and epistemological transformations, the political novel intervened in the relationship between the ideal and real, the imaginary and the political. Novels, it was felt, exalted the imagination at the expense of judgment, and this would be particularly detrimental to the 'weaker' members of society, who had traditionally been excluded from the public sphere: notably the young, the working classes, and women. Hence in the conservative critique of fictional discourse during this period, novels and readers were frequently pathologized in a way that perversely confirms that fiction is the heart, or sinews, of the body politic. One reviewer claimed that "[t]he present state of society is sufficiently corrupt, and stands in need of antidotes rather than emollients," and thus criticized novels like Elizabeth Gooch's *The Contrast* as "[a]n apology for fashionable frailties" (*Critical Review* 13: 345). The same journal recommended Jane West's *A Gossip's Story* as precisely such "an antidote to the pernicious maxims inculcated in most of the modern tales of *sentiment*" (*Critical Review* 21: 228). Again and again, conservative critics denounced novels for polluting, staining, poisoning, or deforming both the individual and the nation.

In the course of the 1790s, first the reformists and then the conservatives came to understand that the literary form is ideological: It comes into being and evolves in response to an inner need, to changes in the consciousness of an ideologically emergent group in society. The rise of the 1790s' Jacobin novel, and the anti-Jacobin reaction it triggered, are therefore apt illustrations of Jameson's observation "that in its emergent, strong form a genre is essentially a socio-symbolic message, or in other terms, that form is immanently and intrinsically an ideology in its own right" (Jameson 140-41). Seen in the first place as historically conditioned discourses that engage in specific and often subversive ways with late-18th-century politics and print culture, both the Jacobin and the anti-Jacobin novel play a key role in deepening our understanding of the 1790s as the site of the birth of modern British political consciousness. The Jacobin novel registered and facilitated a fundamental shift in the awareness of the nation's disenfranchised in regard to the issues of social egalitarianism and the democratic participation in the political process. As the radical political novel's 'significant other,' the anti-Jacobin novel constituted an ideological discourse that was crucially imbricated in the hegemonic political economy of popular conservatism in the 1790s. By disseminating the new partisan political discourse across the lower and middle orders of society, the sociopolitical novel of the 1790s made a significant contribution to "the consolidation of what might be called a plebian or proletarian public sphere" (McCann 2). The genre should for that reason be taken seriously as a historical witness to the French Revolution debate in Britain.

* * *

"It depends not on me," Joel Barlow observed in 1796,

or Mr. Burke, or any other writer, or description of writers, to determine the question, whether a change of government shall take place, and extend through Europe. It depends on a much more important class of men, the class that cannot write; and in a great measure, on those who cannot read. It is to be decided by men who reason better without books, than we do with all the books in the world. (xv)

Barlow was convinced that the will of the people had been made up and that a "general revolution" was at hand, whose progress was "*irresistable*" (xvi). In the end, of course, no such revolution took place—not in Britain, nor anywhere else. And yet, some of the fundamentals of British politics had shifted. There is no denying that the 1790s were marked by a sharp increase in the political awareness of broad sections of the disenfranchised populace (Burke's well-known "swinish multitude"). Simultaneously, among the ruling élite a new awareness emerged that the opinion of the people was henceforth a force to be reckoned with. As a result, a new language of political controversy arose, reflecting the ideological bipolarization that was taking shape. Hereafter there would no longer be any middle ground in the political arena. Although that political arena had not yet bifurcated into fully-fledged oppositional political doctrines at the time, those merely sympathizing with the call for reform were accused by the loyalists of wanting to reduce God's creation into "a mass of ruins" (again in Burke's phrase). By contrast, those campaigning for anything less than a radical overhaul of the system of parliamentary representation were seen by the reformists as enemies of the natural rights of man. In fact, loyalists and reformists became so entrenched in their oppositional political discourse that in the final analysis phrases like 'Revolutionary debate' and the 'war of ideas' have only limited value. Even the initial battle of words between Burke and Paine was not aimed at convincing anyone on the opposite side of the ideological divide to switch allegiances. But from 1793 onward, Jacobin and anti-Jacobin campaigners and pamphleteers were almost exclusively canvassing their own power base. There seems little doubt that the prime objective of both reformists and loyalists in the so-called 'Revolutionary debate' was to legitimize and naturalize their own ideological positions. Rather than a serious exchange of arguments concerning the nature of liberty or the nuts and bolts of parliamentary representation, the 'war of ideas' was therefore fundamentally a kind of discursive performance—yet a performance that, crucially, would from now on take place in the (henceforth bifurcated) public sphere.

As a result of the participatory nature of the Revolutionary debate, the performative discourse of political modernity was structured and choreographed, and hence socially codified and prescriptive. During the early decades of the 19th century it would emerge that the reformists were in retrospect more adept in the new discursive environment than the conservatives. Like all social justice movements, radicalism in Britain was an assemblage of networked communities, whose members had learned to speak the common discourse of individual rights and social equality and justice. Positing that a culture is only collective when it is collectively made, the reformists had thus popularized the notion that a common culture is inseparable from radical social change and full democratic participation at all levels of social life. It is undeniably true that by 1798, radicalism had lost the battle against the forces of political consolidation. Yet, in hindsight, it is also evident that while the reform movement had temporarily lost the debate, it had successfully mobilized the arguments for the future (re-)making of Britain's sociopolitical order, as well as the values and meanings that constitute the common culture.

WORKS CITED

Andrews, Stuart. *The British Periodical Press and the French Revolution, 1789-1799*. Basingstoke: Palgrave, 2000. Print.

Atkinson, William. *An Oblique View of the Grand Conspiracy, Against Social Order; Or, a Candid Inquiry, Tending to Shew What Part the Ana-*

lytical, the Monthly, the Critical Reviews, and the New Annual Register, Have Taken in that Conspiracy. 1798. Detroit: Gale Ecco, Print Editions, 2010. Print.

Barlow, Joel. *The Political Writings of Joel Barlow, Containing "Advice to the Privileged Orders," "Letter to the National Convention," "Letter to the People of Piedmont," "The Conspiracy of Kings."* New York: Printed for Fellows & Adam, Thomas Greenleaf, and Naphtati Judah, 1796. Print.

Bourdieu, Pierre. *Outline of a Theory of Practice*. Trans. Richard Nice. Cambridge: Cambridge UP, 1977. Print.

Burke, Edmund. "First Letter on a Regicide Peace." *Letters on a Regicide Peace*. 1795. Ed. E.J. Payne. Indianapolis, IN: Liberty Fund, 1990. Print.

Butler, Marilyn. *Jane Austen and the War of Ideas*. Oxford: Clarendon P, 1975. Print.

Caspar, Scott E., Joanne D. Chaison, and Jeffrey D. Groves. *Perspectives on American Book History: Artifacts and Commentary*. Amherst: U of Massachusetts P, 2002. Print.

Christie, Ian R. *Stress and Stability in Late Eighteenth-Century Britain: Reflections on the British Avoidance of Revolution*. London: Clarendon P, 1984. Print.

Claeys, Gregory. "Introduction: Political Writings of the 1790s." *Radicalism and Reform: Responses to Burke, 1790-1791*. Vol. 1. London: Pickering & Chatto, 1995. Print.

Cobban, Alfred, ed. *The Debate on the French Revolution, 1789-1800*. London: A. and C. Black, 1963. Print.

Copeland, Thomas. *Our Eminent Friend Edmund Burke*. New Haven, CT: Yale UP, 1949. Print.

Critical Review ns 13 (1795). Print.

Critical Review ns 21 (1797). Print.

Dickinson, H.T. *Politics of the People in Eighteenth-Century Britain*. New York: St. Martin's P, 1994. Print.

---. *Liberty and Property: Political Ideology in Eighteenth-Century Britain*. New York: Holmes and Meier, 1977. Print.

Dinwiddy, John. "Interpretations of Anti-Jacobinism." *The French Revolution and British Popular Politics*. Ed. Mark Philp. Cambridge: Cambridge UP, 2009. 38-49. Print.

Eagleton, Terry. *The Idea of Culture*. Oxford: Blackwell, 2000. Print.

Gallaway, W.F. "The Conservative Attitude toward Fiction, 1770-1830." *PMLA* 55.4 (December 1940): 1041-59. Print.

Gentleman's Magazine 57, II:6 (December 1787): 1048-49. Print.

Godwin, William. *Enquiry Concerning Political Justice, and Its Influence on Morals and Happiness*. 1793. 3rd ed. 2 vols. London: Printed for G.G. and J. Robinson, 1798. Print.

---. "Analysis of Own Character, Begun Sep. 26, 1798." *Autobiography, Autobiographical Fragments and Reflections, Godwin/Shelley Correspondence, Memoirs. The Collected Novels and Memoirs of William Godwin.* Ed. Mark Philp. 8 vols. Vol. 1. London: Pickering and Chatto, 1992. Print.

---. "Thoughts Occasioned By the Perusal of Dr. Parr's Spital Sermon, Preached at Christ Church, April 15, 1800: Being a Reply to the Attacks of Dr. Parr, Mr. Mackintosh, The Author of an Essay of Population, and others (1801)." *Political and Philosophical Writings of William Godwin*. Ed. Mark Philp. 7 vols. London: Pickering and Chatto, 1993. Print.

Grenby, Matthew. *The Anti-Jacobin Novel: British Conservatism and the French Revolution*. Cambridge: Cambridge UP, 2001. Print.

Hamilton, Elizabeth. *Memoirs of Modern Philosophers*. 3 vols. Bath: R. Cruttwell, for G.G. and J. Robinson, London, 1800. Print.

Hazlitt, William. *The Spirit of the Age or Contemporary Portraits*. 1825. Oxford: Oxford UP, 1928. Print.

Jameson, Fredric. *The Political Unconscious: Narrative as a Socially Symbolic Act*. London: Routledge, 1989. Print.

Le Mesurier, Havilland. *Thoughts on a French Invasion, with Reference to the Probability of Its Success, and the Proper Means of Resisting It*. London: Printed for J. Wright, 1798. Print.

McCann, Andrew. *Cultural Politics in the 1790s: Literature, Radicalism and the Public Sphere*. Basingstoke: Macmillan, 1999. Print.

Manogue, Ralph A. "The Plight of James Ridgway, London Bookseller and Publisher, and the Newgate Radicals, 1792-1797." *The Wordsworth Circle* 27 (1996): 158-66. Print.

Orians, G. Harrison. "Censure of Fiction in American Romances and Magazines, 1789-1810." *PMLA* 52.1 (March 1937): 195-214. Print.

Pendelton, Gayle Trusdel. "English Conservative Propaganda during the French Revolution, 1789-1802." Diss. Emory University, 1976. Print.

Philp, Mark. "The Fragmented Ideology of Reform." *The French Revolution and British Popular Politics*. Ed. Mark Philp. Cambridge: Cambridge UP, 2004. 50-77. Print.

---. "Introduction." *The French Revolution and British Popular Politics*. Ed. Mark Philp. Cambridge: Cambridge UP, 2004. 1-17. Print.

Rev. of "The Invasion; or, What Might have Been; a Novel." *New London Review* 1.4 (April 1799): 407. Print.

Royle, Edward, and James Walvin. *English Radicals and Reformers, 1760-1848*. Lexington, KY: UP Kentucky, 1982. Print.

Simpson, David. *Romanticism, Nationalism, and the Revolt against Theory*. Chicago: Chicago UP, 1993. Print.

Thale, Mary. *Selections from the Papers of the London Corresponding Society, 1792-1799*. Cambridge: Cambridge UP, 1983. Print.

The Anti-Jacobin Review 1 (1798/99). Print.

The Anti-Jacobin Review 3 (1799). Print.

Thomas, George Andrew. "The Consequences of a French Invasion, Considered as Motives to Union and Exertion." *An Address to the Parishioners of Woolwich, on Occasion of Their Meeting to Form an Armed Association*. London: Printed for F. and C. Rivington, 1798. Print.

Thomis, Malcolm I., and Peter Holt. *Threats of Revolution in Britain, 1789-1848*. London: Macmillan, 1977. Print.

Thompson, E.P. *The Making of the English Working Class*. London: Victor Gollancz, 1963. Print.

Walker, George. *The Vagabond*. 3rd ed. 2 vols. London: Printed for G. Walker, and Lee and Hurst, 1799. Print.

Western, J.D. "The Volunteer Movement as an Anti-Revolutionary Force, 1793-1801." *The English History Review* 71:281 (1965): 603-614. Print.

Winterbotham, William. *An Historical, Geographical, Commercial, and Political View of the American United States, and of the European Settlements in America and the West-Indies*. 4 vols. London: Printed for the Editor; J. Ridgway, York Street; H.D. Symonds, Paternoster Row; and D. Holt, Newark, 1795. Print.

Wollstonecraft, Mary. *A Vindication of the Rights of Woman: With Strictures on Political and Moral Subjects*. London: Printed for J. Johnson, 1792. Print.

'Success' and 'Failure' of Literary Collaboration between Authors in Belarus in the 1920s

GUN-BRITT KOHLER[1]

INTRODUCTION: BELARUS AS A 'PRECARIOUS SPACE'

In the first third of the 20th century, the Belarus region is marked by a high degree of precariousness. To a substantial extent, this precariousness is the result of a series of antagonistic political shifts and developments, causing massive frictions in the social, cultural and socio-economic spheres.[2]

Since the so called 'Partitions of Poland' at the end of the 18th century the greater area of Belarus was largely incorporated into the Russian Empire as the 'Northwestern Provinces' ('Severo-zapadnyj kraj'). The Russian Revolution of 1905 facilitates first initiatives of explicit formations of national cultural identity between 1905-1915 which are, however, almost entirely disrupted by revolution, civil war and WWI. Between 1918 and

---

1 In accordance with the standard in Slavonic studies, the transliteration of authors' names from Cyrillic script in this contribution strictly follows the spelling used in the original documents. This may result in variant spellings of the same author's name (e.g., Russian: Naumenko, Belarusian: Navumenka; German: Kohler, Russian and Belarusian: Koler etc.).

2 A highly readable general overview of the political, socio-cultural and economic developments can be found in Beyrau and Lindner.

1920 the Belarus region was the site on which the Polish-Soviet conflicts were carried out and was subject to several changing and competing powers.[3] In 1921 the Peace of Riga officially divides the country into two parts for almost two decades (until 1939): the eastern part (BSSR) belongs to the Soviet Union, the western part (unofficially called West Belarus) belongs to the IInd Polish Republic. The ideological border between 'communism' and 'capitalism' runs midway through the Belarus region.

Due to the Soviet Policy on Nationalities, the BSSR flourishes culturally in the first half of the 1920s for a short period of time (the so called Belarusization, part of the policy of 'karanizacyja,' which means 'nativization,' 'indigenization'). Effectively, the establishment of a new social-proletarian society entailed the promotion of the Belarusian language and culture, ethnic minorities (particularly in the cultural realm), but also the marginalization of religion (Orthodoxy, Catholicism, and Judaism equally). Already in the second half of the 1920s any indication of 'national' orientation is aggressively fought; cultural institutions are increasingly controlled by the state or Party. Politico-economic changes are of crucial importance: Lenin's and Trotsky's propagated concept of the New Economic Policy (the so-called NEP) substitutes the economic politics of War Communism. Already in the second half of the 1920s, this economic liberation that had generated a sort of bourgeois prosperity decreases and is more and more fiercely fought. It culminates in a forced collectivization and dekulakization (expropriation and liquidation of all farmers including peasants who do not join the collectivization) which destroys developed structures in the predominantly agricultural Belarus. The cultural and economic nationalization ends in the infamous 'cleansings' ('čistki') of the 1930s.

---

[3] At the beginning of 1918, parts of the country (including Minsk) become occupied by German troops; national forces take advantage of the German occupation in the spring of 1918 in order to proclaim the first independent Belarusian Republic BNR (cf. Michaluk). Only six months later, the country is under Soviet control again: the foundation of the Lithuanian-Belarusian Soviet Socialist Republic in 1919 sets off the so called Polish-Soviet War. Between the summer of 1919 and 1920, the western territory of Belarus (including Minsk) is seized by the Polish Army. In 1920 the Belarusian Soviet Socialist Republic (BSSR) is founded in the country's eastern part.

'SMALL' LITERATURE, PRECARIOUSNESS AND COLLABORATION: LEADING QUESTION

The outlined experiences of precariousness and their consequences are reflected in different Belarusian literary works of the 1920s.[4] Moreover, the very literary scene seems to be affected by the precariousness of the social space in which it is embedded: different specificities of the Belarusian literature that can be understood and described as characteristics of 'smallness'[5] in the heuristic sense are (in)directly linked to the nationwide precariousness. This is even more the case since, properly speaking, a literary field begins to develop in Belarus only from 1905 (followed by a period of reconstitution starting around 1921). It is virtually a provisional field—its

---

4   In the literature between 1905-15 this is expressed in the topos "pakryŭdžanasc'," the social and national 'offendedness' of the Belarusian people (usually represented by the peasant) that is increasingly juxtaposed with the optimistic topos "Maladaja Belarus'" ("Young Belarus"; cf. Bahdanovič). The contradiction of political and sociopolitical developments is, among other things, critically reflected upon in the 1920s. An example *par excellence* is the play *Tutėjšyja* (usually translated as *The Natives*, meaning 'The Locals') of Belarusian author Janka Kupala from 1922: The 'tragic-comical scenes' illustrate the difficult situation of the population that is torn between the changing occupying forces in the Polish-Soviet War. With each change of power, the protagonist Mikita Znosak picks up the respective language of the occupying forces (Germans, Poles, Soviets) in order to assimilate and, ultimately, gets arrested because he cannot longer cope with the shifting powers and discourses. The play was banned already during the 1920s and is not performed in Belarusian theaters until today.

5   'Small' literatures are from a heuristic perspective understood as characterized by, firstly, marginal significance (that is their representation in international reference books and reviews, their presence in the international book market, the nomination for international literary prices etc.) within this international complex of literary fields that Pascale Casanova described as "world republic of letters" (Casanova) and, secondly, a smaller internal organizational capacity in contrast to bigger literatures (cf. van Rees). In order to determine criteria and parameters of literary 'smallness' in general and Belarusian literature in particular see Koler and Naumenko, "Aspekty."

existence and functioning is hardly secured by institutionally established alliances in the early 1920s.

Against this backdrop, the development of alliances between authors seems to be of decisive importance—also in contrast to other field-specific alliances (between authors and readers, editors, literary critics) or extra-literary forms of collaboration (between authors and the Party, jurisdiction, church).[6] Historic reasons, for one, are indicative of this observation in that the constitution of the Belarusian field (1905-1915) first of all implies the institution of the 'author' (indicated, for example, by the emergence of a striking number of literary pseudonyms, which can be understood as "postural indexes" [Meizoz 178] serving as markers of poetological positions; see Kohler, "Strategien"). Starting from this core institution, other field-specific actors or institutions are consciously and explicitly generated (for instance the reader) (cf. Navumenka; see also Vabiščėvič). On the other hand, the importance of literary groups in the literary scene of the 1920s is evident. The affiliation with one of the authors' associations seems to be a *conditio sine qua non* in terms of a literary position: hardly any author of the 1920 is without membership in one of the numerous groups.

Starting from this observation, this contribution investigates when and how literary alliances have developed between authors as well as between authors and magazines in Belarusian literature of the 1920s (which is here heuristically understood as 'small' literature). Furthermore, this contribution will look at how these alliances interact, what functions they perform in the literary system and what parameters in the context of general literary-

---

6 Systematic research on literary collaborations in Belarus has not been undertaken to date. Previous investigations have predominantly focused on the correlation of the newspaper *Naša Niva* (*Our Soil*) and the national identity formation (lastly Unučak; Vabiščėvič). A systematic study from the 1970s on Belarusian literary criticism of the 1920s to 30s, however, is available. It also looks at the interwovenness of literary criticism and literary production with party-political imperatives but is, thus, to be reviewed from a post-soviet perspective (Mušynski, *Belaruskaja*). A recent publication on the interwovenness of literature and power in the 1920s to 30s can only limitedly be used for the current issue as it focuses on the literary production of the Soviet core area—Russia (Liptak and Murašov).

specific precariousness determine their 'success' and 'failure.' These are the leading hypotheses:

- particularly in the first third of the 20th century, the development of alliances between authors is of predominant importance in Belarusian literature: being a 'small literature,' the Belarusian literary scene forms itself largely through the interaction of various literary interest groups;
- in the special case of Belarus, author alliances during the 1920s are expected to overcome the complexity of social reality in the literary field and compensate the weak institutional structures of the field;
- consequently, they constitute a significant dimension of literary positioning and a sort of 'shelter' for the literary production which, however, gets increasingly precarious since it is placed under party-political and state governance.

The heuristic correlation of 'smallness' and precariousness is essentially based on three premises as regards the collaboration between authors and in reference to Bourdieu's field model and several other related studies (primarily Casanova; van Rees/Dorleijn; van Rees; Koler/Naumenko, "Aspekty"): To begin with, literary fields tend to be weakly institutionalized in general and in contrast to other social spheres (Bourdieu, *Rules* 366).[7] Secondly, within this already weakly institutionalized field, authors and readers are usually described as most inadequately organized actors (van Rees 12). Thirdly and finally, Bourdieu conceives of literary group formations as particularly unstable (Bourdieu, *Rules* 424ff.). Although the term precariousness as such is not explicitly used,[8] it is nevertheless conspicuous that Bourdieu, in describing literary groups, foregrounds the aspects of "forma-

---

7 Bourdieu emphasizes the lack of instances that "intervene in struggles for priority or authority and general fights over the defense and conquest of dominating positions and that could grant legal or institutional protection" (*Rules* 366). In the context of Bourdieu's postulation of the 'temporarily' occupied position of areas of cultural production within the field of power (343) one might argue for a basic latent precariousness in each one literary field (see also 358-59).

8 From a sociological perspective, Bourdieu makes a statement on the term 'precariousness' in 1998 in an article called "La précarité est aujourd'hui partout," in which he also refers to the cultural field.

tion and dissolution" and sees them as situational and temporary alliances of convenience between, in fact, "differently motivated" partners.

Consequently, one might now expect that Bourdieu's estimated instability and precariousness of collaboration (and institution) intensifies in the 'small' (and institutionally particularly 'weak') literature. It is thus well conceivable that the 'small' literature and its at least partially inherent precariousness offers specific forms of collaboration in response, virtually as a sort of 'hedging strategy.'

The Belarusian literary field of the 1920s is dominated by a specific tension with respect to this hypothetical scenario—a tension which is at the center of this investigation—because the Belarusian literature of this decade is marked by two antagonistic lines of development: The reconstitution and development of a national Belarusian literature that seeks to build on the period of constitution of 1905-15 coincides with the conceptualization and institutionalization of the Soviet-Belarusian 'proletarian' literature that increasingly puts organization and shaping of the literary sphere under control of central Party organs (Koler/Naumenko, "Aspekty"; Kohler/Navumenka, "Interference"). The state of competition between these two movements is enhanced by the policy shifts that take place as a consequence to the 'Belarusization.' These antagonistic developments thus negotiate the "monopoly of literary legitimacy" and the question of the "legitimate definition of the author" (Bourdieu, *Rules* 354) on a level that ultimately affects the very existence of the field.

The groups of authors that are formed in this context seem, thus, *a priori* to be marked by instability: Organization-wise they reach their endpoint in the centralization of all literary powers in the Union of Soviet Writers;[9] politically, this centralization coincides with the suppression and, ultimate-

---

[9] The extent to which the transition of writers' groups into one central writers' association can be described as an alliance would have to be investigated in a separate study. Hypothetically and on an institutional level, this development could be described as a sign of change from the 'field' to an 'apparatus' (*sensu* Bourdieu, cf. Bourdieu/Wacquant 133). It is also well conceivable that affiliation with the central writers' association serves as a strategic alliance of the partner with the Party that is, in fact, represented by the Association; this is where the author disposes of some freedom, something that remains inaccessible to those who are not affiliated with the Association.

ly, liquidation of many Belarusian authors in the second half of the 1930s.[10] Only very few authors last through this complex process (for instance Kandrat Krapiva, Jakub Kolas, and others). It is these authors who help form the Belarusian literature of the Soviet era (the period since the 1940s) as the system's alliance partners.[11]

AUTHOR GROUPS ACCORDING TO BOURDIEU

As far as Bourdieu's field model conceives of literary conduct as a principally social act—that is conduct that happens in a social space and which is correlated with it—theoretically, one might consider collaborations and alliance formations on all possible levels of this model. Bourdieu discusses different respective aspects in terms of (a) the generation of artists (cf. *Rules* 200ff.); (b) the literary school (cf. 205ff.); (c) the literary group (cf. 422ff.); and (d) the literary magazine (cf. 431-32). Literary alliances can be identified almost exclusively in contexts of struggles for certain positions and legitimation (between generations, schools, groups) as well as contexts of distinction strategies.

In the narrow sense, Bourdieu tends to conceptualize literary groups in terms of the formation and resolution of avant-garde movements and identifies their manifestation and constitution in the act of name giving, manifesttos and programs, initiation rituals, regular meetings etc. He puts emphasis on two main characteristics in these alliance formations: firstly, their 'oppositional unity,' that is, consensus as regards mutual enemies which, at least temporarily, superposes the somewhat differing dispositions of those actors

---

10 In the Belarusian historiography this is described as a sign of an "Executed Literature" ("Rasstraljanaja litaratura"; cf. Savik/Skobla/Cvirka).

11 This is another little-investigated problem: Jakub Kolas und Kandrat Krapiva are indeed authors that become famous in the Soviet Union. It is striking that their specific literary prestige is based on works from the 1920s and early 1930s, but not from a later period. The alliance of these authors with the Party influences their synchronic production, but, paradoxically, their earlier non-compliant works continue to have an effect (see Hockx for the complex interplay of state, Party and literary autonomy in the socialist field from a field-theoretical perspective with the example of Chinese literature).

involved; secondly, the temporary nature of these alliances of convenience between partners "whose temporary adjacent interests ultimately disperse" (422). The level of appreciation or acknowledgement that is awarded those groups is similar to the dispersion of close positions of the alliance partners due to their genuinely different dispositions. The continuous and increasing institutionalization process of the field actually causes original oppositions to intensify. Interestingly, Bourdieu's premise that conceives of the concentration of literary powers as a way to successfully defend or enforce concrete claims to the legitimacy of a particular literary understanding and author profile respectively, seems to be actually confirmed by the very fact that the acknowledged group ultimately dissolves: It becomes obsolete in the literary field.

Bourdieu's conceptualization of a group's magazine—or the magazine as a form of grouping—identifies similar strategies: It usually revolves around one or a few 'leaders'; their table of contents—at least in the first editions—is similarly a "politico-religious determination of position" (431) and the exhibition of symbolic capital that is reflected in the magazine. The magazine that operates skillfully chooses the broadest spectrum in collaborating authors; that is, it tries to avoid an all too obvious and compromising focus to achieve balance (cf. 432). These characteristics convey that the magazine is much more apt to be institutionalized than the group. Rather than focusing on distinction, the strategies at play here—based on similar or comparable dispositions and in compliance with the laws of the market—aim much more on consensus and permanent establishment.

Bourdieu draws the conclusion from this model that, in terms of method, it is not sufficient to merely consider texts and poetological 'label' in order to comprehend the principle that temporarily unifies author and work groups. He advocates an approach that includes actors' dispositions and motivations (cf. 432-33).

This consideration seems to play into this contribution's epistemological interest, but it does so from an opposite perspective. According to Bourdieu, precariousness of groups is based on the (incongruent) dispositions of its collaborating actors. Conversely, then, congruent dispositions would have to secure permanent alliances. If this should not apply, the consequence would be that dispositions are not as permanent as Bourdieu understands them, but that they are, in fact, subject to fluctuation. Another possible conclusion would be that precariousness of alliances might not be based primarily on dispositions of collaborating partners, but might be determined by other parameters, such as aesthetic differences (however, the question would be why this alliance is formed at all). Alternatively, precariousness of alliances might result from the precariousness of a "changed universe of substitutable options simultaneously offered" where "meaning and value" of positions fluctuate (233).

In comparison to Bourdieu's case study France, the observations made here are of particular interest for the investigation of 'small' literatures because the difference marked by 'class-related' dispositions seems to be significantly less distinct (cf. Kohler, "National").[12] Hypothetically, and in the case of Belarus, the precariousness of literary groups correlates with the precariousness of the 'universe' and explains the profile as well as strategies of the magazines which were strongly linked with the respective groups.

AUTHOR GROUPS IN THE BELARUSIAN LITERARY FIELD OF THE 1920S

The Belarusian literary field is marked by a significant institutionalization boost in the beginning of the 1920s that is immensely stimulated and encouraged by a culture-political initiative of the young Belarusian Soviet Republic. A significant factor and central vehicle of this dynamic is the fierce polemic that accompanies the formation of different literary groups. The chronology of their formation, as well as the changing positions of authors that happen within and because of them, implies that the very differentiation of the field itself (that is, the creation of new positions by way of distinction) is the driving momentum in the formation of these groups (cf. Navumenka). Within these processes of alliance formation, then, one can observe a close interaction of these 'types' of groups (i.e., 'generation of art-

---

12 This applies particularly to Belarusian literature; particularly in respect to areal and social origin and as regards educational differences that go along with that, the Belarusian society of the respective era is characterized by a low degree of differentiation.

ists,' 'literary group,' 'literary magazine' and 'literary school'), which, in Bourdieu's model, were generally considered to remain separate.[13]

The central groups of the 1920s and their interactions will be briefly outlined here:

The first decisive group is 'Maladnjak' ('Saplings').[14] Founded in 1923, this author organization functions as a programmatic melting pot and laboratory of the young Belarusian authors.[15] The Revolution gives this generation of authors of 'proletarian' and 'rural' descent opportunities that were formerly denied to them—which is why they are convinced supporters of the new order (Navumenka 156). Their main task is the literary advancement in the constitution of a socialist society (Babarėka 17). 'Maladnjak' may very well be described as a mass organization, and rightly so: it is supported by the Party (Komsomol, the youth organization of KP) and opens branches in all major Belarus cities in only a short period of time (more than 12 in the first two years; cf. Harėcki 10). The central (if not the only) medium of the organization is the eponymic magazine *Maladnjak* (Minsk, 1923-1932). 'Maladnjak' ends with the official integration in the general Belarus writers' guild, BelAPP ('Belarusian Association of Proletarian Writers') in 1928 and finally in the Union of Soviet Writers in 1932.

This first literary organization that was, by the way, under the Party's lead from the very beginning was something of a nucleus from which and in dissociation of which further relevant groups and organs developed. This happened in two thrusts:

In 1926 the so called 'First Split' occurs. Some of the most important members of the organization publicly declare their resignation and found a new group 'Uzvyšša' ('Excelsior,' literally: 'elevation,' 'raising') that has

---

13 Not least due to this fact, groups in particular are the category by which the Belarusian historiography still tries to produce an internal differentiation of the confusing literary process of the 1920s (cf. Navumenka).

14 All titles of magazines and names of groups are translated according to Adamovich (who was a member of one of the groups and later emigrated to Germany and United States).

15 The draft version of the statutes of this association states that the main goal is to support writers with a 'proletarian' and 'poor rural' ideological orientation who wish to propagate a communist culture of Belarus in their work (cf. "Proėkt statutu" 110).

an eponymic magazine (Minsk, 1927-1931). *Uzvyšša*—the group and the magazine—is active until 1931 which is when the group dissolves and simultaneously ceases to publish the magazine.

In 1927/28 'Maladnjak' experiences a 'Second Split' which leads to the loss of its founders and several other main authors. They reorganize in mainly two new groups: 1927 the group 'Polymja' ('The Flame') comes into being and will last until 1931. It allies itself to the eponymous magazine that has already been in existence since 1922—a magazine of this name is still published today. Also in 1927, the 'Belaruskaja litaraturna-mastackaja kamuna' ('Belarusian literary-artistic Commune'), a tiny group, comes into existence and founds the magazine *Roskvit* ('Flowering,' literally: 'blooming'), but will last only a few months before it dissolves (only two issues of *Roskvit* appear during that time). 'Maladnjak's' second split leads to a reorganization of this very group itself in 'BelAPP' ('Belarusian Association of Proletarian Writers').

Apart from those groups mentioned here, there are numerous other mostly short lived groups and magazines in Minsk, the provinces and abroad. These do not get nationwide attention, however, and they are only marginally involved in decisive polemics occupying a rather reporting position (Hužaloŭski 88).[16] In sum, almost every single author of the Belarusian literary field is at some point during the 1920s member of one (or successively several) of the mentioned groups. The positioning in the literary field of the time happens almost exclusively via or within groups.[17]

---

16 The capital Minsk is significant in this context, as it experiences an educational and cultural boost (foundation of the University in 1921, foundation of the Institute of Belarusian Culture in 1922 which is the antecedent of the 1928 founded Academy of Sciences, foundation of the National Library in 1922) that institutionalizes literary forces.

17 The representatives of the 'older' generation who had been associated with the group around 'Naša Niva' and have the status of 'classics' were the exception in the first half of the 1920s (cf. Kohler, "Strategien"). Only in the second half of the 1920s do they join 'Polymja,' see below.

'Successful' Literary Alliances

The increasing number of literary groups that result from each other or tend to reposition may be very well understood as a process of differentiation that seems to be spawned by the originally programmatic uniformity of the group "Maladnjak" which was, however, the only choice at first (cf. Navumenka) and leading to a growing number of different positions in the field. The need for distinction of each and every new emerging magazine is reflected also in the polemic language of their programmatic declarations.

'Young' against 'Old': The Dismissal of 'National Classics'

In early declarations by 'Maladnjak,' young authors try to set themselves apart from the 'old ones,' which is perfectly in line with Bourdieu's model. This is the former generation of authors of the founding and constitution era (1905-15), which produced a pleiad of 'classical' national poets (cf. Kohler, "Strategien"). This former generation is on occasion even excluded in the discourse of the young proletarian magazine *Maladnjak* ("a large number of the old authors remains outside the limits of post-revolutionary literature;" cf. "Usebelaruskae" 93).[18] At best, they are acknowledged as supporters of outdated ('national' and 'bourgeois') ideals:

> There are individual representatives with different affinities in their work, but they are not part of or unified in a group, even if there is some similarity between them. "Maladnjak" takes a relentless opposition and fights against this very similarity that transpires in their work as ideology of rebirth.[19] (*Bjuletėn*' 16)

In any case, the magazine claims to be the only institution that is actually capable of producing adequate literature for society ("new artistic forms that meet the new artistic literary content"; cf. "Zamest dėkljaracyi" 55).

---

18 "І значная частка старых літаратараў апынулася за межамі пасьля-кастрычнікавай літаратуры."

19 "Ёсць асобныя прадстаўнікі з рознымі ўхіламі ў творчасьці, але нязгуртаваныя ў якое-небудзь аб'яднаньне, хаця некаторая агульнасьць між імі ёсьць. Вось проці гэтай агульнасьці, якая выражаецца ў творчасьці праз выяўленьне адраджэнцкай ідэолёгіі, 'Маладняк' заняў позыцыю няпрымірымай барацьбы."

Despite the positioning of the 'Maladnjak' that becomes evident in the key word "у рожкі са старымі" (which means something like 'take the old ones on the horns'), publications by representatives of the pre-revolutionary generation of authors who are not part of the group are still occasionally published in the magazine (cf. 55). Interestingly, this seems to be congruent with Bourdieu's assumption that a magazine's rules and regulations tend to be more liberal than those of groups. Maksim Harėcki, who is the first historiographer of 'Maladnjak,' summarizes the intergenerational conflict as follows:

The young authors begin to understand that it will be altogether difficult for the older generation of writers to produce literature that the readers of the new era need, that only them, the young colleagues, those authors born in the literature of this era will be capable of adequately achieving just that; they will, however, also face difficulty in usurping and establishing their own position in literature and to gather in their own powerfully organized and visible collective if they do not get rid of the older generations authority in the eyes of the readers.[20] (Harėcki 6-7)

Nevertheless, the 'generation-'aspect is probably still fairly irrelevant in the conflict arising from 'Maladnjak': The old generation of authors has, in fact, no more support on the side of literary institutions in this reorganizing and institutionalizing and again 'provisional' field in the beginning of the 1920s than the representatives of 'Maladnjak'—rather the opposite is the case (cf. Kohler, "Strategien" 252-53). The generation gap might be rather understood as a sort of code for the predominantly ideological conflict that, in terms of the new, class-oriented Soviet literature, critically negotiates the prestige of the pre-revolutionary generation of authors that had developed

---

20 "Тады маладыя пачынаюць разумець, што, з аднаго боку, старым наогул цяжка даць тое, што патрэбна чытачу новае эпохі, што даць гэта ў належнай меры могуць толькі яны, маладыя, народжаныя ў літаратуры гэтаю эпохаю, і што, з другога боку, ім таксама цяжка гэта будзе зрабіць, калі яны не адсунуць у вачох чытача аўторытэт старых у бок з свае дарогі, калі яны не адваююць і ня зоймуць у літаратуры сваё асобнае месца, калі яны ня згуртуюцца у свой асобны, можна організаваны і яскрава выяулены калектіў." On the polemics with the 'Olds,' cf. Babarėka.

from the national literary capital in terms of the new, class-oriented Soviet literature.[21]

Struggles for Position, Ideological Agenda, and Rhetoric

In a similar way, the struggles between groups that emerged from 'Maladnjak' in 1928 are not concerned with determining literary-poetological directions proper of the kind Bourdieu has observed in France (for instance Symbolists vs. Surrealists or the like).[22] Rather, aesthetic and poetological questions are reflected upon in an ideological mode; they are concerned with questions of thematic focus and formal character of a 'proletarian' literature, of dispositional credibility of their authors, of conformity with the 'mass reader' and so on and bear witness to the priority of a 'socialist reorganization' over a literary discourse. In this way, there are hardly any different positions identifiable in the manifestos and programmatic declarations of rivaling groups—it remains cloudy where exactly the literary difference lies.

Nine of the authors who resigned from the 'Maladnjak' in 1926 and founded the group 'Uzvyšša' formulate laconically in the newspaper *Saveckaja Belarus'* ('Soviet Belarus'):

---

21 This applies particularly to Janka Kupala and Jakub Kolas who are awarded the status of 'national poets' ("narodny paėt") in 1925 and 1926. This 'ennoblement,' however, coincides with repressions and is thus certainly a strategy to exert ideological control over authors rather than a mere 'honor' (cf. Koler, "Stvarėnne").

22 'Maladnjak' decides against an identification of the magazine with a 'literary school': "The term 'maladnjakizm' cannot universalize the work produced within the context of 'Maladnjak' like a literary school that we do not create. [...] So far, we do not have a mutual form and direction. Each one of us utilizes some elements from former schools of thought selecting the useful and appropriate. Since this is the way it is, there is certainly no direction or movement"; *Bjuletėn'* 20: "Тэрмін 'маладнякізм' ня можа абагульніць маладняцкіх твораў, як літаратурная школа, якой мы не ўтвараем. [...] У нас пакуль што няма адзінай формы і напрамку. Кожны з нас карыстае тыя ці іншыя элемэнты старых напрамкаў, выбіраючы з іх усё карыснае і прыгоднае. А паколькі гэта так, пастолькі нельга гаварыць аб пэўных напрамках і плынях."

We resigned from "Maladnjak" on May 27 because we disapprove of the organization's work methods and its characteristics of the contemporary condition of the Belarusian proletarian literature.²³ ("Tav. rėdaktaru" 6)

The group's program is specified in nine detailed theses, dated to May 26th 1926, and can be looked up in the first issue of the literary magazine *Uzvyšša* from January 1927. As regards the position of 'Uzvyšša,' the polemic language against 'Maladnjak' and the unmistakable literary commitment to the 'older' generation is particularly striking:

The young authors of the post-revolutionary era may have dissociated themselves from achievements (of the 'Old'), but have accomplished only little themselves (they have not produced anything in terms of significant and deep works).²⁴ ("Ad zhurtavan'nja" 168)

Apart from the explicit commitment to the 'Old' ones whose work is acknowledged as 'basis of the national and cultural renaissance of Belarus' by 'Uzvyšša,' the offensive proclamation of the literary work as "single legitimate expression of artistic-literary directions" (168)²⁵ is certainly another blow against 'Maladnjak'—particularly because 'Maladnjak' in fact practices a sort of 'culture of declaration.' Thus, 'Uzvyšša's' program indeed suggests that the crucial poetological disagreement is founded in the shaping of 'proletarian' literature: The group declares a more or less clearly defined 'quality oriented' position and sees itself as supporter of striving 'high' art; its name 'Uzvyšša' may thus be seen as part of the poetological program:

---

23 "Мы выйшлі з 'Маладняка' 27 траўня г. г., не згаджаючыся з метадамі працы арганізацыі і яе характарыстыкай сучаснага становішча беларускай пралетарскай літаратуры."

24 "[…] малад[ыя] пісьменьнік[і] пасьлякастрычніцкай пары, якія, адмовіўшы папярэднія дасягненьні ('старое'), новых дасягненьняў у большасьці не дайшлі (не ўтварылі новага ў сэнсе вялікіх і глыбокіх твораў)."

25 "Мы лічым, што кожны літаратурна-мастацкі кірунак знаходзіць свае выражэньне ў самай творчасьці."

The aim is not to write Odes and Hymns about elevation, but to create elevation out of one's own power. This very goal and awareness is the young generation's impetus and reason why "Uzvyšša" has been founded.[26] ("Ad zhurtavan'nja" 169)

'Uzvyšša' puts this program into reality. Poetological and literary critical reflection takes an important position (in a derogatory way, this is also declared by the 'Maladnjak's' review of *Uzvyšša's* first issue). Another of its main objectives is the support of Belarusian prose that is only fairly little developed (cf. 169) and which it supports to its best abilities: Fictional prose genres take a significant position among published primary works.

Both the perseverance in maintaining a quality standard and the poetological reflection seem to establish 'Uzvyšša' as something close to an autonomistic literary concept. Interestingly, this is counteracted by the magazine's persistent commitment to class struggle, the constitution of a socialist society, the 'mass reader' and the Party (cf. "Statut Uzvyšša" 171). This indicates, however, that already in the 1920s the Party functions as a significant alliance partner a group or magazine cannot go without: 'Uzvyšša' publicly declares 'conformity' with the Party program and admits that the group will not be able to implement its tasks without the Party's support (cf. 170-71).[27]

The case is very similar for *Polymja* and *Roskvit*, for instance. The 'revolutionary Marxist' magazine *Polymja* has already in 1922 explicitly pronounced the dichotomous 'friend-enemy' opposition that will significantly determine the ideological discourse of the 1920s:

Only those who share our view of the national question and generally acknowledge the Soviet authority, only those workers will be accommodated in our magazine. [...] Those who will accept our program may follow our lead. Those who do not

---

26 "Ня оды і гімны складаць пра ўзвышша, тварыць узвышша ўласнымі сіламі — вось тая сьвядомасьць, што становіць сабою 'трэшчынку' між маладымі пісьменьнікамі і выклікае да жыцьця 'Узвышша'."

27 Literary groups have to get official approval for their regulations by the People's Commissariat for Internal Affairs (Narkamunutspraŭ, russ.: NKVD), only then do they also get financial support (cf. Skryhan). Thus, all groups are strictly organized according to the communist model (leadership, meetings, resolutions, minute-taking, audit commission etc.).

have the courage to embrace it are against us. We will accept no intermediate position, because such position must not exist.[28] ("Našy zadanni" 4)

Similarly, the 'Belarusian Literary Artistic Community' according to the statutes

is founded on the principles of revolutionary Marxism and the Communist Party and dedicates itself to the purposes of contributing to the fostering and the construction of life through literature and art and of fighting for the most perfectly organized way of human coexistence—the world commune.[29] ("Statut Kamuny" 79)

In all these cases, manifestoes and programmatic statements define the activities of the groups predominantly in terms of their ideological positions and their contributions to the construction of society.

The disputes between magazines—the polemics between *Uzvyšša* and *Maladnjak* in particular—are thus marked by a predominantly ideological struggle for the legal definition of 'proletarian' literature: Platon Halavač contemplates the differences between both groups from a 'Maladnjak' perspective:

The separation of "Uzvyšša" from "Maladnjak" has profound reasons of social and class-related nature. The literary work of "Uzvyšša" and "Maladnjak" bears witness to it. [...] The creation of "Uzvyšša" [...] shows the detachment from the working class in literature. (This does not apply to all comrades of the group "Uzvyšša", but

---

28 "Толькі тыя, якія прымаюць нашу ацэнку нацыянальнага пытаньня й прынцыпова прызнаюць Савецкую ўладу—толькі гэтыя працоўнікі магчымуць знайсьці месца на баках нашага журналу. [...] Тыя, хто нашу праграму прымуць, пойдуць за намі. Усе-ж, хто ня знойдзе сьмеласьці яе прыняць, пойдуць супроціў нас. Сярэдзіны мы не прызнаем, ды яе й быць ня можа."

29 "[...] грунтуючыся на прынцыпах рэвалюцыйнага марксызму і камуністычнае партыі, ставіць сабе заданьнем, праз літаратуру і мастацтва прымаць удзел у жыцьцёбудаўніцтве, вясці змаганьне за найбольш дасканальна арганізаваную форму чалавечага сужыцьця—камуну сусьвету." The first issue of *Roskvit* is still published under the label of the Polack branch of 'Maladnjak.'

the fact that the magazine does not respond to the publication of such works in their review section attests to the observation that group interests are more important than all this talk about the proletarian characteristics of their works).[30] (Halavač 5-6)

One year later, in 1929, both magazines resort to a clearly hostile rhetoric in expressing their conflicting views. Lukaš Bėnde, one of the most prominent Marxist literary critics from *Maladnjak*, denounces 'Uzvyšša' and their "new theories and methods" as media of a hostile bourgeois ideology hidden underneath a "Marxist phraseology" (Bėnde 101). 'Uzvyšša' hits back in a similar fashion:

> All these people put so much effort not just interfering with "Uzvyšša's" work, but to destroy the organization all together. They had no principles and acted with shallow passion: There was no sign of scruples, scientific nature or sincere interest in founding a proletarian literature. They were bold enough to hide behind the Party's name, but "Uzvyšša" did not believe them [...].[31] ("Try hady" 65)

Differentiation under the Cover of Supplementary Alliances

Despite the party ideological rhetoric, which all magazines and groups seem to have in common, there are also distinctive parameters that show these alliance formations between authors and strategies are to be understood as a way of taking different positions in the field. Despite their

---

30 "[А]дыход ад 'Маладняка' групы 'Узвышша' мае пад сабой глыбокія падставы соцыяльнага, клясавага парадку. Аб гэтым сьведчыць творчасць 'Узвышша' і 'Маладняка'. [...] Творчасць 'Узвышша' [...] паказвае аддаленьне ад лініі рабочае клясы ў літаратуры. (Бязумоўна, сказанае ні ў якім разе нельга аднесьці да ўсіх т.т. з групы 'Узвышша,' але нерэагаваньне аб'яднаньня ў часопісі, рэцэнзіях на зьяўленьне такіх твораў, замаўчваньне іх гаворыць аб тым, што інтарэсы групы ў даным выпадку пераважаюць усякія гаворкі аб пролетарскасьці творчасьці)."

31 "[Г]эта ўсё тыя асобы, якія ўсімі сіламі стараліся ня толькі пашкодзіць Узвышшу працаваць, а нават зусім зьнішчыць Узвышша як арганізацыю. Ня мелі яны ніякіх прынцыпаў і выступалі, як самыя заядлыя верхагляды: ні сумленьня, ні навуковасьці, ні шчырасьці да справы стварэньня пролетарскай літаратуры ў іх выступленьнях ня было й кроплі. Яны мелі сьмеласьць прыкрывацца імем партыі, але Узвышша ім ня верыла [...]."

proclamations the positions taken by both *Uzvyšša* and particularly *Polymja* in relation to the national literary tradition are specific to them and are fundamentally opposed to the party line to which they pledge their allegiance: Both magazines initially appear (at least indirectly) as 'heirs' of the literary founding era of 1905-15 (cf. Navumenka). *Uzvyšša* does so on two levels: support of the national tradition established by the former generation of authors (see above)[32] and poetologically by extending the range of genres and topics.[33] *Polymja*, on the other hand, displays even stronger characteristics of heritage than *Uzvyšša* even in terms of their collaborators: Publishing authors encompass members from the *Naša-Niva*-generation with different political backgrounds (Jakub Kolas, Ciška Hartny, Leapol'd Rodzėvič) as well as former 'Maladnjak' members (Michas' Zarėcki, Ales' Dudar) and future supporters of *Uzvyšša* (Paŭljuk Trus) which means that it does not apply to the proclaimed 'friend-or-enemy' dichotomy on the level of artistic production. The only group that has a strong poetological focus is the 'Litaraturna-mastackaja kamuna': It exhibits (following the Russian organization 'LEF') a 'tabula rasa' sort of disposition of the Russian futurists. Ultimately, however, the group does not follow an aesthetic agenda; it swiftly collapses and disappears in the 'BelAPP' (cf. Žybul').

Faced with the necessity of allying themselves to the Party or demonstrating its conformity with the party line, which they proclaim in their programmatic statements but do not practice convincingly at the level of the literary productions in the magazines, they seem to ensure their political credibility by way of specific supplementary alliances. The literary review section shows a particularly aggressive Marxist attitude in the 1920s which is in stark contrast to the rather soft political and ideological tone of their magazine. This pronounced Marxist orientation in their literary critique is certainly a protectionist strategy to secure the magazine's further existence, despite potential accusation of a nationalist positioning.

---

32 *Uzvyšša*, however, does not publish primary works of the previous generation. An exception is Zmitrok Bjadulja, the only former representative of the *Naša-Niva* era who is an official member of the group 'Uzvyšša.'

33 Mušynski (*Belaruskaja* 174) draws a connection between the aggravated morale of the literary section and the intensified literary fight. He claims that 'narrow dogmatism' und 'propagation of a simplistic, vulgar concept of literature' are the weak points of *Polymja's* literary criticism in the second half of the 1920s.

Uzvyšša develops a similar publication strategy to secure credibility through additional alliances. Despite its clear commitment to proletarian literature, on account of its unconditionally prioritizing the aesthetic quality of literary works, "Uzvyšša" is continually accused of being elitist ('quasi-bourgeois,' 'decadent'). The additional alliance with the reader works against this flaw—this alliance similarly ties in with the tradition of the pre-revolutionary newspaper *Naša Niva*. The second issue already addresses the reader with the proclaimed goal to "transform literary criticism [...] into a real reader's organ in literature" ("ператварыць крытыку [...] у сапраўдны орган чытача ў літаратуры"; ibid). Consequently, its appeal to the reader reads like an echo of *Naša Niva's* call that set the start for a Belarusian literature in 1906 (cf. "Pačynajučy" 1):

For this reason, *Uzvyšša* asks its readers to share their thoughts and views of the magazine's content, single works and the magazine as a whole and, additionally, to send their wish lists for artistic literature. Everything that is send to us will be used by the magazine and meet with a positive response on its pages. Only with help of your active and vital participation in increasing the magazine's creative power and distribution, Comrades readers, the goal of creating a proletarian literature can be reached; a literature that is the soul of each proletarian and peasant, of each working reader and Soviet Belarus' pride.[34] ("Da čytačoŭ" 218)

The alliance with the reader that is aimed at by *Uzvyšša* may be interpreted in different ways: One effect is certainly the rebuttal of the accusation that 'Uzvyšša' was propagating an understanding of art that was out of touch and 'elitist.' Its strategy is then similar to that of 'Maladnjak,' in the sense

---

34 "Дзеля гэтага 'Узвышша' зьвяртаючыся да сваіх чытачоў заклікае ўсіх таварышоў надсылаць да рэдакцыі свае думкі пра матар'ялы часопісі і наогул свае погляды як на паасобныя творы, так і наогул на часопісь уцалку, і свае жаданьні, што да мастацкай літаратуры. Усё надасланае будзе выкарыстана часопісьцю і знойдзе свой адбітак на яе старонках. Толькі пры вашым, таварышы чытачы, жывым і чынным удзеле ў справе творчасьці узвышша часопісі і яе пашырэньні, будзе дасягнута мэта ўтварэньня пролетарскай беларускай літаратуры, якая будзе душою кожнага пролетара і селяніна, кожнага працоўнага чытача і гордасьцю Савецкай Беларусі."

that it generates a somewhat collective art—art that is created 'by a proletarian for a proletarian.' The reader as the magazine's alliance partner guarantees the fulfillment of this concept.

From a field-theoretical perspective, the reader's participation implies a renegotiation of *nomos,* the consensual 'faith in the game' on which depend the boundaries of the literary field (cf. Bourdieu, *Rules* 223). After all, the implication of the reader in the production and valuation process (literary criticism being addressed as a reader's organ) blurs the lines between material and symbolic production (cf. Dorleijn/van Rees; van Rees): each reader is, at least potentially, reader, author and critic alike.

The alliance with the reader gets deliberately reactivated by *Uzvyšša* in 1929. The declared goal is to "break down the Chinese wall between the author and the reader" in order to ensure that the "mass reader's needs" as the 'user' of the literary production gets heard (Krapiva 97-98).[35] An advertisement (1929/2) even claims that the perusal as well as the assistance in *Uzvyšša* is a form of 'civic duty':

Write comments and words of advice concerning the magazine because the creation of a Belarusian proletarian literature is a social matter! Each citizen ought to be subscriber and reader of *Uzvyšša*. Contribute to the section "The reader has the floor!"[36] (*Uzvyšša* 1929/2:102)

The ideological success of *Uzvyšša's* strategy in terms of an additional alliance with the reader becomes evident as *Maladnjak* begins to copy it. In 1929 they also publish an appeal that encourages the "Comrade readers" to send wishes and commentaries to the editorial board. The appeal concludes with a solemnly: "To the alliance of reader and author!" ("За сувязь чытача з пісьменнікам"; cf. "Čytačam" 142). None of this, however, can

---

35 Here, Krapiva critically reflects upon the entire literary system as regards its mediating agents (literary criticism) within the scope of a hermetical division between author and reader.

36 "Пішэце свае заўвагі і парады пра часопіс 'Узвышша,' бо справа стварэньня беларускай пролетарскай літаратуры—справа грамадзкая! Кожны грамадзянін павінен быць падпішчыкам і чытачом 'Узвышша'."

be viewed as a true and solid alliance because the readers show only little if any interest at all.[37]

Still, what should be looked at more closely in terms of an additional alliance is the interaction between literary review and censorship (see below) which could help explain *Polymjas'* striking discrepancy between literary review and primary literature.

However, partial compromise as regards additional alliances in literary production secures the formation of two positions that expedite the differentiation in the literary field and resists the ideologically controlled achievement of uniformity. Apart from *Maladnjak* which represents the ideological-proletarian literary concept that will eventually become established as *nomos*, there are also a national Belarusian position (*Polymja*) and a mostly a-ideological aesthetic position (*Uzvyšša*).

The observations and considerations made here prove according to the hypotheses formulated above that the formation of literary groups in the 1920s from the chief organization 'Maladnjak' (which becomes more ideologically radical) is indeed to be viewed as a strategic formation of alliances between authors. Their necessity results from the impingement of party ideological imperatives in the institutionally poorly secured literary space of a 'provisional' field: The groups and organs seemingly function as collective shelters where authors of similar or close dispositions who do not comply with the legitimate position defined by party ideology and wish to develop other positions may position themselves. Particularly the magazines *Uzvyšša* and *Polymja*, which serve as examples in this contribution, show that additional alliances establish not just credibility but even protect literary productions from ideological absorption.

Until the late 1920s, this is a 'tacit agreement' between all actors of the field—between authors, groups and magazines, but also the officials (after all, they authorize the formation of new groups), literary criticism, subscribers and readers. The described strategies are similarly part of the *nomos* that ensures the differentiation and functioning of this 'provisional' field and counteracts its precariousness.

---

37 Further research remains to be done in this respect. Sources, however, are hard to come by, since only fragments of the archives of relevant magazines have been preserved.

'Failure' of Literary Collaborations between Authors

As yet it is difficult to say at what point and in what way exactly this fragile agreement starts to collapse. The resolution of the central committee of the Belarusian Communist Party from May 27, 1932 might be viewed as an explicit endpoint of literary collaboration in the sense of the above outlined. The resolution plans to establish the Union of Soviet Writers and the factual liquidation of all author groups as well as the consolidation of all literary magazines under the organization committee of the new State union (*Saveckaja Belarus'* 28.05.1932; cf. Sidarėvič; Hužaloŭski 96). By that time, however, the system has in fact already collapsed. In 1931 'Uzvyšša' dissolves ("Pastanova litaraturna-mastackaha" 178-80) and even the minutes of the 1928 founded 'BelAPP' are marked by the awareness of the crisis in 1930. This collapse is usually seen as determined by the radicalized cultural politics after the termination of the 'New Economic Policy' and the aggravation of class struggles caused by Stalin in 1928 because they actually resulted in the exclusion of every 'non-proletarian' forces from arts and cultural resources (cf. Mušynski, *Belaruskaja*; Brigadina 80; Sidarėvič; Hužaloŭski).

The increasing ideological pressure on literature aggravates the 'friend-enemy' dichotomy. Until 1928 authors are mainly valued according to their group affiliation. 'Uzvyšša's' polemic bit on Adam Babarėka (the group's most important theorist) who has once co-founded 'Maladnjak' shows this. In an ironic manner it is pointed out that Babarėka's positions were appreciated by 'Maladnjak' representatives for as long as he had been associated with the group; and that these very positions had become inacceptable since he had left 'Maladnjak' and co-founded 'Uzvyšša' (BDAMLi f.66/1019). Babarėka turns from 'Maladnjak's' friend to 'Uzvyšša's' friend and, thus, automatically becomes 'Maladnjak's' enemy.[38]

---

38 Within only a short period of time, Babarėka becomes also the 'enemy' of 'Uzvyšša'; cf. below.

"Former Friends Become Enemies":[39] The Case of Zarècki

Under reinforced conditions, since 1929 magazines and groups are increasingly forced to state unconditional ideological decidedness—even by paying the price of 'sacrificing' some of their own members; that is, the reassessment where 'friends' become 'enemies' of their own group. The sacrifice of some in order to save the group shows that the alliance model for authors that had functioned as a 'shelter' does not hold any longer.

The case of novelist Michaś Zarècki (cf. Kohler, "Fehlpositionierung") exemplifies the situation: Zarècki, coming from a province, a supporter of the Revolution and soldier of the Red Army as a young man, is one of the leading figures of 'Maladnjak' in the early 1920s. Very soon he starts to cautiously dissociate from the official ideology in his narratives by writing about ethically problematic aspects of the new social order even though, initially, he is viewed as a 'revolutionary-romantic' author (cf. Mušynski, "Michaś"' 505) in contemporary reviews and is member of the Communist Party. Zarècki's position is not endangered by this at first. His affiliation with 'Maladnjak' and his role as editor of *Maladnjak* serve as protection.

His resignation from the group in 1927 (he becomes a co-founder of 'Polymja') deprives him of his loyalty of Marxist critique, however. While *Polymja* tolerates his texts despite its (Marxist) literary-critical stance, *Maladnjak* from now on classifies his works as anti-class and national democratic. Finally, in the second half of 1929, Zarècki publishes two works in two different magazines (*Saveckaja Belarus'* and *Polymja* which is his 'own' magazine) inducing an unprecedented malicious campaign against him.[40] Curiously, it is not just 'external' magazines that partake in this hate campaign. The group 'Polymja' is particularly involved in the literary critique, too.

Both magazines publicly declare that by having published Zarècki's texts they indeed made a "big political mistake." Moreover, they publish harsh condemning reviews of Zarècki's work. In *Polymja*, for instance, it says:

---

39 More accurately: "[...] and previous friends turn into the worst enemies" ("і ранейшыя прыяцелі абарачаюцца ў найлюцейшых ворагаў"). It is the final word from the first part of Zarècki's unfinished novel *Kryvičy* (1931).

40 This is the travelogue *Padarožža na Novuju Zjamlju* (*Journey to a New Land*) and the first part of the unfinished novel *Kryvičy*.

It's the apotheosis of nationalism, it is the most vicious though most cowardly denunciation of proletarian dictatorship and the Socialist construction in the BSSR. Zarėcki mutters cowardly with discontent about Haloŭlit [the central board of censors; GK] and about the fact that Haloŭlit prevented him from revealing the entire corruption of the heroes of 'Kryvičy' and destroying them in the following parts. Poor Zarėcki, callous Haloŭlit who denies Zarėcki 'ruining' his heroes.[41] (Budzinski 231)

As a consequence, Zarėcki becomes the "enemy in his own home" (that is the title of Budzinkis's article in *Polymja*), gets excluded from the Party and sent to the provinces to work.

The question is, then, why an author like Zarėcki, who was very well aware of the possibilities and impossibilities in the contemporary field, opted for what turned out to be the 'wrong' strategies of literary positioning. The only logical explanation for this case seems to be a radical change in the functioning of alliances, a change Zarėcki could not have foreseen because it was him who prompted it. In the aggravated political environment, the magazine loses its institutional protective function. As the quote from Budzinski clearly illustrates, the Party's central board of censors now occupies a position between the magazine and the individual author and thus weakens their ties. Consequently, the magazine is not just unable to protect Zarėcki, the latter even becomes a potential threat to the entire group. Thus, the group has to distance itself from the author in order to maintain its integrity and to secure its existence. The alliance between Zarėcki and *Polymja* collapses.

---

41 "Гэта апофэоз нацыяналізму, гэта самае злое, хоць і трусьлівае выступленьне супроць пролетарскае дыктатуры і соцыялістычнага будаўніцтва ў БССР. Зарэцкі трусьліва мармыча пра галоўліт і пра тое, што галоўліт перашкодзіў яму ў наступных частках выявіць усю гніласьць гэрояў 'Крывічоў' і загубіць іх. Бедны Зарэцкі, жорсткі Галоўліт, які забараняе Зарэцкаму 'загубіць' сваіх гэрояў."

"The End of Friendship":[42] Censorship and Literary Criticism

A central board of censors, the so-called Haloŭlit (Central Administration Board of Literature and Publishing) has existed since 1922 in the Belarusian Soviet Republic. It is organized in a similar fashion to the Moscovite agency and is governed by the Belarusian Commissariat of Enlightenment. Effectively, however, it is governed by the Party's Central Committee (officially so since 1926) (cf. Hužaloŭski 9-10). As censorship has played a role in the Belarusian literary field since the early 1920s, the sheer fact of censorship is not sufficient to account for the failure of literary collaboration between authors around the turn of 1930s, which has been illustrated by the case of Zarėcki. Rather, it seems to be a matter of qualitative changes in the interplay between censorship and authors that are caused by different external factors:

On the one hand, censorship is repeatedly reorganized during the 1920s, its range of tasks expands and work force increases and its control function tightens. One consequence of these reorganizing measures is (in contrast to the practice of the early 1920s when literary scholars and literary critics were appointed members of the body of censors) the increasing employment of officials since 1928 who primarily stand out for their exceptional loyalty to the Party and "are familiar with literary work" (Hužaloŭski 11, 99). Hence, the above described alliances of authors that manifest in magazines and groups up to 1928 encompass alliances with representatives of the body of censors (that is literary scholars and literary critics) that were established until 1928.

A second significant change might be that since 1927 censorship could potentially entail penal procedures (cf. 20). This altered quality of censorship becomes tangible for the first time in 1928 when Ales' Dudar (one of the former leaders of 'Maladnjak' and subsequently member of the group 'Polymja') is exiled due to one of his texts. This very occasion marks the turning point towards a repressive censorship that could, in case of doubt, be directed against an individual author (cf. 104).

---

42 *End of Friendship* (Kanec družby) is the title of a play by Kandrat Krapiva (1934). It deals with the precariousness of personal relations under the requirement of unconditional loyalty to the Party and shows the repressions and public show trials that accompanied the policy of forced collectivization.

Including those mentioned changes, the Central Committee's decision that aimed at terminating the existence of several competitive literary groups is a signal of a far-reaching turn: Unity and decidedness as regards the party line become stipulations that directly subject the individual author (and later even the censor) to the dictates of the Party. This is realized by help of monopoly of the Party governed literary criticism which complements censorship and builds the foundation for literary lawsuits (cf. Hužaloŭski 99-100). Author alliances that are supported in the 1920s by the partial integration of literary criticism that is close to censorship are replaced with the new alliances between literary critic, censorship and Party at the end of the decade, which are in opposition to the author as an 'individual.'[43]

In this final episode of their existence, the magazines tend to state the ideological development of their members and begin to let single members go. This increasing 'exhibition' of single members by their group as regards their adjustment to the ideological discourse of the time shows that the model of author alliances has reached the end of its functionality.

The magazine *Uzvyšša* publishes a detailed statement by the group on political literary 'mistakes' of single members during the past years ("Pastanova Belaruskaha" 9ff.). At the end of 1930, the group dissociates from some of its initial founders (Adam Babarėka, Jazep Pušča and Uladzimir Duboŭka) and demands "unconditional punishment of counter-revolutionary forces" ("Rezoljucija" 167-168). Only several issues later, the magazine publishes an extensive and detailed literary ideological payoff with the former theoretical spokesman Adam Babarėka. While the literary texts themselves remain true to the original, ideologically neutral and autonomic line (representatives are for instance Lukaš Kaljuha und Kandrat Krapiva; cf. Koler/Naumenko, "Aspekty"), works of the former publically vilified members, however, do not get published anymore. Soon after, the rest of the group dissolves and ceases to publish any more issues.

The demise of *Uzvyšša* just like the example of Zarėcki and his relationship with *Polymja* shows that the alliance of authors in the sense of institutionalizing a group and a magazine as a strategy to form new positions

---

43 Following Grüttemeier's analysis (in this volume; see also Grüttemeier/Laros), the link between author alliances and literary criticism, censorship and also the legal system needs to be otherwise further investigated. Results might be referred back to the problem of the 'provisional' field.

under the umbrella of this cooperation does no longer work. Literary groups are substituted by alliances between the board of censors, literary criticism and the Party in the Belarusian-Soviet field. The author may join this alliance and might be even (temporarily) rehabilitated—Zarėcki whose novel *Vjaz'mo* (*Fetters* 1932) is awarded best novel on the subject of collectivization documents this (cf. Mušynski, *Praŭdzivaja*).[44]

In the late 1920s the preservation of quasi-autonomist positions is no longer possible except at the cost of a complete subordination of the individual to the ideological system and in the mode of writing in code. In this way, the disappearance of the groups that had formed in the field and which were the very constitutive feature of the field cause the disappearance of the field itself.

Summary and Outlook

It seems that the formation of alliances between authors in the first third of the 20th century was an effective strategy for the Belarusian 'small' and young literature that was marked by precariousness to overcome the institutional and organizational weakness and produce distinct positions in the 'provisional' literary field.

With regards to the specific complex circumstances of the 1920s (that is in the context of reconstitution or new formation, differentiation and ideologization) the consensus seems to rest in a concept of alliance, according to which alliances have two functions: As they combine or focus on similar interests, dispositions and fundamental political positions of authors in individual groups and magazines, they significantly play into the process of differentiation. One main characteristic is certainly the fact that, to the outside world, these groups only represent very general and little distinctive positions and commit themselves entirely to a proletarian literature that works to build the 'new socialist society.' This subordination, institutionalized in the formal act of approval granted to the group or magazine by the council of people's commissioners constitutes the *conditio sine qua non* of literary

---

44 After all, Zarėcki becomes a victim of the cleansing in 1937 as did nearly all distinctive authors, literary critics and scholars of the 1920s, irrespective of to which group they were affiliated.

groupings of any description and creates in the Belarusian field a paradoxical situation that can be described as a 'uniform diversity.'[45] The literary-poetological differentiation of the field is hardly distinguishable to the outside; it is rather implicitly measurable in terms of the splitting and new formation that come along with the fluctuation of authors who migrate from one group to another. The differentiation happens, in fact, behind the uniformity of public proclamations and manifestoes. This is, then, the second main function of alliances; that is, the somewhat disguising potential of these groups and their magazines that enables authors to take positions which differ from the officially sanctioned and legitimate position. One could go so far as to argue that the groups constitute a space where artistic individuality (also the realization of autonomous positions) remains possible. The strategy of 'additional alliances' (with the reader, literary criticism and thus, hypothetically, with the censorship that was initially and generally loyal) proves the protective function of these groups. These additional alliances attest, moreover, to the outside the groups' and magazines' loyalty to the party line.

The aggravation of the political situation (particularly since 1928) renders the model of alliances between authors (which was meant to lighten the precariousness of the 'provisional' literary field) precarious in itself. Granting artistic autonomous positions becomes a threat to the existence of groups which compromises its function as a 'shelter.' The alliance between authors now becomes displaced (and finally even obsolete) by the powerful 'compulsory alliance' of groups and magazines with the censorship (Haloŭlit) that had been institutionalized since the beginning of the 1920s: The groups begin to virtually dissolve even before they are officially transferred into the Union of Soviet Writers in 1932.

In the case of Belarus, the precariousness of alliances between authors results not just from diverging dispositions of partners who constitute temporary literary interest groups (even if these are the main impetus for group (trans)formations in the sense of the differentiation processes). What adds to the 'failure' of this specific form of alliance is a "change of the universe" (Bourdieu, *Rules* 233) in the second half of the 1920s. To be precise, this change, which can be described in terms of a political-ideological radical-

---

45 This also implies the suspension of the market corrective of 'demand' which usually determines whether a magazine lasts or not.

ization, first manifests itself in a revaluation of positions and positionings in the literary field, and eventually results in the dissolution of inner-literary alliances between authors, who are forced to pact with the alliance of the Party, censorship, and literary criticism instead.

To what extent such possible alliances (mainly the Union of Soviet Writers) work to promote or reduce precariousness and possibly even generate new forms of inner-literary alliances remains an issue for further research.[46] Finally, it is significant that the post-Soviet reconstitution of the literary field after 1991 happens again by way of a brisk alliance and group formation of authors (for instance 'Tutėjšyja' ('Locals,' 'Natives'), 'Bum-Bam-Lit,' 'Schmerzwerk' ('Pain-Work'), 'Tavarystva vol'nych litarataraŭ' ('Cooperative of Free Literati') as well as the existence of competitive writers' guilds) that seems to be expiring for some years again.[47] It seems that (presumably due to the precarious situation of the Belarusian literature itself which is divided into a Russian-speaking and Belarusian-speaking branch) in recent years a new way of alliance formation is gaining in significance and meaning; that is, the alliance between authors and readers who come into face-to-face-dialogue through readings, poetry slams particularly in Minsk, but also through blogs, platforms on the internet.

WORKS CITED

Adamovich, Anthony. *Opposition to Sovietization in Belarussian Literature (1917-1957)*. Munich: Institute for the Study of the UDSSR. Series I/38, 1958. Print.

"Ad zhurtavan'nja": "Ad belaruskaha litaraturna-mastackaha zhurtavan'nja 'Uzvyšša'." *Uzvyšša* 1 (1927): 168-70. Print.

---

[46] It is interesting, for instance, that in the 1970s-80s renowned Soviet Belarusian authors are also recognized as literary scholars. Today, their children often teach at the Belarusian State University or work at the Belarusian Academy of Sciences. It is also interesting that many university lecturers as well as students in Belarusian Literature (more or less known, and more or less published) write poetry or prose or/and are involved in Belarusian literary criticism.

[47] For further information on the development of literature in the recent past see McMillin.

Babarėka, Adam. "Vjasnu radzila vosen'." *Maladnjak* 7 (1925): 1-21. Print.
Bahdanovič, Iryna. "Die belarussische Lyrik der 1910-20er Jahre im Kontext des europäischen Modernismus." *Kleinheit als Spezifik: Beiträge zu einer feldtheoretischen Analyse der belarussischen Literatur im Kontext 'kleiner' slavischer Literaturen*. Ed. Gun-Britt Kohler, Pavel Navumenka, and Ralf Grüttemeier. Oldenburg: BIS-Verlag, 2012. 123-42. Print.
Bėndė, Lukaš. "Mikola Bajkoŭ na litaraturnym fronce (pra knihu M. Bajkova 'Na litaraturnyja tėmy')." *Maladnjak* 5-6 (1929): 101-10. Print.
Beyrau, Dietrich, and Rainer Lindner. *Handbuch der Geschichte Weißrusslands*. Göttingen: Vandenhoeck & Ruprecht, 2001. Print.
Bjuletėn': *Bjuletėn' plenumu cėntral'naha bjuro ŭsebelaruskaha abjadnan'nja poėtaŭ i pis'men'nikaŭ Maladnjak*. Minsk: Vydan'ne CB "Maladnjak," 1925. Print.
Bourdieu, Pierre. "La précarité est aujourd'hui partout." *Contre-feux I: Propos pour servir à la résistance contre l'invasion Néo-libérale*. Paris: Liber-Raisons d'Agir, 1998: 95-102. Print.
---. *The Rules of Art: Genesis and Structure of the Literary Field*. 1996. Cambridge: Polity P, 2011. Print.
Bourdieu, Pierre, and Loïc Wacquant. *Reflexive Anthropologie*. 1992. Frankfurt/Main: Suhrkamp, 2006. Print.
Brigadina, Ol'ga. "Belorusskaja nacional'naja kul'tura 1930-ch gg.: k postanovke problemy—chudožnik i vlast'." *Pracy historyčnaha fakul'tėta BDU: navukovy zbornik, vyp. 3*. Minsk: BDU, 2008: 80-85. Print.
Budzinski, Stanislaŭ. "Vorah u dome." *Polymja* 11-12 (1929): 223-52. Print.
Casanova, Pascale. *The World Republic of Letters [La république mondiale des lettres]*. Cambridge, MA: Harvard UP, 2004. Print.
"Čytačam": "Čytačam 'Maladnjaka'." *Maladnjak* 5-6 (1929): 142. Print.
"Da čytačoŭ": "Ad rėdakcyi 'Uzvyšša' da čytačoŭ." *Uzvyšša* 2 (1927): 218. Print.
Dorleijn, Gillis, and Kees van Rees. "The Eighteenth-Century Literary Field in Western Europe: The Interdependence of Material and Symbolic Production and Consumption." *Poetics* 28 (2001): 331-453. Print.
Grüttemeier, Ralf, and Ted Laros. "Literature in Law: *Exceptio Artis* and the Emergence of Literary Fields." *Law and Humanities* 7 (2013): 204-17. Print.

Halavač, Platon. "Pjac' našych hod." *Maladnjak* 11 (1928): 3-7. Print.

Harėcki, Maksim. *'Maladnjak za pjac' hadoŭ, 1923-1928.* Minsk: Belaruskae dzjaržaŭnae vydavectva, 1928. Print.

Hockx, Michel. "The Literary Field and the Field of Power: The Case of Modern China." *Paragraph* 35.1 (2012): 49-65. Print.

Hužaloŭski, Aljaksandar. *Čyrvony alovak: Narysy pa history cėnzury ŭ BSSR. Kniha I: 1919-1941.* Minsk: Zvjazda. Print.

Kohler, Gun-Britt. "National Disposition and the Author's Trajectory: Reflections on Polish and Croatian Literature." *Authorship Revisited: Conceptions of Authorship around 1900 and 2000.* Ed. Gillis Dorleijn, Ralf Grüttemeier, and Liesbeth Korthals Altes. Leuven: Peeters, 2010. 11-38. Print.

---. "Strategien von Posture und Positionierung in 'kleinen' Literaturen: Das Pseudonym in der belarussischen Literatur des ersten Drittels des 20. Jahrhunderts." *Kleinheit als Spezifik: Beiträge zu einer feldtheoretischen Analyse der belarussischen Literatur im Kontext 'kleiner' slavischer Literaturen.* Ed. Gun-Britt Kohler, Pavel Navumenka, and Ralf Grüttemeier. Oldenburg: BIS-Verlag, 2012. 235-63. Print.

---. "Fehlpositionierung und Autopalimpsest: Michas' Zarėckis Romanfragmente *Kryvičy* (1929) und *Smerc' Andrėja Berazoŭskaha* (1931) im Kontext der Entautonomisierung des belarussischen Literaturfeldes." *Zeitschrift für Slawistik* 58.1 (2013): 3-30. Print.

Kohler, Gun-Britt, and Pavel Navumenka. "Interference of Autonomization and Deautonomization in the Belarusian Literary Field: Indication of 'Smallness,' or Something Different?" *Vestnik BGU. Seryja 4: Filal., Žurn., Ped.* 2012/3 (dekabr'), 3-11. Print.

Koler, Gun-Bryt. "'Stvarėnne stvaral'nikaŭ': Aspekty simvaličnaj pradukcyi 'narodnaha paėta' i nacyjanalnaj klasiki." *Mova—litaratura—kultura.* Minsk: Vyd. Cėntr BDU, 2012. 389-97. Print.

Koler, Gun-Britt, and P.I. Naumenko. "Aspekty i strategii institucional'noj i ėstetičeskoj avtonomizacii v 'malych'literaturach (na materiale belorusskoj literatury pervoj treti XXst.)."*Belorusskaja literatura kak model' razvitija 'malych' (slavjanskich) literatur: materialy k tematičeskomu bloku na XV Meždunarodnom s"esde slavistov.* Ed. Gun-Britt Koler and Pavel Naumenko. Minsk: Biznesofset, 2013. 7-90. Print.

Krapiva, Kandrat. "Slova—čytaču." *Uzvyšša* 1 (1929): 97-99. Print.

Liptak, Tomáš, and Jurij Murašov, eds. *Schrift und Macht: Zur Sowjetischen Literatur der 1920er und 30er Jahre*. Wien: Böhlau, 2012. Print.

McMillin, Arnold. *Writing in a Cold Climate: Belarusian Literature from the 1970s to the Present Day*. London: Maney Publ. for the Modern Humanities Research Association, 2010. Print.

Meizoz, Jérôme. "Die Posture und das literarische Feld: Rousseau, Céline, Ajar, Houellebecq." *Text und Feld: Bourdieu in der literaturwissenschaftlichen Praxis*. Ed. Markus Joch and Norbert Wolf. Tübingen: Max Niemeyer Verlag, 2005. 177-88. Print.

Michaluk, Dorota. *Białoruska Republika Ludowa 1918-1920: U podstaw białoruskiej państwowości*. Toruń: Wydawnictwo Naukowe Uniwersytetu Mikołaja Kopernika, 2010. Print.

Mušynski, Michas'. *Belaruskaja krytyka i litaraturaznaŭstva (20-30-ja hady)*. Minsk: Navuka i tèchnika, 1975. Print.

---. "Michas' Zarècki." *Historyja belaruskaj litaratury XX stahoddzja: U 4 t. T.2.* Minsk: Belaruskaja navuka, 2002. 504-49.

---. *Praŭdzivaja historyja žyccja i tvorčasci Michasja Zarèckaha*. Minsk: Belaruskaja navuka, 2005. Print.

"Našy zadanni": "Našy zadanni." *Polymja* 1 (1922): 3-6. Print.

Navumenka, Pavel. "Konsolidierungszentren literarischer Kräfte im Hinblick auf die Autonomisierung des belarussischen Literaturfeldes: Literaturvereinigungen im ersten Drittel des 20. Jh." *Kleinheit als Spezifik: Beiträge zu einer feldtheoretischen Analyse der belarussischen Literatur im Kontext 'kleiner' slavischer Literaturen*. Ed. Gun-Britt Kohler, Pavel Navumenka, and Ralf Grüttemeier. Oldenburg: BIS-Verlag, 2012. Print.

"Pačynajučy": "Pačynajučy wydavac'..." *Naša niva* 1 (1906): 1. Print.

"Pastanova Belaruskaha": "Pastanova belaruskaha litaraturna-mastackaha zhurtavan'nja 'Uzvyšša'." *Uzvyšša* 1 (1930): 9-11. Print.

"Pastanova litaraturna-mastackaha": "Pastanova litaraturna-mastackaha zhurtavan'nja 'Uzvyšša'." *Uzvyšša* 11-12 (1931): 178-80. Print.

"Proèkt statute": "Proèkt statutu Ŭsebelarusk. ab'jadnan'nja poètaŭ i pis'men'nikaŭ 'Maladnjak'." *Maladnjak* 7 (1925): 110-11. Print.

"Rezoljucija": "Rezoljucija ahulnaha schodu 'Uzvyšša'." *Uzvyšša* 9-10 (1930): 167-68. Print.

Savik, Lidzija, Michas' Skobla, and Kastus' Cvirka, eds. *Rasstraljanaja litaratura*. Minsk: Belaruski knihazbor, 2008. Print.

Sidarėvič, Anatol'. "'Ličyć pažadanym...'. (Jak paŭstaŭ arhkamitėt Sajuza pis'mennikoŭ BSSR)." *Litaraturnaja Belaruś* 6 (2012), 20-21. Print.

Skryhan, Jan. *Vybranyja tvory*. Minsk: Belaruski knihazbor, 2005. Print.

"Statut Kamuny": "Statut Belaruskaj Litaraturna-Mastackaj Kamuny." *Roskvit* 2 (1928): 79-80. Print.

"Statut Uzvyšša": "Statut Belaruskaha litaraturna-mastackaha zhurtavan'nja 'Uzvyšša'." *Uzvyšša* 1 (1927): 171-72. Print.

"Tav. rėdaktaru." *Saveckaja Belarus'* 154 (10.07.1926): 6. Print.

"Try hady": "Try hady pracy Uzvyšša." *Uzvyšša* 5 (1929): 64-66. Print.

Unučak, Andrėj. *'Naša niva' i belaruski nacyjanal'ny ruch (1906-1915hh.)*. Minsk: Belaruskaja navuka, 2008. Print.

"Usebelaruskae": "Maladnjak: Usebelaruskae abjadnan'ne poėtaŭ i pis'men'nikaŭ. Jaho napramak, umovy pracy, forma tvoraŭ, praca." *Maladnjak* 5 (1924): 93-97. Print.

Vabiščėvič, Taccjana. *Stanaŭlenne nacyjanalnaj paėtyčnaj tradycyi (1900-1910-ja hh.): faktary, mechanizmy, ėtapy*. Minsk: Belaruskaja navuka, 2009. Print.

van Rees, Kees. "Field, Capital and Habitus: A Relational Approach to 'Small' Literatures." *Kleinheit als Spezifik: Beiträge zu einer feldtheoretischen Analyse der belarussischen Literatur im Kontext 'kleiner' slavischer Literaturen*. Ed. Gun-Britt Kohler, Pavel Navumenka, and Ralf Grüttemeier. Oldenburg: BIS-Verlag, 2012. 15-26. Print.

"Zamest dėkljaracyi": "'Maladnjak'. (Zamest dėkljaracyi)." *Maladnjak* 6 (1925): 55. Print.

Žybul', Viktar. "Futurystyčnaja mara belarusaŭ: Dzejnasc' 'belaruskaj litaraturna-mastackaj kamuny' va ŭspaminach i dakumentach." *Arche* 9 (2008): 106-48. Print.

Profession and Ideology: Cultural Institutions and the Formation of Literary Circles in the Soviet Occupied Territory and the Early GDR

ARVI SEPP

STUNDE NULL AND LITERATURE

The situation in the German literary field after 1945 was by no means characterized by a unity of authors or by a *Stunde Null* or 'zero hour.' In fact there was virulent competition between different groups of authors. The conflict between literary emigrants and the authors who went into inner emigration broke out already in August 1945 with the contributions of Frank Thiess and Walter von Molo and the reaction of Thomas Mann. The return of exiled authors to the Soviet Occupied Territory contributed much to the polarization in German literature after 1945. After all, the literary field was dominated virtually without competition by authors who returned from exile and whose understanding of literature was canonized as the decisive influential force, whereas the public in the Western occupied zones largely ignored the exiles (cf. Heukenkamp 130). On the other hand, the indubitable anti-fascism of the exiled authors became the symbol of a committed literature and for decades enjoyed the status of symbolic capital for the following generation of writers. In the publishing house of the Soviet Military Administration (SMAD) and soon afterwards in the Berlin Aufbau-Verlag, their books were published and literary journals such as *Aufbau, Ost und West* or *Heute und Morgen* were open to them. In addition, aesthetic positions of the Weimar Republic were reactivated among these authors in the years immediately following the war. Younger authors distanced themselves from the older generation of established writers. In view of this apparent split the aim was to redefine the role of literature and of the authors in social space.

My contribution addresses the question how the literary field in the Soviet Occupied Zone and the early GDR was organized and structured. As the literary field after the end of National Socialism had to be newly occupied, the attempt was undertaken to achieve symbolic power over competing groups in the East and the literary field in the West. Without ignoring the weight of the ideological conditions, this article endeavors to present a plausible argument that relatively independent relationships arose between authors, publishing houses, periodicals, and writers' associations which were not always directly politically determined. The first part will give an idea of the tension between unity and separation of the East and the West in the German literary field in the first years after 1945. In the second part, the complex situation of the East German literary field in the Soviet Occupied Territory and the Early GDR between autonomy and heteronomy will be closely scrutinized. Finally, in the third and main part, I will analyze the formation of a specific literary circle in a case study of the literary journal *Sinn und Form* (cf. Parker/Philpotts).

THE GERMAN LITERARY FIELD BETWEEN UNITY AND SEPARATION

At first, the East-West confrontation was not as omnipresent and decisive as has often been assumed. Particularly in Berlin, the occupying powers endeavored to provide a framework for the revival of cultural institutions. Theater life and the abundance of art exhibitions were owed, not least, to a competition between them. Moreover, as licensors, they ensured that a diversity of opinions could arise as long as the views expressed were antifascist (cf. Heukenkamp 121). The establishment of the institutions themselves, in which literary relationships took on material shape, will be examined in what follows.

In Pierre Bourdieu's field theory, which will theoretically guide the analysis in this article, literature is primarily seen as a means to power, symbolic recognition, and social differentiation. Literature is thus demystified and analyzed as a tool with which the social actor interacts with institutions, groups and individuals within the literary field:

> The process in which works are caught up is the product of the struggle between those who espouse conservatism because of the dominant position they temporarily occupy in the field (by virtue of their specific capital), that is to say, they defend routine and routinization, the banal and banalization, in a word, they defend the established symbolic order, and those who are inclined to a heretical rupture, to the critique of established forms, to the subversion of the prevailing models and to a return to the purity of origins. In fact, only knowledge of the structure can provide the tools of a true knowledge of the processes which lead to a new state of the structure and which thereby also comprise the means of comprehending this new structure. (Bourdieu 205-6)

The discussion on the role and function of German literature in East and West Germany after the Second World War can be read in the light of Bourdieu's field theory and his assertion of the 'struggle' between the 'new' and the 'established.'[1]

Indeed, the German literary field after 1945 was intrinsically open and in this temporary void literature had to be re-defined all over. Younger authors such as Hans Werner Richter, Werner Kolbenhoff and Alfred Andersch differentiated themselves on the one hand from exiled authors such as Thomas Mann, who had already been widely acclaimed in the Weimar period, and on the other hand from authors of the *Innere Emigration*, such as Frank Thiess and Walter von Molo (cf. Gansel, "Gruppenbildung" 65-74). The quick constitution of literary groups in the aftermath of the Second World War was a strategic way to position and orient oneself in the wide open field of culture and acquire symbolic power over the definition of legitimate literature.[2]

In Berlin in the aftermath of the war there was a movement supported by authors from all four sectors who attempted to bring German authors

---

[1] For more information on the applicability of Bourdieu's field theory on the terrain of GDR literature, cf. the insightful study of Leon Hempel (13-18).

[2] On the question of the constitution of literary groups in the Soviet Occupied Zone and the early GDR, cf. Gregor Ohlerich (130-35).

from all occupied zones together. These efforts were associated with the conviction that Berlin could again become the literary centre it had once been. One of the protagonists of the Berlin group was Günther Weisenborn, at the time co-editor of the periodical *Ulenspiegel*, which was licensed by the American authorities, and a member of the executive of the *Schutzverband Deutscher Autoren* (Protective Association of German Authors). A second, more influential person was Johannes R. Becher, who became the first GDR Minister of Culture in 1954. The *Kulturbund* (Cultural Association) he founded is often associated with a line true to the party principles of the SED, the Socialist Unity Party of Germany. But this view must, to a certain extent, be qualified, as the publications of the *Kulturbund* in fact represented a wide concept of culture which had little in common with socialist realism. Above all, the *Kulturbund* remained open to West European culture (cf. Ohlerich 124).[3] Accordingly, on the occasion of the first all-German congress of German authors in 1947, Becher affirmed in his contribution "Wie kämpft der Schriftsteller für den Frieden?—Was heißt 'Für den Frieden sein'?" that

> there is [...] no West German and East German literature, no South German and North German, but only one literature, a German one, which does not allow itself to be isolated within the borders of the zones, but for whom soon, we hope, the gates to the world, across the borders of Germany, will be opened again. (Becher, *Vom Anderswerden* 240-41)

But this unity soon turned out to be an unfulfillable hope. The authors of the *Kulturbund* did not stand alone in their endeavors to promote the dialogue between German authors. From 1946 onwards preparatory committees in Berlin and Munich began to work for the establishment of an all-German PEN-organization (International Association of Poets, Essayists and Novelists). Amongst others, Günther Weisenborn, Ricarda Huch and Elisabeth Langgässer were active in this context. The most important project, however, was initiated by the *Schutzbund Deutscher Autoren*. In 1946, Weisenborn proposed to Becher the organization of a German writers' congress,

---

3 For more information on the concept and policy of the *Kulturbund* between 1945 and 1949, cf. also Gerd Dietrich (24-35).

uniting both East and West.[4] While the political reproaches and accusations at the congress were made loudly, little was heard of the literary rivalries.

The commitment to the European avant-garde and the self-confident judgment on the given situation implied a vote against the realism of the authors in exile and could have been the starting point for a literary debate, which did not, however, take place. The group of authors connected with *Der Ruf* (including Walter Kolbenhoff), from which the *Gruppe 47* later arose, were hardly concerned with literary programmes at the conference in West-Berlin. They mistrustfully registered the influence of the Soviet occupying power on cultural life in Berlin and they encountered those German authors who in their opinion had adopted Soviet aesthetic-political models with particular animosity.

Their intervention against any kind of representation of German literature by East German authors marked the opening of the Cold War in literature. In the controversy at the congress who could be counted as a part of German literature, the notions of the incompatibility of East and West, of aesthetics shaped by ideology and of plurality of opinions came to light earlier than elsewhere. Not only the honesty of the commitment of the authors of the *Kulturbund* to non-partisanship and democracy was denied; an author who attempted to mediate, such as Günther Weisenborn from the SDA, was also suspected and attacked at the conference (cf. Heukenkamp 127). In view of such centrifugal forces, the division of German literature into two camps seemed inevitable. The breakdown of the contacts between East and West indeed led to the creation of two separate literary fields.

But the presence of Brecht in the GDR, for example, demonstrates that the development of East German literature cannot be considered as a mere appendix to the cultural politics of the SED. From 1949 onwards, the literary landscape was enriched by a theatre of world reputation, the *Berliner Ensemble*, which continued to influence literary history after Brecht's death. The intensive relationship with classical German literature was also more than the result of a policy imposed by SED cultural politics. In view of the great veneration for Goethe shown in the Soviet Occupied Zone, an outsider like Thomas Mann wished to participate in the honour paid to Goethe in Weimar no less than in Frankfurt am Main. He accepted an appear-

---

4   For more detailed information on the preparation and content of the first German Writers' Congress in 1947 (cf. Gansel, *Parlament* 41-92, esp. 44-46).

ance together with Johannes R. Becher, because he did not see him as a political representative but as a worthy author. Another author from outside, Lion Feuchtwanger, on the other hand could not understand why Arnold Zweig was unable to admit the presence of symptoms of anti-Semitism in the GDR. These two examples reveal that literary life in the Soviet Occupied Zone and the early GDR were clearly registered outside of Germany (e.g., by both Mann and Feuchtwanger in the U.S.), but scarcely at all in the Federal Republic in the 1950s (cf. Heukenkamp 128).

The variety of regional activities revealing a certain degree of pluralism gradually came to an end after 1949. The establishment of a national prize at the same time as the foundation of the GDR, which was critically received by some writers, was the symbolic sign of the end of this phase and of the onset of the centralization in the literary field. There are marked differences in the cultural-political interventions of the occupying power in the step-by-step process of unification of the writers' organizations, which began with the dissolution of the pan-German oriented SDA and the generalization of the principle behind the distribution of literary commissions. These were now no longer issued to the so-called 'party authors' but quite simply to all writers.

The politicization of authors was certainly more striking in the Soviet Occupied Zone because it was demanded in official expressions of opinion. But the statements made at cultural conferences and plenary assemblies did not have a direct impact on the distribution of reputation, furtherance and publicity for authors. Ultimately there were other powers which could further unpopular writers, and the secret fame of those who despised official recognition. The decisive autonomous instances of literary life were never entirely eliminated. In this context, the situation of the literary journal *Sinn und Form* in the Soviet Occupied Territory and the GDR is quite striking in that it seemed to operate in a relatively autonomous manner in spite of the ideological foundations of the period. I will argue that the tensions of the early Cold War cultural field and the increasing pressures imposed on the journal by SED cultural policies in the early 1950s was also the making of the journal. If, as Bourdieu in *The Rules of Art* suggests, new artistic endeavors establish themselves through an initial period "full of asceticism and renunciation" (255)—that is a renunciation of material profits in favor of the symbolic capital of cultural prestige—the capacity of *Sinn und Form* in the first half of the fifties to apparently renounce the heteronomous political interests of the SED show that by then the journal had already acquired substantial reserves of symbolic capital which were invested in its distinctive all-German mission to promote the values of a progressive cultural restoration.

BETWEEN AUTONOMY AND HETERONOMY: GERMAN COMMUNISM AND THE LITERARY FIELD

In *The Rules of Art*, Bourdieu invites literary sociology to situate cultural objects within agents of the literary field, and these agents are not only the authors themselves, but also agents of transmission and reception, such as critics, publishing houses, professional organisations, and editors. In Bourdieu's terms, in his analysis of the *Nouvelle Revue Française*, edited by André Gide, the literary journal becomes a central institution in the field, a site "in which intellectuals adopt positions in that field and through which they exercise agency in their transaction of capital" (Parker/Philpotts 5). In this context, as Parker and Philpotts continue, the concept of symbolic capital is most important:

While cultural capital [...] is essential in equipping agents to participate in the intellectual field, it is the 'symbolic capital' of 'accumulated prestige, celebrity, consecration or honour' which is the most sought-after currency of the intellectual and literary world. (5)

In this context, the 'precarious alliances' between these agents can be exemplified through an analysis of the literary journal *Sinn und Form*.

When the journal was founded in late 1948 and in the first years afterwards (under the editorship of Johannes R. Becher and Paul Wiegler and thereafter of Peter Huchel), a number of factors ensured the relative 'autonomy' of literary values in the East German literary field in which *Sinn und Form* was active. This had partly to do with the incomplete implementation of totalitarian rule in the Soviet Occupied Zone and the early GDR. Cultural continuities across both the geographical and temporal boundaries of any political regime act as one of the most important restrictions on the exercise of dictatorial power, and the autonomous values of the literary field constitute one significant set of such cultural continuities. In the early GDR, the inability to exercise total control over the cultural sphere was exacerbated not only by the necessarily uncertain nature of cultural policy and its associated institutions during the crystallisation phase of the regime, but also by a set of political and geo-political factors bound up with the fragile power of the SED and its fundamental lack of legitimacy in this early period. Most importantly, German political division could not so easily partition German cultural space, still less so when Stalin's policy on the German Question was oriented not towards revolutionary strategy, but towards securing Soviet interests through negotiation with the Western allies and the unification of Germany (cf. 18). Even after Stalin's death and until 1955, priority in Soviet policy was given to unification rather than the separate development of a socialist state.

As GDR Minister of Culture, Johannes R. Becher emphasizes the importance of the "indivisible humanist culture" of both Germanys in the "Programmerklärung des Ministeriums für Kultur zur Verteidigung der Einheit der deutschen Kultur," published in the second issue of *Sinn und Form* in 1954 (315). In the manifesto, the "free circulation of humanist works of literature and art in the whole of Germany" (316) and the "cooperation between German academies, universities [...], artists' and writers' organizations [...] that foster Germany's collective humanist culture" (316-17) are declared of utmost importance to the defence of German literary and artistic heritage. However, the apparent tension between a focus on a common German culture and the ideology of a separate socialist state led to a particularly contradictory cultural policy by the SED before 1955 (cf. Parker/Philpotts 19). Of course, many committed authors found themselves in a dilemma because the East German government who should have been defending a unified German culture with a sincere approach to the legacy of Nazism, seemed to be developing into the other direction, the direction of anti-Western Cold War ideology, inimical to the relative aesthetic autonomy of the *Kulturbund* and with it of the journal *Sinn und Form* (cf. 19-24).

In the years to come, primarily after 1955, the insistence on the humanist tradition of Weimar Classicism by the SED cultural officials, their exclusion of Western modernism (with authors like Joyce, Proust, Beckett, Gide, Kafka, or Camus),[5] and the advocacy for a more proletarian focus of

---

5 On the anti-formalism campaign and the reception of Western modernist authors in the GDR, cf. Wolfgang Emmerich (11).

Socialist Realism posed serious problems to *Sinn und Form*, but fundamentally there was no contradiction between an elite literary journal and official German Marxist aesthetics, as we will also see in the next section on autonomy and the literary field in the context of *Sinn und Form*.

SINN UND FORM:
AUTONOMY AND THE LITERARY FIELD

Sinn und Form bears values which can also be discerned in the wave of new journals that saw the light immediately after 1945. In all of them a strong sense of urgency and agency in this period of transition can be seen. In this period, the sense of a moral and material rebirth also cleared the way for a new definition of literature and the re-establishment of positions in the literary field (cf. Parker/Philpotts 14).

A vehement struggle between continuity and innovation in the literary field becomes apparent directly after the Second World War. This tension can on the one hand be seen in relation to notions of autonomy and heteronomy of literature. The positions taken in this period defend political and moral engagement in the wake of Nazi dictatorship and literary *Gleichschaltung* or, on the contrary, suspicion of ideology, as they hold on to the need of the apolitical literariness of literature.[6] On the other hand the tension is to be seen in relation to established and heretical positions in the field: the former occupied by agents rich in symbolic capital (such as exile authors), the latter by a new generation wanting to usurp those established positions (Parker/Philpotts 5). Before the foundation of the journal in late 1948 we can see in the correspondence between the future editors Huchel and Becher with other intellectuals that the question of autonomy was explicitly debated.

In a letter to Johannes R. Becher, Heinz-Wilfried Sabais comments upon a conversation with Peter Huchel in mid-1948. Sabais approvingly emphasizes how the autonomy of *Sinn und Form* bears strong similarities with the formalist ideas of Stefan George's aestheticist literature journal *Blätter für die Kunst*:

---

[6] Arnold Zweig emphasizes that in the journal's programme "the Moral and the Just are necessarily part of the conditions of the Beautiful" (5).

I believe that this journal will fulfil a great and demanding mission, and in saying that I am reminded of Stefan George's *Blätter für die Kunst*, not in their function, and of course without their soullessness and reactionary line. If I understand it correctly that function was to [...] unite tradition and progress. (Sabais qtd. in Parker/ Philpotts 16; translation by Parker and Philpotts)

It is significant, too, that originally Johannes R. Becher intended to call the journal not *Sinn und Form*, but rather *Maß und Wert*, after the exile journal which was published by Thomas Mann and managed by Ferdinand Lion in Zürich between 1937 and 1940 to counter the cultural barbarity of National Socialism by emphasizing—with reference to Goethe—the enduring classicistic measure and value of the autonomous bourgeois institution of literature.[7] The founding of *Sinn und Form* meant a clear intervention in the literary field in the Soviet Occupied Territory, in that it was internationally focused on Western literary traditions and distanced itself from both aestheticism and socialism (cf. 15).[8] A look at the publicity flyer of 1948 shows the journal's precarious balancing act between autonomous and heteronomous values:

In *Sinn und Form* we are presenting a literary journal, the publication of which can only be justified if—far removed from aestheticism—it serves the spirit of language and poetry. For only by meeting this condition can it become one of the essential and representative literary publications that appear as periodicals in Germany. First and foremost, the selection of contributions will proceed according to the principles that ought always to have applied to such a review: to grant a hearing to all those voices that, through artistic means, shape the word in the cause of human and social progress, in the interests of humanism and of intellectual profundity or that, through critical means and with meticulous knowledge, evaluate literary publications from the intellectual realm, both in Germany and abroad. (13)

---

7   For more information on the programme of *Maß und Wert* as a token of the conviction that the modern German literary tradition could oppose National Socialist barbarism (cf. Parker/Davies/Philpotts 94-106, esp. 97).

8   It is interesting in this respect to note that from the foundation of *Sinn und Form* until Stalin's death in 1953, only one explicit reference to Stalin can be found, suggesting a relatively high degree of aesthetic and political autonomy of the journal in the literary field of the early GDR (cf. Stalin 7).

Thanks to the official Soviet policy promoting pan-German cultural unity, the literary field in the early GDR possessed a certain degree of artistic autonomy. This made it possible for the journal to accumulate literary and ideological prestige through its all-German agenda (cf. 60). The journal was indeed being founded with a focus on famous writers in the field of autonomous literary production.

In order to elucidate the accumulated capital of the journal after merely five years of existence, when many other journals founded in the years 1945-49 had already ceased to exist, the structure of the journal's contributors in the well-known 1954 double issue will be briefly analyzed. The publication of leading East German intellectuals who were highly acclaimed in the West (like Bertolt Brecht, Ernst Bloch and Hans Mayer) as well as the publication of influential western writers (like Thomas Mann and Alfred Döblin) and other established authors (e.g., Hans Henny Jahnn), *Sinn und Form* accumulated a large amount of symbolic capital in a relative short period of time, as Parker and Philpotts rightly point out (cf. 44). The canonical writers who gave their names to the journal contributed to its consecration and offered it an aura of intellectual liberalism, literary modernism, anti-fascist humanism, and a pan-German cultural conviction. The authors in *Sinn und Form* thus helped establishing the collective aesthetic and cultural-political programme of the journal.[9]

In this sense, the establishment of symbolic capital of *Sinn und Form* in the GDR literary field can be compared to the significant portion of capital donated to the literary journal *Les Temps Modernes*, founded by Jean Paul Sartre in 1945, by esteemed authors such as Michel Leiris, Raymond Queneau, Simone de Beauvoir. In this respect, Bourdieu writes:

The 'intellectual review,' as the composition of the editorial board shows, gathers under Sartre's banner the living representatives of all the intellectual traditions integrated in the oeuvre and person of the founder, and allows the Sartrean project of

---

9 Already in the first issue of *Sinn und Form* in 1949, established international authors like Romain Rolland, Oskar Loerke, Hans Reisiger, Hermann Kasack, Charles-Ferdinand Ramuz, Wladimir Majakowski and Vítězslav Nezval were published to emphasize the journal's programmatic interests of literary internationalism, unity in German culture, anti-fascism, and modernism.

thinking through all aspects of existence to be established in a collective programme […]. (211)

As is the case for *Les Temps Modernes*, the collective programme of *Sinn und Form* clearly shows its aesthetic and intellectual profile. Most of the contributors were Western-oriented and only Johannes R. Becher and Ludwig Renn were SED loyalists. Moreover, orthodox communist writers such as Willi Bredel and Konrad Wolf were only marginally represented in *Sinn und Form* under Huchel's editorship. The journal's symbolic capital was thus clearly defined by the international intellectual and literary field, not by the official GDR cultural policy makers (cf. Parker/Philpotts 44). On the other hand, there were also a number of lesser known, non-GDR authors in the 1954 double issue. Here, the exchange of capital which normally takes place between contributor and journal is reversed in that the younger authors' symbolic capital significantly increased thanks to the presence of influential writers. Yet, also these respected contributors (e.g., Döblin and Brecht) profited from being published in *Sinn und Form* because of the following increase of their symbolic capital in the West. Equally, by publishing lesser known authors, the journal highlights its commitment to the autonomy of the literary field, where a lack of recognition may lead to the accumulation of prestige (cf. 44).

An analysis of *Sinn und Form* shows the various precarious relations between intellectuals and power. Writers and artists, as a dominant fraction within the class of intellectuals, in turn dominated by politics, possess cultural capital that allows them to obtain symbolic and material privileges in the GDR. The internal legitimacy of the literary field stands in a chiastic relation to the field of power, as Joseph Jurt has it.[10] The literary field indeed defines itself through the autonomy vis-à-vis political authority (cf. Jurt 90). As Bourdieu suggests in *The Rules of Art* in his discussion of André Gide and the group of authors around him:

The gathering together of the authors and, secondarily, of the texts which make up a literary review has as its genuine principle […] social strategies close to those governing the constitution of a salon or a movement—even though they take into account […] the strictly literary capital of the assembled authors. (273)

---

10 On the relation between the literary field and the field of power, cf. Jurt (88-93).

These "social strategies" can be seen as the sum of resources and profits that can be derived from group membership and mutual acquaintance (cf. Parker/Philpotts 219). Indeed, the journal's primary act of exchange is the offering and acceptance of texts for publication. This act functions as the criterion for entering into the group, limiting group membership and thus determining the volume of social capital of the journal through its network of contributors.

In the early years after the journal's founding, authors such as Theodor W. Adorno and Max Horkheimer, Nelly Sachs, Frederico Garcia Lorca and Pablo Neruda published in *Sinn und Form* (cf. 221). Significantly, the journal's relationship with Neruda was also institutionalised when he was elected corresponding member of the Literature Section of the *Akademie der Künste* in 1955. The Academy was able to fulfil its mission as an elite cultural institution, and the *Sinn und Form* network was often at the origin of it. Later on, largely free from domestic political considerations, also Thomas Mann, Alfred Döblin, Louis Aragon, Peter Weiss and other contributors of *Sinn und Form* were elected into the Academy. On the other hand, as Parker and Philpotts note with regard to the number of subscribers, we can see that in 1953 the journal had only 2,400 subscribers and a total print-run of just 5,000 in the mid-1950s. The selective nature of the readership is a key element of their acquisition of symbolic capital. Discussing the articles of *Sinn und Form* with other readers meant a kind of political and intellectual sign of alternative in-group membership (cf. 60).

Conclusion

In her essay "The Literary Field between the State and the Market," Gisèle Sapiro emphasizes that the professional organization is an important instrument of ideological control: "[T]he major instruments of control are the centralization of the means of production, unification of the profession, surveillance of professional institutions, and ideological supervision" (445). From the latter half of the 1950s onwards, the GDR Writers' Union controls the channels of publication and the major means of consecration of authors, such as prizes, literary journals, and presence in academies and juries. Indeed, in 1955, in Leipzig the Institute of Literature Johannes R. Becher (*Literaturinstitut*, later on called *Literaturinstitut Johannes R. Becher*) was founded. The creation of this school of writers illustrates the will to develop a corporative structure of the writing profession and the policy of ideological control and training. The year 1955 meant an important turning point in the development of the East-German literary field, which definitively abandoned the idea of an all-German literary culture. Yet, as has been shown with the case of *Sinn und Form*, there was still, in some cases, the possibility of a precarious literary *Ersatzöffentlichkeit*, a compensatory public sphere which was allowed thanks to the accumulated symbolic capital of the journal in the early years of its existence.

WORKS CITED

Becher, Johannes R. *Vom Anderswerden: Reden, Aufsätze, Briefe.* Berlin: Aufbau, 1952. Print.

---. "Programmerklärung des Ministeriums für Kultur zur Verteidigung der Einheit der deutschen Kultur." *Sinn und Form* 6.2 (1954): 279-321. Print.

Bourdieu, Pierre. *The Rules of Art: Genesis and Structure of the Literary Field.* Trans. Susan Emanuel. Stanford, CA: Stanford UP, 1996. Print.

Dietrich, Gerd. *Politik und Kultur in der Sowjetischen Besatzungszone Deutschlands (SBZ) 1945-1949.* Bern: Lang, 1993. Print.

Emmerich, Wolfgang. "Holzwege, gelegentlich Lichtungen: Ostdeutsche Literatur 1945-55." *Doppelleben: Literarische Szenen aus Nachkriegsdeutschland.* Ed. Bernd Bisch and Thomas Combrink. Göttingen: Wallstein, 2009. 107-16. Print.

Gansel, Carsten. *Parlament des Geistes: Literatur zwischen Hoffnung und Repression 1945-1961.* Berlin: Basisdruck, 1996. Print.

---. "Für eine 'wirksame ideologische, fachliche, und berufliche Unterstützung'—Literarische Gruppenbildung und Schriftstellerorganisationen nach 1945 in der Sowjetischen Besatzungszone und der DDR." *Doppelleben: Literarische Szenen aus Nachkriegsdeutschland.* Ed. Bernd Bisch and Thomas Combrink. Göttingen: Wallstein, 2009. 65-74. Print.

Hempel, Leon. "Die agonale Dynamik des lyrischen Terrains: Herausbildung und Grenzen des literarischen Feldes der DDR." *Literarisches Feld DDR: Bedingungen und Formen literarischer Produktion in der DDR.* Ed. Ute Wölfel. Würzburg: Königshausen & Neumann, 2005. 13-29. Print.

Heukenkamp, Ursula. "Ein Anfang ohne rechte Hoffnung: Versuch einer analytischen Beschreibung der Nachkriegsliteratur in der sowjetischen Besatzungszone (SBZ)." *Internationales Archiv für Sozialgeschichte der deutschen Literatur.* 18.2 (1993): 121-44. Print.

Jurt, Joseph. *Das literarische Feld: Das Konzept Pierre Bourdieus in Theorie und Praxis.* Darmstadt: Wissenschaftliche Buchgesellschaft, 1995. Print.

Ohlerich, Gregor. *Sozialistische Denkwelten: Modell eines literarischen Feldes der SBZ/DDR 1945 bis 1953.* Heidelberg: Winter, 2005. Print.

Parker, Stephen, Peter Davies, and Matthew Philpotts. *The Modern Restoration: Re-thinking German Literary History 1930-1960.* Berlin: de Gruyter, 2004. Print.

Parker, Stephen, and Matthew Philpotts. *Sinn und Form: The Anatomy of a Literary Journal.* Berlin: de Gruyter, 2009. Print.

Sapiro, Gisèle. "The Literary Field between the State and the Market." *Poetics* 31 (2003): 441-64. Print.

Stalin, Joseph W. "Über den Frieden." *Sinn und Form* 3.4 (1951): 7. Print.

Zweig, Arnold. "Zur Übernahme der Zeitschrift durch die Deutsche Akademie der Künste." *Sinn und Form* 2.5 (1950): 5. Print.

Precarious Alliances between Literature and Law: A Tentative Account of the Case of Australia

RALF GRÜTTEMEIER

Australia's history of censorship is an interesting case, especially from a comparative point of view. It is one of the few democratic countries, with an independent jurisdiction, in which a writer actually had to serve a sentence of 10 days in prison, due to obscene libel found in his novel. This happened on instigation of the Victorian Supreme Court in June 1948 to Robert Close for publishing *Love me Sailor* (1945). According to Nicole Moore (2012), author of a thorough account of Australian censorship based on her discovery in 2005 of *The Censor's Library* in the National Archives, this harshness is exemplary: Australia's censorship was "trumped in its severity only by Catholic Ireland and Apartheid South Africa" in the Western world (cf. Moore 3). One of the main questions of her study therefore is to explain why, even though this question finally turned out "hardest to answer" (cf. 346-47). Moore mentions several reasons such as "extensive campaigning by religious organizations" and other pressure groups throughout the 20th century, "a conservative Australian constituency," "Australia's physical isolation," concluding:

Australia's import culture, patrollable borders, expansive Customs bureaucracy, weak domestic publishing industry and powerful legal regimes, strengthened by overlaps between state and federal powers, make the case that Australia was a severe censor simply because it could be. (347)

While all these observations seem plausible as such, taken together they leave a somewhat arbitrary and circular impression: Australia was severe because it could be severe. Would that not be true for every 'strong' state? Furthermore, how can one account, on the basis of the reasons given, for the fact that not only severe censorship, but prohibitive censorship altogether came to an end in 1973, eventually being replaced by an age-classification system in the 1980s (cf. 288, 307ff.)? Why "could" Australia be no longer a severe censor from 1973 onwards though at least some of the factors given above definitely did not change? Against this background, the following article will argue that a more systematic explanation for the relative severity *and* the abolishment of Australian censorship can be given when they are related to the rather late emergence of an *Australian* literary field. The article will focus especially on the role of the legal elites, whose relationship with the literary field will be characterized as a precarious alliance. Australia's "powerful legal regimes" did more than contribute to prosecuting literature and even handcuffing writers. One can argue that the dynamics triggered off by this legal system trying to deal reliably with literature in a young and democratic country as Australia, finally resulted in a relatively high degree of institutional autonomy for literature within the field of law—a kind of legal exemption or *exceptio artis*. In that sense, the legal elites seem to be enemies as well as allies of actors within the literary field. The autonomy with regard to legal prosecution, however, is not stable in the sense that once it is reached, literature will be free from any legal interference forever: Legal prosecution of literature cannot be excluded completely, in Australia nor anywhere else in the world, and therefore this alliance remains a highly *precarious* one.

The paper will start off with some remarks on its theoretical framework inspired by Bourdieu, which will then be illustrated with the case of the Netherlands. After having sketched the most important literary trials in Australia, a hypothesis on the emergence of the Australian literary field will be outlined, before some general conclusions are drawn.

THE EMERGENCE OF LITERARY FIELDS ACCORDING TO BOURDIEU

Les règles de l'art (1992; English translation 1996) is generally seen as the sum of Pierre Bourdieu's work on the literary field, especially concerning its historical genesis (cf. Dorleijn/van Rees 21ff.). A crucial notion for Bourdieu in this respect is the concept of autonomy. It is institutional autonomy that allows the literary and artistic fields to function primarily according to their own rules, and not to those of economy ("loser wins," cf. Bourdieu 113-40). Bourdieu is quite explicit on the historical moment of birth of a relatively autonomous literary field in France. This phenomenon must be situated in the second half of the 19th century, more specifically at the end of it, around the Dreyfus-affaire, in which Zola intervened with his famous *J'accuse* in 1898 (cf. Bourdieu 61, 114). The localization within a specific decennium is surprising if one considers other suggestions for the birth of a literary field in France as Alain Viala's (1985)—who pleads for the 17th century because of the rise of independent authorship around the *Académie*—or Siegfried Schmidt's (1989)—who from a Luhmannian system-theoretical point of view sees the 18th century as the cradle of the 'literary social system' in Germany, England and France.

Although Bourdieu states that the routes of autonomy are "complex, if not impenetrable" (52), he seems to possess rather reliable criteria for his judgment. However, when looking more closely at these criteria, there is some reason for doubt. In a direct answer to Viala, Bourdieu criticizes Viala for taking only one criterion (authorship) as sufficient for the birth of the literary field. According to Bourdieu, a combination of a number of aspects is necessary: "And it is only at the end of the nineteenth century that the system of characteristics constitutive of an autonomous field is found assembled together" (367). This view is in tune with Bourdieu's argument elsewhere that the emergence of the literary and artistic field "reached its culmination only at the end of the nineteenth century" (387). But one is left to guess what this "system of characteristics constitutive of an autonomous field" exactly consists of, how one has to decide whether a "culmination" is reached or not, and how to account for "de-autonomising" tendencies (cf. Kohler/Navumenko). The book lacks an explicit and systematic discussion of these aspects. There seems to be a historical problem in Bourdieu's theory on how to assess the moment when fields come into being and which actors do participate with what specific actions to contribute to this crucial period of establishing a literary field.

A possible starting point for tackling this problem might be the observation that Bourdieu's 'history-problem' could be connected to the fact that in most of *The Rules of Art*, his overall analytical perspective on autonomy lies *within* the literary institutions themselves and their interaction—not on the way the 'outside' deals with literature. However, the view from 'within' seems to be a reductive perspective since Bourdieu explicitly frames the literary (or more generally: the cultural) field within the field of power. For him, the field of power—politics, law and economy—not only dominates the cultural field, but at the same time they are connected by a structural homology of positions and dispositions. In this hierarchical constellation, one would expect a significant contribution of the field of power to the emergence of the literary field, too. Against this background, the present contribution will explore whether one might achieve a clearer diagnosis on the historical rise of literary fields by contrasting the view from the inside with one from the 'outside.' This would involve paying attention also to institutions and agents from outside the literary field in order to assess their participation in the formative process of a literary field. From this perspective, indications that the literary field is recognized as relatively autonomous by the field of power or the 'societal' field as a whole, may be seen as a constitutive step in its coming into being. A possible tool to assess this recognition can be found in juridical procedures that deal with literature.

Literary trials seem to be part of most national literary histories. A list of leading trials can easily be drawn (cf. Ladenson), reaching from the famous Flaubert and Baudelaire trials in France (1857), via the *Lady Chatterley's Lover* trial in England (1960) to the *Esra* trial in Germany (2003-2007) which went all the way up to the Highest German Court, the *Bundesverfassungsgericht*. An interesting phenomenon from the perspective of cross-participation—i.e., agents of one field participating in professional activities in another field, and vice versa—is that, at least in some countries, professional juridical actors from a specific point in history onwards seem to award to literature a certain exceptional status in these trials, often conceptualized as the *exceptio artis* (cf. Knies). The concept basically relates to the idea that certain utterances seen as breaking the law could be judged differently when those utterances are considered to be part of a work of art or literature. Once art and literature are accorded such a special status within jurisdiction, they are treated differently from utterances such as newspaper articles or political pamphlets when it comes to juridical procedures that have to deal with the freedom of speech and its limitations by the law, for example in case of libel, obscenity, blasphemy and so on. This special status might be seen as an indication for the fact that a relatively autonomous literary field has come into being, whose existence is consecrated by the juridical field, as part of the field of power. In other words, an alliance between very different and heterogeneous actors—in this case, at least those of the literary and the juridical field—seems to be crucial for the constitution of a literary field.

Such a relatedness between the legal and the literary elites would offer another theoretical challenge for field theory. For Bourdieu (cf. 127), "permanent struggles" are the motor of the literary field and its fundamental law is the war of everyone against everyone fighting for positions, going along with the exclusion of outsiders (cf. 204). The concept of alliances however—taken here as strategic joint activities of different actors with different agendas—is touched upon by Bourdieu only in passing (204). Against the background outlined above, it seems worthwhile to consider whether alliances, be it infra-field or inter-field, might have played a larger role in the constitution of the literary field than field-theory has accounted for.

THE CASE OF THE NETHERLANDS

By way of illustrating these theoretical reflections, the case of the Netherlands is helpful because existing research on both the rise of the Dutch literary field (cf. Dorleijn/van Rees) and on Dutch literary trials (cf. Beekman/ Grüttemeier; Grüttemeier/Laros) has produced data which allow one to assess a connection between both phenomena. Sociologically speaking and in comparison to surrounding countries, the Netherlands show a much slower pace of pre-field-development until the beginning of the 20th century and in some respects even until after the Second World War. The growth of the number of pupils in Higher School Education—the group with the highest potential as book consumers—grows from less than 8,000 in 1880 to about 30,000 by 1920 (compared to about 255,000 in 1998) (cf. Dorleijn/van Rees 36-37). A professionalization of journalistic literary criticism for example can only be detected from the 1910s onwards, as Nel van Dijk shows (in Dorleijn/van Rees 123-42). Nevertheless, in research on the different Dutch literary institutions it is generally held that around 1900 in the Netherlands a literary field has come into being (cf. 27).

Around the same time, the legal system started to interact with the changing societal status and functioning of literature in a new way. In the

Netherlands, the first explicit reference to a special position and protection of works of art in law can be seen around 1900 in a memorandum on a stricter law on pornography, though in the end, it did not make its way into the Act (cf. Schalken 36). But the memorandum definitely was not an isolated event in Dutch jurisprudence. The highest Dutch court, the *Hoge Raad*, referred to a special status concerning art in the prosecution of the presentation of obscene images on postcards for the first time in 1908. And in 1920 Dutch jurisdiction concerning literature received some guiding principles from the *Hoge Raad* in a trial against a bookseller who had the Dutch translation *De Hel* (1919) of Henri Barbusse's *L'enfer* (1908) in stock. The way to give literature a certain degree of protection and autonomy was the requirement that works of art had to be judged as a whole and not on isolated passages (cf. Grüttemeier/Laros 206ff.).

This verdict from April 12, 1920 brought to an end not only a series of different trials, but also a broad societal protest against the prosecution of a book of this internationally renowned socialist writer and figure in the European intellectual life, famous for his anti-war novel *Le feu* from 1916 (translated into English as *Under fire* in 1917) and his pacifist activities with other leading intellectuals such as Romain Rolland, Anatole France and Heinrich Mann. Interestingly enough, these protests not only arose in literary circles by the leading journal for booksellers, *Nieuwsblad voor den boekhandel*, by the author himself (in the socialist newspaper *Het Volk* on June 2, 1919) or the libertarian society *De Dageraad* in The Hague on May 27, 1919. The affair soon had made its way into the political field, too.

Within four weeks of the confiscation, the juridical action became the subject of a substantial debate in the Dutch parliament, the *Tweede Kamer*. This debate, which was held on June 12, 1919, was initiated by a formal interpellation, brought forward by the leader of the Communist Party of the Netherlands (CPH) David Wijnkoop, in which several questions were being posed to Minister of Justice, Heemskerk, from the Calvinist party ARP. In the debate, Wijnkoop brought in a resolution expressing the *Tweede Kamer*'s disapproval of the confiscation of *De hel*. The resolution was defeated by 36 against 27 votes, with the majority consisting of the Catholic party (i.e., RKSP), the Calvinist parties (i.e., ARP and CHU), and the liberal parties in parliament. But it was striking that nearly all participants of the debate agreed on one point, which was that "one should not subjugate art," as the Minister himself phrased it. Yet, to decide whether or not a crime had been committed was the task of the court, he said—and therefore the *Tweede Kamer* should refrain from commenting on an ongoing juridical procedure. The liberals agreed with the Minister on this point, and therefore the resolution failed to obtain a majority (cf. Grüttemeier/Laros 207-10).

However, what this parliamentary debate shows from a broader perspective, are several alliances that are surprising. To start with, the conviction of an institutional autonomy of the literary field is shared in the Netherlands around 1920 by all literary institutions and actors on the one hand and the largest part of the political elites on the other. Literature, including modern literature, is seen as something valuable for the nation-state, and should not be bothered by state- or juridical interferences, in order to be able to develop its specific potentials for the good of the state. Except for the large catholic party RKSP and some smaller confessional groups, this conviction turned out to be common sense around 1920. The other side of this conviction was the belief in the authority of literary expertise. This expertise was regarded as crucial for judging adequately about literary matters, including the translation of Barbusse's novel. Again, a central stake in the battle for positions in the literary field—literary expertise—is not only accepted by the political elites in the parliamentary debate, it is at the same time reinforced and even consecrated by Parliament, one might say. To act professionally as a Member of Parliament with regards to literature seems to require accepting the view of literary experts on literature as the adequate view. What seems to be an act of suppression of literature by the state at first, on a closer look turns out to be a mutual reinforcement of professionalism of the literary and the political elite, revealing a homology of positions in the field of power and the literary field. This alliance between literary and political elites around the birth of the literary field in the Netherlands in 1920 regarding institutional literary autonomy and literary expertise seems crucial for the consecration of that field.

A final interesting dimension of the debate from the perspective of precarious alliances regards the role of the socialists. Socialists and Communists had taken a leading role in the protests, ranging from literary critics to their members in Parliament. An evident explanation for this is of course to be sought in the socialist sympathies and activities of Barbusse at that time—from the perspective of the socialists, Barbusse was one of their troops. However, what is striking: at the core of the socialist line there was not a political argument but the relative institutional autonomy of literature and of literary expertise. By this, the socialist critics and politicians find themselves in this affair fighting side by side with *l'art pour l'art* critics who plead for the poetic and institutional autonomy of literature. While it is generally acknowledged that the focus on more autonomous aesthetics and the institutional autonomy of literature by authors as Flaubert and Baudelaire led to a breach with bourgeois morals, which in turn could lead to legal procedures (cf. Bourdieu 75-76), the same road obviously can be taken in the other direction, too. Breaking with bourgeois morals, as in the case of Barbusse, can be defended in public debates around 1920 in the Netherlands basically with stressing the institutional autonomy of literature, and without stressing the ethical or political side. This line of argument is unlikely to be only a conscious tactical manoeuvre on the part of the socialists—the consensus which shows in their main arguments indicates the existence of broad systemic alliances at the bottom of the rise of the Dutch literary field between politicians and literary experts as well as between socialists and other political groups concerning the relative institutional autonomy of arts and literature.

In this alliance, finally, also the legal elites participated, if one is to judge from the published juridical debate that started shortly after the confiscation, especially in the renowned juridical weekly *Weekblad van het recht*. The juridical experts maintained right from the start that it takes literary expertise to judge literature, and that jurisdiction on obscenity should stay away from the prosecution of literature as far as possible. In fact, already in their coverage of the Parliamentary Debate, the weekly made a highly accurate prediction of the trials to come: at the court of The Hague on October 6, 1919; the Appeal Court on January 7, 1920; and that of the *Hoge Raad* on April 12, 1920. This prediction of the editors turned out to represent precisely what was described as *exceptio artis* above: the juridical acknowledgment of a relative institutional autonomy of literature (cf. Grüttemeier/Laros 211-12). This greater autonomy is not absolute, but autonomy to a greater degree. In front of the court it is definitely not enough to claim that a certain text is literature and any prosecution will stop. There seems to be no doubt that literature is subjected to law—but it can count on benevolence, because it is given a certain degree of institutional autonomy.

Concerning the case of the Netherlands, it seems that from the perspective taken here, 1920 is a constitutive moment of the emergence of the Dutch literary field and the 1920 judgement of the *Hoge Raad* seems the final consecration of its existence by the political and juridical elites. The major achievement of these alliances has not only been maintained during the formative years of the Dutch literary field, but—given the jurisdiction in the Netherlands on literature—until today. Especially the blasphemy trial against Gerard Reve's *Nader tot U* (Nearer to Thee) 1966-1968 and the libel trial against Peter Waterdrinker's novel *Danslessen* (Dancelessons) 1999-2001 show this continuity. Both trials made their way up to the *Hoge Raad* in The Hague, and in both cases the highest jurisdiction in the Netherlands confirmed a relatively high degree of autonomy of literature (cf. Grüttemeier 186-88).

However, the broad strategic alliance described above remains a precarious one, since the stability of the achievement of the *exceptio artis*-alliance did not mean that the elites of both fields could not find themselves on different sides of the trenches at some future point. In each of the court cases on literature after the 1920 Barbusse-trial the judiciary itself has been the target of many protests from the literary field. Basically, the actors of literary institutions often see in each possible verdict against a literary author, even in each prosecution, a threat to the very existence of literature as we know it—which implies seeing the judicial and state agents as repressive forces who lack the right to speak about literature—and an opportunity to demand absolute autonomy for art and literature. In these generally fierce protests, the relatively high degree of institutional autonomy already reached as well as the unchanged embeddedness of the literary field within the field of power seems to be lost out of sight, at least from the view of literary circles.

Another conclusion from the case of the Netherlands could be that the precondition for the rise of the concept of *exceptio artis* within jurisdiction obviously is a substantial development of literary institutions on their route of specialization and professionalization in the past. A development, which in turn was legitimated and further stimulated by the introduction of the concept in the legal field. Still, one might wonder whether the synchronicity of the literary field coming into being in the Netherlands at the beginning of the 20th century and the binding introduction of the *exceptio artis* within jurisdiction in 1920 is just a Dutch coincidence or whether our data really corroborate the need for a structural extension of the field-theoretical model. Which brings us back to our initial question: in how far can this approach be applied to the data available concerning Australia?

Literary Trials in Australia

Australian censorship was initially set up as a system to control the importation of publications of all kind, on the basis of the Australian Customs Act of 1901 which did not make any reference to public opinion or expert advice. However, from 1933 onwards, suspicious items with a possible claim to literary or scholarly merit were to be transferred to a newly inaugurated board of experts—since 1937 this was known as the Literature Censorship Board (LCB)—to advise the minister on banning (cf. Moore 31ff.). From the field-theoretical approach taken in the present article, this measure could be seen as the first indication for a special status given to literature (and science) by the field of power, though it was a very weak exemption. This can be illustrated with regard to obscene literature.

In the whole of Britain, the Commonwealth and South Africa, the background of the juridical view concerning obscenity was the so-called Hicklin test from 1868, determining until far into the 20th century the way jurisdiction dealt with obscene texts. The decisive criterion for obscenity was whether the tendency of the item was "to deprave and corrupt those whose minds are open to such immoral influences" (qtd. in McDonald 294). The test did not make any references to scholarship or arts, but it did include the sentence "and into whose hand a publication of this sort might fall." According to Peter McDonald, the intention of the 1857 Act, as explicitly stressed by judge Blackburn in the Hicklin case and the press reports on that case, was, among others, to make sure that works of classical literature containing matter definitely obscene—as works by Ausonius, Juvenal or Aristophanes—would not fall under the Act. When these texts were, for example, distributed in their original language and/or in expensive editions, it was implied as unlikely that they might fall into the wrong hands (cf. McDonald 298-99). The special status for literature given here can therefore be seen as a kind of *exceptio artis* referring to classical or canonized literature, not to contemporary one. Evidently the Hicklin-test is a rule based on and at the same time reproducing social inequality, protecting art "as a resource of the elite" (cf. Beisel 151 *et passim*).

It seems likely that the very same elitism and classical expertise can be found in the circles of the Australian LCB: Nicole Moore (12) explicitly points to "its members' classicism and legal training," leading to the appointment of the retired Solicitor General Sir Robert Garran as the first chairman of the Board in 1933, until 1937. Garran was appointed to the new position of Appeals Censor in 1937 and held it until his death in 1957. The classics scholar Dr. Leslie Holdsworth Allen—who got his PhD at Leipzig university with a thesis on P. B. Shelley—succeeded Garran twice, once in 1937 as Chair of the LCB and then in 1957 by becoming Garran's successor as Appeals Censor—a position he held until 1966 (cf. Moore 34-35). The continuity and homogeneity of the Australian elites in this role as censors over more than 30 years is striking, while their societal function seems clear: to grant a certain degree of special freedom within the censorship procedure to classical and canonized literature—not to modern literature. It was on this point that the juridical (Garran) and the literary (Allen) elite stood side by side.

This situation forms the background for the first series of trials against literary texts in Australia in which state obscenity legislation was used regarding literature. The three most prominent of these trials took place between 1944 and 1948. The first was the South Australian case against an issue of the avant-garde magazine *Angry Penguins* for obscene Australian poetry. In September 1944, the editors Max Harris and John Reed were sentenced by an Adelaide Court under South Australia's Police Offences Act for, in the end, two poems being "indecent," for which they had to pay a fine of 5 pounds (cf. Moore 164-67). Second, Lawson Glassop's novel *We were the rats* on the 1944 siege of Tobruk, published by Angus & Robertson was accused of containing obscene material in New South Wales under the Obscene Publications act. The appeal case of June 13, 1946 confirmed the banning in the earlier trial in April of the same year (cf. Moore 157-60, 168-70, 173-74). The most notorious of the three major cases, however, was the Victorian case of obscene libel against Robert Close for his novel *Love me Sailor*, telling the story of a *femme fatale* on board of a merchant navy windjammer and her effects on the crew. The jury trial ended with the verdict of the Victorian Supreme Court in June 1948 mentioned above: Justice Fullagar committed Close to jail for 10 days (cf. 176-91).

When looking more closely at these trials, the first thing that strikes one is the heterogeneity of the juridical situation: three different states with three different kinds of laws and legal procedures establishing ethical borderlines in and around Australian literature. However, despite all differences, these trials have at least two dimensions in common. The first is the impossibility for the judge or the jury to accept a claim to literary merit as a defense. Therefore, expert evidence did not play any role in these trials either. Moore (164) concludes laconically with regard to the absence of the literary merit-criterion in the *Angry Penguins*-trial: "This troubled Clarke, the magistrate, before he declared the issue of *Angry Penguins* to have insufficient claim to art or merit in any case." Clarke is not explicit about the reasons for his literary critical judgement, but there is some circumstantial evidence concerning his poetics.

This evidence can be derived from a second dimension shared by these trials: All verdicts basically relied on isolated words or passages that were regarded as an offence to public morals. The already quoted Clarke stated that "words" could be indecent, and this was his criterion in fining the editors for two incriminated poems within the magazine (cf. 167). It seems likely, especially in view of the classicist preferences of the elites in the field of power referred to above and generally ascribed to Oxbridge-education far into the 20th century (cf. Dale 19), to infer an idealist, platonic aesthetics of 'the good, the true and the beautiful' dominating the Australian juridical system around that time—as one could also hold for Germany (cf. Knies) and the Netherlands (cf. Grüttemeier/Laros 212-16) until at least the middle of the 20th century. From this poetics, it is a specific kind of realism that the courts object to. An example may be the heroine of Close's novel who is described as "the sort sailormen tear out of magazines and stick over their bunks." It seems to be this suggestiveness that the Victorian courts found corrupting (cf. Moore 183). Certain domains of human life should not be dealt with in written text, let alone in literature, as Justice Studdert in the appeal trial on Glassop's novel *We Were the Rats* states explicitly:

I have borne in mind the life of the soldier in Tobruk for which I imagine no-one could get a better picture than from the book itself [...] but it seems to me that not everything a man says or does can be the subject of publication to the general public. (qtd. in Moore 159)

Looking back at Clarke's critical judgement quoted above, it seems as if the mere existence of elements as swear-words or passages with explicit reference to sexuality undermines a possible claim to being art, since in an idealist platonic poetics there is no room for such passages or words. In this regard it is telling that in *We Were the Rats*, the incriminated elements leading to a conviction were stemming from other texts: stanza's from the 19th century popular ballad "Bastards in the Bush" and passages from the American pulp magazine *Saucy Stories*.

To sum up, it turns out that the degree of institutional autonomy of literature is very weak around the end of the 1940s in Australia. Literary merit and expert advice do not play a role for the jurisdiction in these cases and the concepts of literature at stake point towards a classical idealist aesthetics of transformation (of reality into art), which clashes with forms of contemporary modernist poetry and realist prose. This attitude seems to have been dominant until the end of the 1960s, as one can tell from the influence of the Victoria Supreme Court trial about *Love me Sailor*, still quoted by Judge Levine in 1970 as precedent in a New South Wales District Court (cf. 177, 272-73). Nevertheless, there are first indications that parts of the juridical elites began to think differently already in the 1940s. New South Wales for example passes new legislation—to be precise, in May 1946, exactly in between the first trial on *We were the rats* and the appeal in June, which was still held under the old law—which establishes a new clause in the Obscene Publications Act, making literary or artistic merit possible as a means of defence. For the English speaking world, this is a very early introduction of a special status for literature, comparable with Woolsey's famous New York District Court judgement on *Ulysses* in 1933 (cf. Ladenson 95-98), but placing New South Wales still 13 years ahead of the British Obscene Publications Act of 1959 (cf. McDonald 299-300). Though the public debate in Victoria around the Close trial tried to push legislation in the same direction, these efforts failed, and in 1954 amendments in New South Wales fundamentally weakened the possibility of a literary-merit defence again (cf. Moore 170, 216).

This was roughly the legal context when, in 1968, censorship substantially changed. Whereas the Literature Censorship Board had been dealing with imported books only, the newly established National Literature Board of Review taking over in 1968 was also responsible for the censorship of domestic books, i.e., books produced in Australia. Taking censorship to a federal level meant at the same time making censorship uniform in the sense of leaving censorship of Australian-made literature no longer to the legislation and jurisdiction of the different states only. This also gave a new national dimension to all kind of protests against censorship. Seen from this perspective, it comes as no surprise that within two years after the introduction of the new rule, Australia had its first trial ever for wrongful seizure, triggered by university lecturer and gay activist Dennis Altman who wanted to regain his US paperback copies of Gore Vidal's *Myra Breckenridge* (including, for example, a dildo rape scene of a man) and of Sanford Friedman's *Totempole*, a minor gay novel banned already in 1966. The trial in a NSW District court ended with a draw: Judge Levine found Friedman's *Totempole* not offensive. With regard to *Myra Breckenridge*, however he motivated his different judgement with a reference to the *Love me Sailor*-case:

If, in relation to this book, I was to pose the question suggested by Fullagar J. in R. v. Close, namely, 'Do you think there are passages in it which are just plain dirt and nothing else, introduced for the sake of dirtiness and from the sure knowledge that notoriety earned by dirtiness will command for the book a ready sale?', my answer would have to be 'Yes'. (qtd. in Moore 273)

The other side of the verdict of Judge Levine, however, was that a judge had to be absolutely sure that there was no artistic dimension in the incriminated passages at all ("just plain dirt and nothing else," written for the "sake of dirtiness" "from the sure knowledge" that sex-scandal sells). From an idealist aesthetics-view, this would have been only stating the obvious in case of *Myra Breckenridge*—just like in the case in Fullagar on Close, for example. However, the fact that Judge Levine in his trial some 20 years after the Fullagar trial released *Totempole*, might be taken as an indication that something had changed in the poetics of parts of the juridical elite: The more or less explicit dealing with gay sexuality in a novel is in the eyes of Levine an acceptable form of literature. Which in turn gives a new dimension to using the Fullagar criterion at the end of the 60s, forcing the judge to be absolutely sure that the incriminated passages are "plain dirt and nothing else." This interpretation can be corroborated by the view of some press articles which saw the release of *Totempole* as a historic victory against censorship (cf. Moore 269-74).

Even more so, the impression that the judicial system was about to change its view on literature is corroborated by the outcome of the first full legal test of a uniform State and Federal judicial practice. These trials—characterized as "a watershed case" by Nicole Moore—started already in the same year 1970 and were based on Philip Roth's *Portnoy's Complaint*, a novel often referred to as a comic novel about masturbation (cf. 274-278).

After the banning of the American edition of *Portnoy's Complaint* in June 1969, Penguin printed an Australian edition of 75,000 copies in Melbourne and started distributing them at the end of August 1970. While the South Australian Labor government immediately decided not to ban the book, legal procedures started in all other states from October 1970 onwards. With only a symbolic conviction of Penguin Australia to pay $100 in Victoria, a decision not to ban by the Queensland Literature Board and the book free on sale in three states (apart from South Australia also in Western Australia, after a clearance by the Perth Court of Petty Sessions, and in New South Wales after two trials with two hung juries in the first half of 1971), the minister of Customs, Don Chipp, removed the import ban on *Portnoy's Complaint* completely on June 16, 1971. After these trials, no fiction book was to face an Australian court until today. How did this dramatic change, compared to the 1940s trials, come about?

From our perspective, two similarities of the prosecutions are striking: First and foremost, the introduction of literary merit as a possible defense into the laws of many States, as for example into the New South Wales legislation on obscenity in 1967 or into the Queensland Objectionable Literature Act or the Western Australian Indecent Publications Act. In Perth, the result was that although the magistrate found the book to be "patently and often nauseatingly obscene," he could not legally do anything against it because of the literary merit clause built into the law. Even the Melbourne Magistrate who fined Penguin $100, acknowledged that the book had literary merit.

The second difference between these procedures and those of the 1940s is directly related to the more widespread and more solid introduction of literary merit into many laws and proceedings: the possibility for literary experts testifying in court. This role was taken for example by writers such as Patrick White as well as by renowned university professors or younger academics in the Melbourne court. White also testified, among others, in the Sydney courts while a group of Western Australian writers was introduced by the defense in the Perth trial. It seems that the role of a suppressor is not the only one that can be attributed to the judicial system. At this moment in history, at least from a field theoretical perspective, legislator and jurisdiction seem to have turned into allies, too, who gave literature a high degree of institutional freedom, enough to be exempted from state intervention after the Roth trial until today.

When one holds these findings against the theoretical frame of our introduction and the analysis of the case of the Netherlands summarized above, there are strong indications to confirm the characterization of the *Portnoy's Complaint* cases indeed as 'watershed' cases in legal respect which gave to literature a relatively high degree of institutional autonomy within jurisdiction. When at the end of this battle the elites of the field of power and the elite of the literary field found each other side by side protecting literary merit from further prosecution—and, as we can add in retrospective: successfully so to date—this alliance nevertheless remains a precarious one. For, as Nicole Moore makes compellingly clear, what the state has not granted to the literary field is absolute autonomy: "[C]ensorship remains an arm of governmental power" (340). Nevertheless, from the beginning of the 1970s onwards, literature seems to have reached a degree of institutional autonomy in Australia very much comparable to that in most other Western countries.

Supposing this diagnosis on the basis of an analysis of legal procedures to be correct, it leaves us with several questions. What changed the rules of the game drastically between trials of the 1940s and those around 1970? How come that *exceptio artis*—in the form of the literary merit defense and admissibility of literary expertise in court—was introduced so late in Australia? And finally, of course, our introductory question: Why was censorship so harsh in Australia before the end of the 1960s? I think there is ample evidence that a plausible answer to some of these questions can be given when one takes into account the historical emergence of the Australian literary field.

INDICATIONS FOR THE RISE OF AN AUSTRALIAN LITERARY FIELD IN THE 1960S

A full-fledged history of the Australian literary field has still to be written. However, quite some work has been done already in relevant chapters of literary histories (from a field-theoretical approach for example Carter), book history (mostly Munro/Sheahan-Bright) and the history of specific institutions (for example Dale). This should suffice to present from existing data plausible views on the emergence of the Australian literary field from a historical perspective.

The most striking feature of Australia's literary history in the 19th and 20th centuries from a field-theoretical perspective has already been referred to above: The book trade in Australia has been dominated by massive and growing imports, mostly from Great Britain. The British book imports doubled in the period between 1893 and 1914 (leading to 3.5 million imported books sold in the 1920s as an annual average, and another million sold second hand), only to treble between 1919 and 1939 (cf. Moore 22). Even though the import had suffered from war-time restrictions on non-essential goods—which in turn gave a relative boost to Australian publishing on "anything resembling paper"—post-war Australia remained a colonial market, once more "swamping local publishers with a veritable flood of imported product" (cf. Munro/Sheahan-Bright 4). When in 1948 the Australian Book Publishers Association (ABPA) was founded, only 15% of the books were of local origin, with very few publishers producing more than a handful of titles each year, forming a "sideline undertaken by enterprising printers and booksellers" (Munro/Sheahan-Bright 4; cf. Bode 27-56). This situation basically lasted until at least 1960. At that time, the membership of the ABPA consisted of 37 publishing firms for the approximately 10.5 million English speakers of Australia, of which only nine companies had a national profile, distributed over five educational/academic publishers and only four publishers producing books for a general public (cf. Munro/Sheahan-Bright 31).

Especially what is generally known as the Australian baby boom between 1946 and 1961 explains the upcoming and relatively strong position of educational Australian publishers at that time (cf. Carter 378; Salt). In the field of higher education the baby boom led to "a rapid expansion in the number and size of universities" in the 50s and 60s (cf. Dale 92) and had in the end consequences for general books, too: In 1971, the majority in the membership of the ABPA had shifted. Of its 67 members, nearly 40 were Australian owned (cf. Munro/Sheahan-Bright 34). The shift was part of a new dynamics in the field of fiction, triggered off by a doubling of the value of Australian publishing from 1961-65, doubled again by 1970, and again by 1979 (cf. Carter 371). This explosive growth attracted not only local lists of British firms and multinational publishers from the 1960s onwards (cf. Buckridge 184; Bode 75-78) but also involved small publishers playing a greater role in the distribution of creative writing (for example with the Jacaranda Press in Brisbane, cf. Carter 371). This in turn led to the founding of the Australian Independent Publishers Association (AIPA) in 1975, which was joined by one of the largest Australian publishers, Angus & Robertson and others who did not feel well represented in the ABPA (cf. Munro/Sheahan-Bright 57). Looking at the Australian publishing houses, it seems as if they have crossed a quantitative threshold and developed new strategies towards further professionalization and institutionalization in the course of the 1960s.

Many indications regarding other institutions of the literary field corroborate this historical view. Regarding literary criticism, it is generally held that it increased and professionalized from the mid-60s onwards in major newspapers such as *Australian*, the *Sydney Morning Herald* and the *Age* (cf. Bennett 249). Concerning academic literary criticism, it was not before 1962 that the first Chair in Australian Literature was appointed, at the University of Sydney, though this position would not be seen as a specialist one for many years to come, but rather one in which candidates would be judged on their expertise in English literature, too, if not mostly (cf. Dale 122-42). The first purely scholarly journal on Australian literature *Australian Literary Studies* was launched in August 1963, aiming at teachers and students of Australian literature (cf. Munro/Sheahan-Bright 141, 251) and it took until May 1978 for the inaugural conference of the Association for the Study of Australian Literature (ASAL) to be held (cf. Dale 177).

The organization of the writers themselves also changed in this period, showing "the increased professionalization of the business of writing" for example in the erection of the Australian Society of Authors in 1963 and of state-based writers centers (cf. Munro/Sheahan-Bright 139, 146-50). An important role in subsidizing writers was played by the Literature Board of the Australia Council which was founded in 1973, giving major grants to writers to write new work (cf. 159ff.). It replaced the Commonwealth Literary Fund of 1908 by making the stimulation of good Australian literature a national project. This project was based on literary expertise in the form of peer group assessment methods and had a budget four times larger than that of its predecessor (cf. Carter 377; Bennett 247). The literary awards also show increasing differentiation and quantity. While traditionally the Miles Franklin Literary Award (since 1957) was the most prestigious literary prize, with only two major elder prizes next to it, the number of prizes increased significantly at the beginning of the 1970s, with three prizes added to the scheme of competition and national awards in one single year, 1974 (i.e., the *Age* Book of the Year Awards, the National Book Council Awards and the Patrick White Award, cf. Munro/Sheahan-Bright 142-45).

Finally, the growing stimuli and options in the fight for positions in the literary field seem to go along with a differentiation in the field of poetics. From the 1960s onwards, different groups raised their voices on the Australian poetic battlefield to get attention and recognition. The first anthologies by authors with a migrant background were published from 1963 onwards (cf. Munro/Sheahan-Bright 269ff.; Mycak/Sarwal), followed for example by feminist writings from the 1970s on (cf. Munro/Sheahan-Bright 263-68; Bode 131-53). Patrick Buckridge (in Munro/Sheahan-Bright 346) puts this poetic differentiation in more general terms, which according to him got a new dynamics since the mid-1970s, signaling "the rise of various new 'schools' of fiction and life-writing focused, for example, on the experience of women, Aboriginal Australians, young adults, migrants, gays and other group."

To conclude this point, one can best quote the summary of David Carter's (360) contribution to *The Cambridge History of Australian Literature*: "By the mid-1970s Australian literature was defined through a set of relatively autonomous institutional sites in universities, publishing, criticism, book selling and professional associations." One could add: In contrast to the 1950s—which would make the 1960s the period in which the institutional foundation for a relatively autonomous Australian literary field was laid.

Conclusion

Taking all the parts of our argument together, it seems that the effectuation of the *exceptio artis* rule within an Australiawide series of trials and in a national debate in 1970/71 is a strong indication for the emergence of an Australian literary field having come to completion and for its consecration by the field of power at that specific historical moment. The structural analogies with the case of the Netherlands (cf. above) are striking. The interconnectedness between the guarantee of an exceptional status given to literature by law and jurisdiction on the one hand, and the substantial professionalization of literary institutions basically in the preceding decade on the other, allows for plausible answers to the questions posed above. The most important structural reason for the rather late introduction of an *exceptio artis* guideline into most Australian jurisprudence around 1970 seems to have been the rather late emergence of an Australian literary field and its relevant institutions—publishers, criticism, state subsidies, prizes etc.—in the course of the 1960s. Starting off from a recognition of and participation in this development, the establishment of a uniform nationwide censorship system in 1968 intensified within 5 years the already growing field-dynamics and led to the end of censorship of literature in Australia.

Precursors of this development were scandals in which the debate on censorship grew into a public, national debate, as in the case of banning of Salinger's *Catcher in the Rye* in 1957 (cf. Moore 222-25), resulting in the regular publication of the list of all banned books. In Bourdieu's view, growing societal protest against state interference with literature is an indication for growing autonomy of the literary field, and the protest against censorship took on a new quality in Australia in the 1960s, when in 1964 the discussion of the *Lady Chatterley* ban "censorship was the hottest issue of the year" (245-50, 255). However, what at first glance seems to be a clear-cut question of them or us, on a closer look turns out to be more complex, as I hope to have demonstrated: when the government and the judiciary strived for a uniform system to control literature, they not only met with institutional needs of the literary field on the point where publishers also claim the urge for a uniform and reliable framework for publishing activities. Furthermore the elites of the field of power and the literary field were bound together in the 1960s and 1970s by the view that modern Australian literature is a national project that needs a reliable judicial framework and has to be protected from unwanted and disturbing interference in order to develop its value for the nation. The achievement of this common goal is, at least to a large extent, made possible by the legal system with the introduction of the *exceptio artis* as a kind of relative institutional autonomy given to literature within the law.

Finally, what seems, in international comparison, to have been a very severe system of censorship turns out to be the other side of the coin of the absence or at least the weakness of an Australian literary field before the 1960s. With crucial professional and specialized literary institutions largely lacking until the 1960s in Australia, important actors in the fight for the autonomy of literature and against censorship were missing. The elites of the field of power saw, for many decades, no corresponding elites of an emerging Australian literary field of contemporary literature. In this situation, the influence of literary elites formed by a traditional education based on a classical canon and an idealist aesthetics was substantial and lasting, personified in the long reign of Garran and Allen in the Literature Censorship Board from 1933 until 1967. However, the fact that this censorship-system could be dismantled completely within five years after its uniform nationalization in 1968 reveals that from a field theoretical perspective Australia is not structurally different from other Western countries—it was only particularly late in the development of a literary field of its own.

These Australian-based remarks allow for a more general formulation: To a large degree, the rise of literary fields seems to be the result of a consensus between the literary, political and juridical elites. This consensus considers literary expertise to be a necessary condition for gaining the legitimation to talk about modern (and other) literature in a way that is regarded as adequate by the cultural and literary field as well as by the field of power. The other side of this conviction is the mutual participation of different institutions and actors in each other's professional activities. The political and juridical elites rely on what established—and this means mostly: academic—literary experts tell them to be adequate ways of dealing with literature. At the same time, making use of external expertise reinforces the professionalism of the political and juridical elites, being responsible for steering the nation state and the legal system as a whole. The recognition of the literary experts by other experts from outside literary circles stabilizes their own emerging positions by adding a source of extra symbolic capital to the 'field of their own' as such and to some positions within. At the same time, the consecration of the literary field by the elites of the field of power makes them specialists that participate in a national endeavor. In this constellation, literature is conceptualized by both fields as a relevant domain that can fulfil its function for humans and the state best when state and jurisdiction refrain from interfering as far as possible within a relatively reliable legal framework. The foundation of this alliance however lies in the precarious relativity of the autonomy given to the literary field by the field of power that does not give up its judicial and legislative power in favor of its ally, neither in Australia, nor in the Netherlands, nor, as far as I know, elsewhere in the World Republic of Letters.

The author would like to thank Nicole Moore for her valuable comments on an earlier version of this paper.

WORKS CITED

Beekman, Klaus, and Ralf Grüttemeier. *De wet van de letter: Literatuur en rechtspraak.* Amsterdam: Athenaeum-Polak & Van Gennep, 2005. Print.

Beisel, Nicola. "Morals Versus Art: Censorship, The Politics of Interpretation, and the Victorian Nude." *American Sociological Review* 58.2 (1993): 145-62. Print.

Bennett, Bruce. "Literary Culture since Vietnam: a New Dynamic." *The Oxford Literary History of Australia.* Ed. Bruce Bennett and Jennifer Strauss. Melbourne: Oxford UP, 1998. 239-64. Print.

Bode, Katherine. *Reading by Numbers: Recalibrating the Literary Field.* London: Anthem P, 2012. Print.

Bourdieu, Pierre. *The Rules of Art: Genesis and Structure of the Literary Field.* Trans. Susan Emanuel. Cambridge: Polity P, 2008. Print.

Buckridge, Patrick. "Clearing a Space for Australian Literature 1940-1965." *The Oxford Literary History of Australia.* Ed. Bruce Bennett and Jennifer Strauss. Melbourne: Oxford UP, 1998. 169-92. Print.

Carter, David. "Publishing, Patronage and Cultural Politics: Institutional Changes in the Field of Australian Literature from 1950." *The Cambridge History of Australian Literature.* Ed. Peter Pierce. Cambridge UP, 2009. 360-90. Print.

Dale, Leigh. *The English Men. Professing Literature in Australian Universities.* Toowoomba: ASAL, 1997. Print.

Dorleijn, Gillis J., and Kees van Rees, eds. *De productie van literatuur: Het literaire veld in Nederland 1800-2000.* Nijmegen: Uitgeverij VanTilt, 2006. Print.

Grüttemeier, Ralf. "Law and the Autonomy of Literature." *The Autonomy of Literature at the Fins de Siècles (1900 and 2000): A Critical Assessment.* Ed. Gillis J. Dorleijn, Ralf Grüttemeier and Liesbeth Korthals Altes. Leuven: Peeters, 2007. 175-92. Print.

Grüttemeier, Ralf, and Ted Laros. "Literature in Law: *Exceptio Artis* and the Emergence of Literary Fields." *Law and Humanities* 7 (2013): 204-17. Print.

Knies, Wolfgang. *Schranken der Kunstfreiheit als verfassungsrechtliches Problem*. München: C.H. Beck, 1967. Print.

Kohler, Gun-Britt, and Pavel I. Navumenka. "Interference of Autonomization and Deautonomization in the Belarusian Literary Field. Indication of 'Smallness,' or Something Different?" *Vestnik BGU. Seryja 4: Filal., Žurn., Ped.* (2012): 3-11. Print.

Ladenson, Elisabeth. *Dirt for Art's Sake: Books on Trial from* Madame Bovary *to* Lolita. Ithaca: Cornell UP, 2007. Print.

McDonald, Peter. "Old Phrases and Great Obscenities: The Strange Afterlife of Two Victorian Anxieties." *Journal of Victorian Culture* 13 (2008): 294-302. Print.

Moore, Nicole. *The Censor's Library*. St. Lucia: U of Queensland P, 2012. Print.

Munro, Craig, and Robyn Sheahan-Bright, eds. *Paper Empires: A History of the Book in Australia 1946-2005*. St. Lucia: U of Queensland P, 2006. Print.

Mycak, Sonia, and Amit Sarwal, eds. *Australian Made: A Multicultural Reader*. Camperdown: Sydney UP, 2010. Print.

Salt, Bernard. *The Big Shift*. South Yarra, Vic.: Hardie Grant Books, 2004. Print.

Sapiro, Gisèle. *La responsabilité de l'écrivain: Littérature, droit et moral en France (XIXe-XXIe siècle)*. Paris: Le Seuil, 2011. Print.

Schalken, Tom. *Pornografie en strafrecht: Beschouwingen over het pornografiebegrip en zijn juridische hanteerbaarheid*. Arnhem: Gouda Quint, 1972. Print.

Schmidt, Siegfried J. *Die Selbstorganisation des Sozialsystems Literatur im 18. Jahrhundert*. Frankfurt/Main: Suhrkamp, 1989. Print.

Viala, Alain. *Naissance de l'écrivain: Sociologie de la litterature à l'âge classique*. Paris: Editions de Minuit, 1985. Print.

Literary Movements as Precarious Alliances? Observations and Propositions on Movement Discourse and Cultural Participation

ANTON KIRCHHOFER

OBSERVING MOVEMENTS IN LITERATURE AND LITERARY THEORY

The movement holds a singular position in the vocabulary of literary criticism. While other fundamental critical concepts—such as the text, the subject, the author, the reader—have been subjected to intense theoretical inquiry, the movement has enjoyed a largely unquestioned position in our critical terminology.

The critical concerns associated with movements in literary studies are typically centered around a familiar set of questions: What are the essential features of a particular movement, which ideas or textual traits are characteristic of it? Does it have subdivisions, variations, precursors, successors? Who belongs to the movement, and in what particular manner do they belong to it?

A wide selection of reference works offer surveys of literary, artistic and intellectual movements, describing their main features and representatives, arranging movements in chronological succession, highlighting as far as possible the connections or confrontations that exist between them (cf., e.g., Henderson; Turner *Renaissance*; Turner *Expressionism*; Bradshaw/ Dettmar). References to movements abound in the context of interpreting individual texts as well as in the writing of literary history, they can be central to the definition and differentiation of entire periods as well as to the study of individual authors.

The discourse about movements at the same time extends far beyond the sphere of academic criticism. As an example for their relevance to the public discussion of literature, I would like to quote a passage from a conversation between Scottish novelist A.L. Kennedy and literary journalist Stephanie Merritt which was published in a British Sunday paper:

AL Kennedy: […] I'm a Scottish writer because I live there and I was born there, and my books will relate to other books that are Scottish, but it's not my job to do that. That's up to journalists, or the marketing people if they feel that will help sales by creating a Scottish movement.
Observer: So you don't see yourself as part of a Scottish movement?
AL Kennedy: If you talk to anybody who's in a 'movement' unless they're with Andy Warhol or something very few artists, particularly writers, really manipulate the media and create the idea of it. I see some of the other Scottish writers sometimes, but we're presented as always being in the pub together or sharing needles together we meet probably every two years, that's not a movement (laughs). (Merritt n.pag.)

This dialogue is remarkable not least because it does not produce any tangible result. Is there a "Scottish movement"? What might be its main characteristics? And is A.L. Kennedy part of the movement? At the end, the reader is hardly any wiser about these questions, or about the participants' views on them. While both interlocutors accept the relevance of the issue, and both contribute to the discussion, it seems that neither the writer nor the journalist is ready to take the risk of suggesting a definitive view. Neither position appears to have the authority to do so, though at the same time neither seems able to elide the relevance of the category of the 'movement.'

Even in literary theory—no doubt the field of literary discourse which has been most consistently reflexive and self-critical—the situation is hardly any different. Instead of engaging in a theoretical examination of the movement and of its role in critical discourse, literary theory has been the site of a proliferation of theoretical movements since the 1960s. It is true that theoretical movements have resisted taxonomy, as Jacques Derrida has pointed out, and that no one would be able to give an exhaustive list of theoretical movements. Still the progress of literary theory is often captured as a succession of movements and approaches whose main contours are familiar even though the list is capable of many variations and shifts in emphasis. The category has formed the basis for numerous introductions and surveys, where, for instance, New Criticism, Structuralism, Reader Response Theory, Deconstruction and Poststructuralism, or New Historicism are likely to figure along with older, contemporaneous and more recent theoretical movements. Instead of producing a theory of the movement, then, literary theory has offered us so far an insistent and untheorized practice of movement discourse.

Alongside this practical predominance of a movement discourse in theory there also exists a pronounced dissatisfaction. Jacques Derrida has spoken of theoretical movements as "'theoretical' monsters" (67), and has vehemently condemned the critical concern with their rise and decline as the "boring game of applying the most worn-out schemes of the history of ideas to the specificity of what is happening now" (79). In the field of introductions to literary theory, Andrew Bennett and Nicholas Royle have drawn the consequence of presenting "brief essays on a range of key critical concepts" instead of what they programmatically reject as "potted summaries of *isms*" (vii). "*Isms*," Bennett and Royle explain, "inevitably encourage generalization, abstractness, and lack of critical clarity and of historical awareness" (205). Jonathan Culler's *Literary Theory: A Very Short Introduction* also is structured around "shared questions" and "important debates," rather than divided into chapters on 'movements and approaches.' If theory is presented in the form of "a set of competing approaches or methods of interpretation," Culler argues, one loses sight of the fact that the "theoretical movements that introductions identify [...] have a lot in common" ([v]). Much theory, whatever the approach, is "a pugnacious critique of common-sense notions," "an attempt to show that what we take for granted as 'common sense' is in fact a historical construction" (4).

Movement discourse itself, however, has not merely escaped this "pugnacious critique," it also appears to have a way of imposing itself even on those who have dismissed it as inadequate. Rather than abandoning the movement pattern completely, Jonathan Culler's *Very Short Introduction* preserves it in a substantial appendix where "a brief description of modern theoretical movements" is included because "readers have a right to expect an explanation of terms like *structuralism* and *deconstruction* that appear in discussions of criticism" (117, original emphasis). Bennett and Royle concede that their "theoretical reasons for feeling wary of *isms*" are not sufficient to simply "make *isms* go away" because *isms* "are convenient, as well as deadly" (205). At certain points, it turns out, they are also inevitable: A "chapter on the postmodern," Bennett and Royle admit, "may seem inappropriate" in a book which "does not attempt to introduce different critical schools or historical periods of literature," but there seems to be no choice: The term "involves ways of thinking which are unavoidable at the start of the twenty-first century" (231). And even as Derrida denounces the "boring game" of speaking in movements, he joins it, for instance by insisting that "a *concern with history* [...] was already active, present and fundamental [...] in the very poststructuralism which the supporters and promoters of new historicism think it is absolutely crucial to oppose" (68, original emphasis).[1]

How can it be that in spite of the imprecisions and the discontents, which accompany the discourse on movements, there is no appearance of its being abandoned? Instead of theorizing movement discourse, we have so far been largely faced with the alternative of engaging in the practice of movement discourse or seeking to avoid it more or less successfully and consistently. In consequence, a theory of the movement should be able to account for this situation as well as to take us beyond this alternative. I suggest that the first step towards such a theory can usefully take the form of an analysis of the discourse on movements that will provide a more structured view of the enigmatic and contradictory discursive presence of the movement. What are

---

1   Derrida's own propositions describe the contradictions of movement discourse in literary theory rather than offering a theoretical account of it. Employing the French term "jetée" in its double meaning, Derrida speaks of movements as "theoretical jetties." On the one hand, "the force of the movement which throws something or throws itself (jette or se jette) forwards and backwards at the same time, prior to any subject, object, or project, prior to any rejection or abjection"; on the other hand "its institutional and protective consolidation, which can be compared to the jetty, the pier in a harbor meant to break the waves and maintain low tide for boats at anchor or for swimmers" (84). Derrida attributes the "difficulties of analysis," "confusions" and "ambiguities" that surround the discussion of movements to "the difficulty of an effective principial distinction between the two jetties," but also to "the strategic interests involved—for all sides and for various reasons—in confusing or creating a certain interdependence between the two" (84).

the settings and locations where this discourse is practiced? What are the subject positions of the speakers who participate in this discourse? What are the characteristic elements of the concepts of 'movement' which appear in this discourse?

I will begin my exploration of movement discourse with a survey of the theoretical conceptions as they exist in other disciplines in which movements are studied, and complement it with a sample survey of the occurrence of the term in the media of public information and debate, before formulating a set of propositions that could form part of a theory of the movement.

OBSERVING SCHOLARLY DISCOURSE ON MOVEMENTS

Movement Theory in Political Philosophy: Giorgio Agamben

In 2005 Giorgio Agamben noted that "movement" is "a word everyone seems to understand but no one defines." He went on to draw attention to ethical and political risks resulting from this fact: "[W]e must think about the movement because this concept is our unthought and so long as it remains such it risks compromising our choices and strategies" (n.pag.). Political philosophy is thus the only academic field in which the absence of a theory of the movement has been emphatically described as a problem. Agamben noted, too, that the term has importance beyond "the political realm": "When Freud wants to write a book in 1914 in order to describe what he is part of, he calls it a psychoanalytical movement," he points out. On the factors that produce this wider spread of the concept, Agamben has little to suggest: "Evidently, in certain historical moments, certain codewords irresistibly impose themselves [...], without needing to be defined" (n.pag.). Freud's decision to speak of a "psychoanalytic movement" thus remains to a large extent situational and enigmatic.

As for political movements, Agamben reviews the few examinations of the concept in the field of political science (Lorenz von Stein's 1850 *Geschichte der sozialen Bewegung in Frankreich von 1789 bis auf unsre Tage*; Carl Schmitt's 1933 *Staat Bewegung Volk* as well as selected passages from Hannah Arendt's 1951 *The Origins of Totalitarianism*) and raises the question of the historical trajectory of the concept. He dates one of its first significant occurrences "to the French July Revolution of 1830 [when the progressive party called itself 'parti du mouvement']." In the early 20th century, he declares, movements became the dominant phenomenon in politics, exceeding the importance of political parties: "Fascism and Nazism always define themselves as movements first and only secondly as parties" (n.pag.), he states with reference to Hannah Arendt's analysis in *Origins of Totalitarianism*.

Agamben's own theoretical proposition casts the movement as a correlative of a type of power which Michel Foucault has identified as characteristic of modern societies: the notion of biopower. The historical appearance of the movement in the 19th century coincides with the emergence of this type of power, and Agamben posits an essential link between the two: "[T]he movement became a necessity" when the "people ceased to be a political entity and turned into demographical and biological populations," he states—apparently conceptualizing the movement as a social force that operates outside the categories of the conscious rationality of the political subject—and sums this up in the remarkable and no doubt controversial claim: "Democracy ends when movements emerge."[2]

Compared to the positions in literary theory, Agamben's contribution opens up additional perspectives for the discussion of movements. Emphasizing the view of movement discourse as a widespread practice which has been little theorized, he explicitly stresses the existence of a 'transdisciplinary' dimension of the phenomenon as well as to its distinctly 'modern' character. Agamben does not in fact discuss in what ways his conception of the biopolitical character of the (political) movement and his account of the emergence of the movement in the political field might connect to phenomena such as the 'psychoanalytic movement' or indeed to the movements in literature and literary theory. But by its very scope, his approach issues an invitation to examine the enigmatic but insistent presence of the 'movement' in our critical discourse, by way of an investigation of the historical depth as well as of the synchronic thematic spread of the concept. What is the genealogy of the movement, and what are the historical dimensions of movement discourse? What distinguishes literary, political or intellectual movements, over and above their topical differences, and what do they have in common? Are there distinctive differences between the types of

---

[2] Agamben reiterates his claim in a qualified form: "Substantially there are no democratic movements (if by democracy we mean what traditionally regards the people as the political body constitutive of democracy)" (n.pag.).

movements in each field, and would it be possible to produce a typology of movements? Clearly an investigation of these questions would be required in order to test the validity of Agamben's theoretical proposition on the conditions which made the emergence of the concept possible.

Social Movement Theory: Movements as Precarious Alliances

There is one field of study in which the claim that there is no theory of the movement would cause as much surprise as the claim that "democracy ends when movements emerge." The social sciences have produced an extensive body of research on social movements, extending from the classical and paradigmatic phenomena such as abolitionism, the labour movement or the women's movement, to the 'new social movements' which have changed the faces of societies in North America and in many other areas of the world since the 1960s and which continue in new formations and with new types of action and agendas in the contemporary world. The extent and the dynamic with which social movements have pervaded and shaped modern societies has been described as the "movementisation" of society (cf. Melucci; Johnston, *States* 67), as a result of which modern western societies have become "social movement societies" (Meyer/Tarrow; Johnston *Culture* 10). Social movement studies is then a well-established and dynamic field of research in the social sciences (cf., e.g., Della Porta/Diani; Ruggiero/Montagna; McAdam/Snow; Snow/Soule/Kriesi) and it has been accompanied by a sustained theoretical reflection on the phenomenon dating back at least to the 1970s.

My look at this extensive field will necessarily be selective and will focus on the contribution social movement theory can make towards a theory of movements as such. Which aspects of social movement theory can be helpful in order to theorize 'movements in general'? Are movements always essentially social movements? Or if not, how do social movements differ from other types of movements?

It would appear that definitional issues have not been at the forefront of social movement theory. This does not mean that there is a lack of definitions of the phenomenon. The *Blackwell Companion to Social Movements* defines social movements as

collectivities acting with some degree of organization and continuity outside of institutional or organizational channels for the purpose of challenging or defending extant authority, whether it is institutionally or culturally based, in the group, organization, society, culture, or world order of which they are a part. (Snow/Soule/Kriesi 11)

In another contemporary reference work, the authors list four characteristic aspects of social movements: "(1) some degree of organization; (2) some degree of temporal continuity; (3) change-oriented goals; and [(4)] at least some use of extra-institutional forms of action (e.g., street protests, vigils)" (McAdam/Snow 1). They go on to combine these into a similar definition:

[W]e define a social movement as a loose collectivity acting with some degree of organization, temporal continuity, and reliance on noninstitutional forms of action to promote or resist change in the group, society or world order of which it is a part. (1)

Hank Johnston's recent *What is a Social Movement* lists a similar set of defining elements, complemented by a fifth: "collective identity," arising from "an ideational-interpretative element" (25). In spite of accentuating differences in aspect, however, contemporary scholarship tends to emphasize the consensus about the characteristic features of social movements rather than problematize the differences between the various definitions which have been proposed.

The vagueness of the concept, the essential difficulty of pinning it down which I have described as troublesome in the context of literary discourse, does not give rise to similar contradictions and discomforts in social movement theory. Rather, these aspects are simply incorporated and given explicit and definitional recognition. Movements appear to possess no single characteristic structure. Instead they are "structurally diverse" (Johnston, *What is* 24). Similarly, they need "some degree of organization" and of "continuity"—"some degree," but evidently not too much! As soon as the structure of a collective becomes too defined, it seems, they are no longer a movement. Once this characteristic lack of organization disappears, they must be seen as "social movement organizations" (cf. Johnston, *What is* 7 *et passim*).

In these definitions the specific relevance of the concept of movement in relation to the theme of this volume becomes evident. Social movements are a type of alliance. They "are composed of individuals and their interacttions" (Jasper 965), and this implies that they have certain forms of social and cognitive cohesion. At the same time, as we have seen, these alliances do not conform to one particular model or format, and neither must they become too well-defined, too organized, too structured. Movements are understood as loose, spontaneous, diverse and even disparate actual or virtual alliances between agents, whose one essential point of cohesion lies in the fact of a perceived collective agency—however loose or stable, however spontaneous or durable the structure that allows it to emerge, and however well-defined or conceptually explicit its goal might be. In this sense, I will suggest that social movement theory conceptualizes social movements as 'precarious alliances,' and defines its own task as that of accounting for the fact that these collectivities exist despite their lack of a definite and clear structure, and despite all those other factors whose persistent vagueness and openness make them precarious.

Moreover, the different approaches in social movement theory specifically understand it as their role to address this precariousness. They accept the comparative openness of the format as that characteristic which creates the question that theory has to address: How do these alliances exist in spite of the instability of the ties and the structures which hold their various participants and adherents together and regulate their capability of acting as a collective. What is it that allows these unstable formations nevertheless to have an impact, and sometimes a very decisive impact, on the ideas, developments and course of events in societies? In response to these issues, the theory of social movements has focused on the conditions for the emergence and the chances of mobilization of movements. What are the factors that condition the success or failure of movements? How do movements recruit and mobilize adherents to their cause and how do the actions of movements find resonance in society at large and manage to reach the aims they set themselves? A number of approaches have been developed in order to address these issues (for a recent survey cf. Johnston, *What is*, see also Klandermans or Jasper).

By contrast, little progress has been made in the direction of a typology or taxonomy of movements. How similar or how different are, for example, religious movements, political movements, literary movements or what are sometimes called 'cultural movements' to social movements and to each other? As Johnston (*What is* 72-93) points out, the question has come to be recognized in social movement studies, but no sustained lines of inquiry have as yet been proposed. The only exception here is the distinction between 'new social movements'—those which have arisen since the 1960s—

and the classical and paradigmatic social movements such as abolitionism, the labour movement, or the women's movement which date back to the early and mid-19th century. But even here, the idea that these new movements are characterized by new types of action and self-definition has been challenged, e.g., by Calhoun who has argued that the distinction "is specious" (360) and that the features that are usually taken to be specific for the new social movements were equally characteristic for social movements in the early 19th century.

More Precarious Alliances: Sociological Perspectives beyond the Social Movement and Social Movement Theory

In concluding this cross-disciplinary survey of movement discourse and movement theory, I would like to single out two essays which explicitly apply a sociological perspective beyond the sphere of social movements. These essays introduce aspects that not only widen the scope of sociological inquiry but also indicate that the definition of movements as precarious (loosely structured and essentially unstable) alliances between the various agents which may be considered members, supporters, or adherents of the movement offers only a partial view, once it is a question of analysing the general conditions of possibility of movements.

The "general theory of scientific and intellectual movements" proposed by Frickel and Gross (204-32) expresses this limitation through what is excluded by the analogy with social movement theory which they adopt as their basis. It is their guiding assumption that "scientific and intellectual movements [...] are similar in certain respects to social movements" (205). Consequently, the authors raise questions similar to those asked in social movement theory: Their "theory seeks to answer the question, under what social conditions is any particular scientific/intellectual movement, or SIM [...] most likely to emerge, gain adherents, win intellectual prestige, and ultimately acquire some level of institutional stability" (205). As in social movement theory, the goal is to identify the factors that give cohesion and focus, as well as a limited stability (always potentially volatile, never quite stable) to this formation.[3]

---

3 The success of the precarious alliance between a number of emerging and established academics—in relation to their case study of poststructuralism in the U.S. and, as their theory claims, in intellectual movements in general, rests on a com-

In passing, Frickel and Gross exclude a type of intellectual movement which they nevertheless explicitly recognize as a discursive fact: "[W]e would restrict our definition of a SIM to a movement towards whose knowledge core participants are consciously oriented, regardless of their understanding of it" (206), they point out, and add in a footnote: "We leave it to others to explain diffuse changes in thought that few observers at the time recognized as a movement, but which have been so recognized later through historical scholarship" (206, FN 3).

The limitation is worth dwelling on, partly because it points towards the reason why a simple generalization of social movement theory to other types of movements will be insufficient, but even more so because it indicates an added perspective which has the potential to take us into the direction of such a 'general theory of movements.' Within the framework of their argument, the limitation appears to be necessary in order to sustain the parallelism to social movements on which their approach is based. By the same token, it makes explicit a tacit limitation implied in social movement theory. In relation to social movements it apparently goes without saying that some persons, including some of those who are counted as participants, should be consciously oriented towards it. The limitation expressed by Frickel and Gross however indicates that in the field of 'scientific and intellectual movements' this is by no means always the case. Hence, the parallelism which Frickel and Gross posit as their point of departure can only be sustained, if those other kinds of movements are excluded from consideration. At the same time, however, their caveat renders visible the limits of applying social movement theory to movements in general. In the history of ideas, of philosophy, of literature, of art, scholars have identified and stud-

---

bination of four factors: (1) the degree of dissatisfaction among "high-status intellectual actors" with "the intellectual tendencies of the day" (209); (2) the degree of access to "key resources" (213), such as employment and prestige; (3) the degree of access to "micromobilization contexts" such as conferences (219); and (4) the effective framing of "movement ideas" (221). Plausible as this account is, it basically rests on the idea that 'intellectual movements' resemble social movements, except that they have to succeed under the conditions of academic research and academic institutions, while social movements have to succeed under the conditions of society and its media in general. The distinction is thus an effect of different circumstances rather than different structures.

ied movements whose participants may have never been consciously oriented towards a knowledge of that movement. These movements, one might suppose, exist *as* movements only in a discourse whose location is rather distant from the time and setting where the phenomena thus redescribed may be taken to have existed. To the extent that a "general theory of movements" should also offer some guidance on the perspective in which we should perceive these 'movements,' we may conclude that such a general theory has not been proposed to date.

The way to extend the sociological theory of movements as precarious alliances and of the conditions that enable their more or less transitory appearance is to take into account the discourse on movements, which may concern itself both with the movements that are consciously in existence and those which have been recognized later through scholarship. In other words, we may need to extend the notion of the movement as a precarious alliance beyond the circle of those who may be thought to belong to the movement in some way, and to include those who discuss the movement— from whatever position they do so, and in whatever temporal relation to the movement they may stand. And indeed independently also of the question whether the particular movement ever had any self-identified adherents or representatives in the past or present. A precarious alliance among those who have any kind of discursive position enabling them to assert or deny, define or redefine, in short to discuss in any particular way the existence of the movement.

In a pioneering essay in the field of the sociology of literature, Wouter de Nooy has drawn attention to the fact that this angle of analysis has not been widely recognized in literary and cultural studies: "Studies on movements in art usually pay attention to the relations between artists," he observes, "but the position of the critics tends to be ignored" (516). Yet he points out that the critics play a vital role in relation to the ways in which writers and their works are perceived: "The study of literature has its own organizations, practitioners and public. Furthermore it has a product of its own, viz. the artistic image of texts" (509). De Nooy's repeatedly insists on the *productivity* of the discourses on literature. The "study of literature [...] can be seen as a production process," he argues, because it results in "the establishment of an artistic image" (509). Moreover, the writers themselves are not excluded from participation in the production of their "artistic image": "[A]uthors and critics are interdependent" and "the power relations are continually shifting" (510). It follows from this, as de Nooy points out, that the attribution of a writer to a group or movement is in essence a collaborative phenomenon, not primarily between different authors, but between critics and authors. The groups and movements described by de Nooy can indeed be appropriately described as precarious alliances. But as de Nooy shows, these are not necessarily and primarily alliances among authors who share certain ideas about how to write literature, but among critics (who choose to classify authors under a certain label) and authors (who choose to offer themselves to such classification or to reject the label). De Nooy thus contributes to movement theory the explicit recognition of the need for a *discursive alliance* between the observers of a movement on the one hand, and its potential representatives on the other.

Coming from this presentation of de Nooy's and Frickel's and Gross's approaches, I propose that it will be useful (1) to retain the idea that movements can be thought of as precarious alliances; and (2) explicitly to expand the circle of participants in this alliance beyond the self-identified adherents of a particular movement, and to include those who speak about those movements—as critics, journalists, or indeed as members of the movement—as potential participants in the precarious alliance which sustains the movement.

I propose, then, that we should conceptualize the existence of a discourse about movements as a vital ingredient in the existence of movements themselves. It is in the course of this discursive practice that the precarious alliances are formed between those who participate in the discourse that helps to establish the existence of a movement. It may be the self-identified or attributed 'members,' 'leaders' or 'representatives' of the particular movement in question who participate in this discourse, but it may also be, in any combination, a range of supportive or critical observers, and even of opponents and members of different movements. To generalize the observations of Wouter de Nooy in this manner, I suggest, will allow us to move beyond the theoretical limitations in the study of movements stated by Frickel and Gross, and take us towards a more general theoretical approach to (the discourse on) movements.

Towards an Analysis of the Discourse on Movements—Some Samples

The foregoing review of selected approaches towards movement theory has served, hopefully, to elucidate both the requirements such a theory would have to meet, and the difficulties which it is likely to encounter at present. In order to address the open questions we have encountered around the definition, the emergence, the historical as well the synchronic and thematic spread of movements in modern societies, and ultimately also in order to raise the question of the function of movements in modern societies, I suggest that it will be useful to conceptualize movement discourse as a productive site for the emergence and existence of movements. In this context, I will understand movement discourse not just as the discourses employed within and around movements, in order to promote mobilization and identification, i.e., as part of the movement culture. Instead, we need to take into account the existence of discursive practices whose role it is (among other things) to 'recognize' movements and, by giving them recognition, to contribute to their emergence and existence.

The goal of the following selected samples is then to give a sense of the occurrence and distribution of the term 'movement' in the discourse of public media, past and contemporary, in order to explore the thematic range and the chronological span of the term, as well as the range of (non-academic) speakers and subject positions who contribute to movement discourse. While the findings from these probes are likely to add rather than reduce the variety of components of movement discourse, I propose nevertheless that by placing them alongside the state of debate on movements which we have encountered in the various academic disciplines, it becomes possible to formulate a number of propositions or working hypotheses on movement discourse that can serve as points of departure for a theory of the 'movement.' With these propositions I will conclude my contribution.

The first observation to be drawn from the set of samples I am about to present is that the scope of different types of movements extends even beyond the kinds that we have encountered in the preceding survey of disciplinary approaches to movements. The range and variety of movements which have become the object of academic research and theoretical inquiry thus does not necessarily offer a representative selection of the movements which are being or have been discussed in public media. In fact, given the spread of movements across the range of discourse in public, it seems possible to conclude that the academic attention to movements has been selective and has been driven a great deal more by the questions and interests of the various disciplines than by the structure and history of the discourse.

The first two samples of movement discourse are taken from one of the leading British newspapers, and the goal is to gauge the different movements which come to be discussed in the daily coverage of events and developments in society. In the online edition of *The Guardian* for June 11, 2012 (a date chosen quite at random), one will notice, first of all, a range of political movements—there is mention of "an anti-junta resistance movement" in Greece out of which the party Pasok was created, of a "neo-Nazi movement in Greece," and of the "Tea Party Movement" in the U.S. Next, there are also some more or less spontaneous or well-established social movements, such as the "Occupy Wall Street Movement" and "the Fair Immigration Reform Movement (Firm)." Also mentioned on that day were movements in music—in popular music, this is "the early-70s prog-rock movement," in classical music "the period-instrument movement" which is credited with being able to "produce wonderful, eye-opening surprises" "more than 50 years after it all began."

Looking specifically at the book review sections of *The Guardian* and *The Observer*, and widening the time span to include the first half of the year 2012, the chronological and thematic diversity of movements is even greater. Here is a selection of them in contextual quotes:

Stephen King's digital publication of *Riding the Bullet* in 2000 made him one of the pioneers of the ebook movement [...] (Alison Flood, "Stephen King reverts to type with new book Joyland," *The Guardian* 30 May 2012)

[T]he speed of electronic retrieval can work against good thinking. "Should we [...] start a slow-thinking movement like slow cooking?" (Frances Spalding, "All in a Don's Day by Mary Beard," *The Guardian* 11 May 2012)

Thanks to a modern "rewilding" movement, we may be living in an age where "wolf love" for once greatly outweighs "wolf hatred." (Steven Poole, "Steven Poole's nonfiction choice—reviews," *The Guardian* 20 April 2012)

Sam Harris is the most pugnacious of the New Atheists, a movement he helped launch (Glenn Greenwald, "The Moral Landscape by Sam Harris—review," *The Observer* 15 April 2012)

Factories, mines and mills are spreading the sooty sores of manufacture over English fields and groves. But the Romantic movement would not have been born without them. (Carol Rumens, "Poem of the week: Lines Written in Early Spring by William Wordsworth," *The Guardian* 12 March 2012)

the Olympic movement (David Goldblatt, "The Spirit of the Game: How Sport Made the Modern World by Mihir Bose," *The Observer* 12 February 2012)

Iran's 2009 opposition green movement (Roland Elliot Brown, "The Ayatollahs' Democracy: An Iranian Challenge by Hooman Majd," *The Observer* 22 January 2012)

the suppression of the Tiananmen student movement in 1989 (Isabel Hilton, "Under the Hawthorn Tree by Ai Mi," *The Guardian* 20 January 2012)

Jarry is seen increasingly as a major influence on contemporary writing as well as the most important precursor of the dadaists, the surrealists and the British pop art movement (Michael Moorcock, "Alfred Jarry: A Pataphysical Life by Alastair Brotchie," *The Guardian* 4 January 2012)

This sample includes familiar types of movements, but extends the range even further. Along with political movements such as "Iran's 2009 opposition green movement" or "the Tiananmen student movement in 1989," we now also find movements familiar from the context of the history of literature and art ("dadaists," "pop art movement," "the Romantic movement"). Other thematic areas include sports (the Olympic movement), animal ecology (the rewilding movement), or contemporary publishing practices ("the ebook movement"). In addition, there is talk of movements which combine aspects of intellectual life with lifestyles: The "new atheists" are a movement seeking to limit the influence of religion on contemporary society; the slow cooking movement sets up to counter the tendency towards 'fast food,' and the critic draws an analogy between fast food and the thinking that keeps pace with the "speed of electronic retrieval" and correspondingly, between 'slow cooking' and an as yet hypothetical "slow-thinking movement."

In respect of thematic range, while political and social movements are at the forefront of coverage (no doubt in keeping with the nature of news media), the variety among the other movements corresponds to the range of the newspaper's different sections. We may conclude from this that movements occur in any area of human activity which has a critical or journalistic discourse to accompany it.

One may also notice that the range includes movements of very different 'magnitudes' and durations. At one end, we find established and long lasting movements, some affecting many areas of culture—such as the Romantic movement, well known as one of the major movements in European literary and cultural history—, others located in a particular field —such as the Olympic movement, dating back to the late 19th century, or the period-instrument movement which is described as being strong and productive after fifty years of existence. At the other end of the spectrum there are *ad hoc* coinages of movements which are not only ephemeral but hypothetical movements, such as the "slow-thinking movement" of which the critic simply asks whether there might be a demand for its existence. Although in this particular case it does not appear to have happened, the critical observer evidently has the liberty not only to identify movements that may not have been identified before, but even to suggest the creation of movements. We may infer from this the potentially productive nature of the critical discourse on movements.

Historically, it is apparent that contemporary movements predominate (again no doubt in keeping with the nature of news media), but the discussion equally concerns itself with movements from the past—and so do the materials which are reviewed in the book review section. The historical span of movements discussed in this sample again reaches back to the turn of the 19th century, the Romantic movement being the oldest on this list. Of course, since the discourse is not confined to contemporary phenomena, there is nothing in principle to prevent critics from describing or discussing older movements, and no doubt a wider sample would also include such movements.

By contrast, at least in the Anglophone context, it is hard to find any evidence of movement discourse that reaches back further than the 19th century, either in the *Oxford English Dictionary* or in full text collections or bibliographical databases. The earliest entries in the *British Library Catalogue* which carry the term in their title are these:

Anon. [William Cale Townley.] *A Sermon occasioned by the Late Chartist Movement.* London, 1839.

Benjamin Carvosso. *Drunkenness, the Enemy of Britain, Arrested by the Hand of God in the Recent Temperance Movement. A Sermon Preached at a Teetotal Festival.* 2nd ed. Barnstaple: W. Avery, 1841.

Joseph Rathbone. *Are the Puseyites Sincere? A letter [...] on the Oxford Movement.* London, 1841.

Hon Arthur Philip Perceval. *A Collection of Papers connected with the Theological Movement of 1833.* London, 1842.

G. J. Holyoake. *The Movement. Anti-Persecution Gazette and Register of Progress.* Vol. 1, 1843-1845. London: Holyoake.

Francis Wyse. *Federalism. Its Inapplicability to the Wants and Necessities of the Country,* [...] *with Remarks and Observations on the Rise and Progress of the Present Repeal Movement in Ireland; in reply to J. G. V. Porter.* Dublin, 1844.

William Leask. *The Philosophy of the Early Closing Movement. A Lecture.* London, 1849.

George Robinson. *On Education, as Connected with the Sanitary Movement at Newcastle-upon-Tyne and Gateshead. A Lecture.* Newcastle-upon-Tyne: M.A. Richardson, 1849.

Prior to the 1830s, the term occurs rarely in any related sense, and never with a defining epithet (such as "Romantic movement" or "Chartist Movement").

At least in the Anglophone context, the establishment of a discourse on movements is clearly a Victorian phenomenon. From the late 1830s onwards, it appears that various movements are sufficiently in the public eye to warrant coverage in various genres which libraries classify as ephemeral, such as the (printed) sermon, the open letter, the pamphlet, or the public lecture.[4] The chronological suggestion made by Giorgio Agamben, who dated the rise of the concept at around 1830 (in France), appears thus to be borne out.

What is not confirmed by these examples is Agamben's proposition that it will take until the early 20th century for movement discourse to proliferate widely and become dominant. In fact, the thematic range of mid-19th-century movements is quite as diverse as that in the 20th or 21st centuries. There are differences, of course. In part, these can no doubt be attributed to the selective rather than comprehensive character of the samples taken, and in part also to social and cultural changes that have occurred since the early 19th century. *Mutatis mutandis*, then, the thematic range of movements in this last sample is similar to that in our contemporary sample. There is a substantial share of social and political movements (Chartism, the "repeal [of the union between Great Britain and Ireland] movement in Ireland"). Movements which aim for social reform are particularly well-represented, and it is remarkable, too, that alongside an 'oppositional' movement such as Chartism there are several others which aim for the improvement of the moral and practical living conditions of the population (against the consumption of alcoholic beverages, in favor of shorter working hours for shop assistants, for improved sanitary conditions). Equally remarkable is the strong presence of a religious component, especially in the earliest items of this sample. This is in part thematic: The Oxford movement stands out as a significant and controversial religious movement of the 1830s and 1840s. It is manifested above all in the fact that even when the movements under discussion are not predominantly religious—as is the case in the first two items on the list, which deal with Chartism and the Temperance movements respectively—the text type in which they are discussed is of religious origin: namely the sermon.

As was noticeable in my contemporary sample, the critical discourse in the newspapers and periodicals of the time displays an even greater variety

---

4   A survey search in the Library of Congress online catalogue yields even fewer entries which feature the term 'movement' in their titles. It does include, however, a substantial number of ephemeral publications which were retrospectively classified as 'publications associated with the women's movement, abolitionist movement, etc.' by 20th-century librarians.

of movements. In addition to the religious, political and social movements we have already come across, we find:

- movements in literature and art, such as the "much-talked-of pre-Raphaelite movement" (A. Y., *Fraser's Mag.* 53, 686),
- movements in lifestyles and dress, such as the gender specific "beard movement" ("Modern Dress," *London Review* 112) and "crinoline movement" ("Modern Female Dress," *Saturday Review* 696) respecttively,
- movements in the publishing world, such as the "'cheap' or 'penny paper' movement" ("Political Press of America," *Fraser's Mag.* 681), as well as
- movements in which citizens seek to supplement the activities which existing institutions (such as the British Army or the various Churches in Britain) appear to exercise in a too limiting fashion—examples range from "the rifle volunteer movement" ("Modern Periodical Literature," *Dublin Review* 302), which trains its members in the armed defence of their country against potential invaders, and which runs its own journal, to the "Lay Sermon Movement, exemplified in the resolution to give Sunday Evenings to Science and General Knowledge, instead of an exclusive devotion to Theology" ([Lewes,] *Fortnightly Review* 646).

There is a second aspect on which Agamben's propositions offer only a partial account of the phenomena. The suggested connection between movement discourse and biopolitics is borne out by some of the samples, but is arguably contradicted by the samples as a whole. The 'temperance movement'—campaigning against the consumption of alcohol—, the 'early closing movement'—advocating shorter working hours for shop assistants—, and no doubt also the 'sanitary movement' can certainly be described as biopolitical projects. Their aim is to regulate and thereby improve the living conditions of large proportions of the population. But how about the Oxford Movement, the Pre-Raphaelite movement, the beard or crinoline movements, the ebook or the cheap or penny paper movements? Reserving the results of a more extensive inquiry, it seems appropriate to conceptualize movement discourse as an embracing critical practice which is tied to the observation of human social, cultural, intellectual activity.

A more comprehensive view of the range of movements which is thus produced can take its cue from Wouter de Nooy and the understanding of movements as emerging by the means of precarious alliances involving critics who are prepared to discuss the movement in one respect or another (asking questions such as, Does it exist or should it be brought into existence? Who belongs to it? What are its goals, its characteristics, its likely effects?) and thus combine to create a focus of attention in which any self-identified or supposed adherents or representatives of the movement are optional, but not requisite participants. In other words, it is the productivity of movement discourse itself which creates the conditions in which movements—of very different shapes and descriptions—may emerge.

Once we posit the productivity of movement discourse (as suggested above, and arising from the fact that movements are precarious alliances which consist of the readiness of critics to turn their attention to the question of the existence, the characteristics, and so on, of a given movement), we will no longer need to look elsewhere for the fundamental conditions that make the existence of movements possible. The productivity of movement discourse will account for the fact that movements, of very different characters, very different magnitudes and very different durability can potentially emerge in any thematic field to which movement discourse is applied. It will also account for the problem raised by Frickel and Gross, when they speak of "diffuse changes in thought that few observers at the time recognized as a movement, but which have been so recognized later through historical scholarship" (206, FN 3). The productivity of movement discourse can be exercised in retrospect, and the question whether phenomena of the past come to be 'recognized' depends on the question whether a more or less precarious alliance will be formed among those who are observing and assessing these phenomena in retrospect.

Whether the reference is contemporary or past, or even a hypothetical future development, it is a critical privilege to propose that a particular movement exists, that it has this or that quality and that this or that effect, benefit, or danger may come to result or have already resulted from this. It is a critical privilege to identify and name movements, to 'recognize' movements which have not yet been so described or 'recognized'—movements for whose existence no previous claim has been made, and for which there are no active campaigners presenting themselves as leaders, members or representatives. As cases in point, I refer to the Victorian "beard movement" or the hypothetical "slow thinking movement" to be formed in order to counter the speed of digital information processing.

'Recognition' in the case of such 'movements' means, as a minimum requirement, the practical decision on the part of several observers to accept a debate about the existence of the movement, and perhaps about its members and its particular features and qualities. The fulfilment of this minimum requirement effectively amounts to the establishment of a *precarious alliance* between those who ensure this fulfilment—an alliance which may either be lasting or transitory and ephemeral; into which few or many may enter, and which may or may not involve those who are seen as members or participants of the movement itself.

I suggest that this will finally allow us to recognize that the elusiveness of any definition based on structural features, the very imprecision and vagueness on which the definitions of social movements insist—in other words, the very features that have appeared both characteristic and troublesome in relation to the concept and the phenomena it refers to—are essential and constitutive elements of the concept. They are the correlatives and preconditions of the productivity and dynamic openness of movement discourse.

Against this background, I would like to return to the literary interview from which I quoted an extract at the outset of this paper in order to illustrate the puzzling vagueness and indecisiveness that may attend discussions of movements. With the foregoing reflections in mind, I suggest, this dialogue can now be read as something quite different: as an illustration of the essential and characteristic features of movement discourse. For the reader's convenience, I reproduce the quotation here:

AL Kennedy: […] I'm a Scottish writer because I live there and I was born there, and my books will relate to other books that are Scottish, but it's not my job to do that. That's up to journalists, or the marketing people if they feel that will help sales by creating a Scottish movement.
Observer: So you don't see yourself as part of a Scottish movement?
AL Kennedy: If you talk to anybody who's in a 'movement' unless they're with Andy Warhol or something very few artists, particularly writers, really manipulate the media and create the idea of it. I see some of the other Scottish writers sometimes, but we're presented as always being in the pub together or sharing needles together we meet probably every two years, that's not a movement (laughs).

First of all, then, one will notice that the author declares it is "not [her] job" to make claims about her own participation in a particular movement, or about the existence of the movement in question. In the same breath, however, she points out whose "job" this is: that of critics—"journalists"—on the one hand, and of "marketing people" on the other. All the same, in this conversation, it is the author, and not the journalist who introduces the term. Moreover, it is also the author who explains that there are certain artists and writers who are in the position of "manipulating the media" and inducing them to link the particular artist to a particular movement. In spite of the author's claim that she herself does not have this power, the journalist does pick up the cue and accepts the topic of a "Scottish movement." The author goes on to offer the "raw materials" for the critic's job: "I live there and I was born there," "I see some of the other Scottish writers sometimes, [...] we meet probably every two years." And while she appears to withdraw from the task of interpretation, she does in fact contradict the image already created by journalists by ridiculing it ("we're presented as always being in the pub together or sharing needles together") and finally issuing a flat contradiction: "[T]hat's not a movement." Suddenly, it appears as though the author has both the authority and the knowledge which she has just rejected, by declaring it was not her job: namely to pronounce on the existence of a "Scottish movement." We do not have to go so far as to attribute a manipulative intention to the author—in fact the author's intention does not make any difference here—but we can be sure that irrespective of the author's and indeed the journalist's attitudes, neither has the power to end the discussion on the "Scottish movement," should anyone else be moved to continue it.

As by the evidence of this dialogue, the "Scottish movement" has a precarious existence. Of the two partners in dialogue, neither is prepared simply to assert that it exists. At the same time, neither of them is prepared to issue an unequivocal denial of its existence either. The contradictory position taken by the author allows her to keep both options open: on the one hand, to distance herself from those who have asserted that a "Scottish movement" exists and avoid taking responsibility for such a claim; but on the other hand, to define her 'Scottishness' and phrase her deprecation of the idea of a 'movement' in a way that would allow critics still to describe her as a member of that movement, should they choose to. In the present dialogue, the journalist declines to do so, preferring at the same time to retain both of the options as well, rather than forcing the issue in the other direction. At the end of this brief exchange, the issue remains unresolved, and both participants have tacitly worked together in order to adjourn the decision and maintain the possibility that some other speaker might take a more outspoken view. The work mapped out, but left undone in this dialogue is equally clear: the critical work of defining the movement and its significance for contemporary literature, or contemporary society.

What we have witnessed in this passage, then, is an incidental practice of movement discourse, which can be indicative of the discursive practice that maintains movements in existence. It is indicative precisely because of its incidental character. Neither speaker is ready to completely commit to the discursive alliance that could form the basis for a Scottish movement in contemporary British writing; nor are they prepared entirely to reject the possibility. Nevertheless they enter into a precarious alliance which leaves all options open to either of them. The precarious existence of this movement is then founded on an equally precarious alliance whose members are neither fully committed to participate nor ready to abandon it. I have no wish to argue that all potential members of potential movements, and all potential critics observing these potential movements and their potential members, behave exactly like these two speakers. No doubt, many will be far more decisive either in their commitment or their rejection. But I propose that the very vagueness and openness of the movement operate so as to keep the existence, the precise quality and character, the magnitude and significance of all movements, permanently in the balance: always up for redescription and redefinition.

And these constitutive vaguenesses—in respect of its form, scope and structure as well as in respect of its quality and significance—are, in turn, essential to the function of movement discourse.

TOWARDS AN ANALYSIS OF THE DISCOURSE ON MOVEMENTS—SOME PROPOSITIONS

In order to offer a preliminary generalization from the foregoing discussion, I will conclude with a set of propositions on movement discourse, on its salient features, its modes of operation and finally on its function in modern societies. I suggest then, that the following aspects have emerged from the foregoing discussion:

1. *Chronology*: Movement discourse (sustained by a range of media, ephemeral, periodical or scholarly) has existed in the Anglophone public sphere since around the 1830s or 1840s.

2. *Range*: Movement discourse comprises potentially all fields of society—or more accurately: movement discourse exists for all fields of human activity for which there is a public critical discourse whose role it is to monitor the state of this field of activity, to assess actual or possible developments and to analyze the roles of particular agents within them.

3. *Productivity*: Movement discourse is productive. Movements emerge from this discursive practice, and they do not exist independently of it. The existence of movement discourse is a prerequisite for the existence of movements.

4. *Openness of participation*: Participation in movement discourse is open, in principle, to all who are capable of gaining a voice in critical public debates.[5] Within movement discourse, discussions of subject-positions tend to focus on those who are variously described as agents (participants, adherents, representatives or leaders) in the given movements. For participation in movement discourse, however, the adherence or affiliation to any particular movement is not a necessary requirement. Speakers may instead be identified as observers, opponents, critics, or historians of the movement in question. And while it is, of course, possible that those who have identified themselves with a particular movement or who have been so identified by others, will also participate in movement discourse, it is just as possible that this may not be the case. Individual movements emerge into existence with the formation of (dynamically evolving and more or less precarious) discursive alliances—some of which may involve self-identified members or representatives, while others may not. Even movements for which there are no self-identified participants or adherents at a particular time may come to attract self-identified adherents or participants at any future point.

---

5   It may be worth stressing that this does not imply that participation in movement discourse, in contrast to any other form of discursive participation, should be considered as an egalitarian matter. On the contrary, the positions of speakers who participate in movement discourse require the same analysis as those of all other participants in discourse.

The participation of movement representatives is by no means an indispensable element in movement discourse, but rather a particular aspect, deserving due consideration.

5. *Prestige*: Since the 19th century, the movement has been widely introduced as the more prestigious alternative to whatever more concrete types of organisation had already been current in these various fields:

- in political contexts to parties;
- in wider social contexts to clubs, leagues, associations and organizations of various types;
- in religious or confessional contexts to sects or heresies;
- in academic context and in the arts to schools.

There has been symbolic capital associated with diagnosing, identifying, describing, critically assessing movements and even with predicting future movements. There has been a corresponding symbolic capital associated with gaining recognition as a movement, because this recognition translates into acceptance of the power of one's claim that one represents a "key force" (Johnston, *What is* 1) in the particular field.

6. *Openness of definition*: As a result of the conditions under which movement discourse is practiced (and movements are produced in the process) movements display a *constitutive indefinition*. In contrast to the various more concrete types of formations just referred to, which are also tied to particular fields rather than being general, movement discourse is on principle without closure, both in relation to their exact quality and significance, and in relation to the exact circle of persons belonging to them.

7. *Function*: Movement discourse concerns the forces which are supposed to shape any social or cultural setting, any given area of human activity and makes them available for permanent negotiation and renegotiation. The vagueness and the imprecision that invariably attend discussions on movements and which may give rise to the puzzlement and discontent we have come across, thus take on significance as the correlatives of the structural and definitional openness, that has allowed movement discourse since before the middle of the 19th century to become an essential mode in the social negotiation of the forces and developments that shape any area of (creative, social, cultural, intellectual etc.) human activity. The definitional and structural imprecisions attendant on movements are therefore not to be seen as a deficit, a lack of thinking deep and hard and long enough. They

should rather be recognized as indispensable elements, which enable a variety of subject positions to participate in movement discourse and enter into the precarious alliances to which movements owe their existence and recognition. In short, there is much that suggests that we should understand movement discourse as a medium of the participatory metaphysics of the modern secular society.

WORKS CITED

A.Y. "Pre-Raphaelitism from Different Points of View." *Fraser's Magazine* 53 (June 1856): 686-93. Print.

Agamben, Giorgio. "Movement. Uni.Nomade. Seminar War and Democracy." *The European Graduate School.* N.pag., 8 March 2005. Web.

Arendt, Hannah. *The Origins of Totalitarianism.* New York: Harcourt, 1951. Print.

Bennett, Andrew, and Nicholas Royle. *An Introduction to Literature, Criticism and Theory.* 2nd ed. Harlow: Prentice Hall, 1999. Print.

Bradshaw, David, and Kevin J. H. Dettmar, eds. *A Companion to Modernist Literature and Culture.* Oxford: Blackwell, 2006. Print.

Calhoun, Craig. "'New Social Movements' of the Early Nineteenth Century." *Social Science History* 17 (1993): 385-427. Print.

Chesters, Graeme, and Ian Welsh. *Social Movements: The Key Concepts.* New York: Routledge, 2011. Print.

Culler, Jonathan. *Literary Theory: A Very Short Introduction.* 1997. Oxford: Oxford UP, 2000. Print.

de Nooy, Wouter. "Social Networks and Classification in Literature." *Poetics* 20 (1991): 507-37. Print.

Della Porta, Donatella, and Mario Diani. *Social Movements: An Introduction.* 2nd ed. Malden: Blackwell, 2006. Print.

Derrida, Jacques. "Some Statements and Truisms about Neologisms, Newisms, Postisms, Parasitisms, and other Small Seismisms." *The States of "Theory": History, Art, and Critical Discourse.* Ed. David Carroll. New York: Columbia UP, 1990. 63-94. Print.

Frickel, Scott, and Neil Gross. "A General Theory of Scientific/Intellectual Movements." *American Sociological Review* 70.2 (2005): 204-32. Print.

Henderson, Helene, ed. *Twentieth-Century Literary Movements Dictionary*. Detroit: Omni-graphics, 2000. Print.

Jasper, James M. "Social Movement Theory Today: Toward a Theory of Action?" *Sociology Compass* 4.11 (2010): 965-76. Print.

Johnston, Hank. *What is a Social Movement?* Cambridge: Polity P, 2014. Print.

---. *States & Social Movements*. Cambridge: Polity P, 2011. Print.

---, ed. *Culture, Social Movements, and Protest*. Farnham: Ashgate, 2009. Print.

Johnston, Hank, and Bert Klandermans, eds. *Social Movements and Culture*. 1995. London: Routledge, 2003. Print.

Klandermans, Bert. "Theories of Social Movements." *The Social Psychology of Protest*. Oxford: Blackwell, 1997. 199-211. Print.

[Lewes, George Henry.] "Causeries." *Fortnightly Review* 3 (January 15, 1866): 646-49. Print.

McAdam, Doug, and David A. Snow, eds. *Readings on Social Movements: Origins, Dynamics and Outcomes*. 2nd ed. New York: Oxford UP, 2010. Print.

McAdam, Doug, and David A. Snow. "Social Movements: Conceptual and Theoretical Issues." *Readings on Social Movements: Origins, Dynamics and Outcomes*. Ed. McAdam and Snow. 2nd ed. New York: Oxford UP, 2010. 1-8. Print.

Melucci, Alberto. *Nomads of the Present: Social Movements and Individual Needs in Contemporary Society*. London: Hutchinson Radius, 1989. Print.

Merritt, Stephanie. "'What's it like being a Scottish writer?' 'I don't know. I've never been anything else.'" *The Observer* 23 May 1999: N.pag. Web.

Meyer, David S., and Sidney Tarrow, eds. *The Social Movement Society: Contentious Politics for a New Century*. Lanham, MD: Rowman & Littlefield, 1998. Print.

"Modern Dress." *London Review* 11 (July 29, 1865): 112-13. Print.

"Modern Female Dress." *Saturday Review* 20 (December 2, 1865): 696-97. Print.

"Modern Periodical Literature," *Dublin Review* 51 (May 1862): 275-308. Print.

"The Political Press of America." *Fraser's Magazine* 52 (December 1855): 678-85. Print.

Ruggiero, Vincenzo, and Nicola Montagna, eds. *Social Movements: A Reader*. London: Routledge, 2008. Print.

Schmitt, Carl. *Staat Bewegung Volk*. Hamburg: Hanseatische Verlagsanstalt, 1933. Print.

Snow, David A., Sarah A. Soule, and Hanspeter Kriesi, eds. *Blackwell Companion to Social Movements*. 2nd ed. Malden: Blackwell, 2009. Print.

Snow, David A., Sarah A. Soule, and Hanspeter Kriesi. "Mapping the Terrain." *Blackwell Companion to Social Movements*. Ed. Snow, Soule, and Kriesi. 2nd ed. Malden: Blackwell, 2009. 3-16. Print.

von Stein, Lorenz. *Geschichte der sozialen Bewegung in Frankreich von 1789 bis auf unsre Tage*. 3 vols. 1850. Hildesheim: Georg Olms, 1959. Print.

Turner, Jane, ed. *From Renaissance to Impressionism: Styles and Movements in Western Art, 1400-1900*. New York: St. Martin's P, 2000. Print.

---, ed. *From Expressionism to Post-Modernism: Styles and Movements in 20th-century Western Art*. London: GroveArt, 2000. Print.

Notes on Contributors

Anna Auguscik is a Lecturer at the Institute of English and American Studies at the University of Oldenburg, where she recently completed a dissertation on the role of literary prizes and book reviewing for the literary marketplace, *Prizing Debate in Literary Interaction: The Fourth Decade of the Booker Prize and the Contemporary Novel in the UK*. A member of the interdisciplinary research project *Fiction Meets Science* (funded by the VolkswagenStiftung), she is currently working on the critical and public reception of contemporary science novels.

Christoph Bläsi is Professor of Book Studies at Johannes Gutenberg University Mainz, Germany (since 2009; main research areas: digital publishing, book business / management) and permanent visiting professor at the University of St. Gallen, Switzerland (since 2011). In 2014, he was Caledonian Research Fund Fellow at Edinburgh Napier University and the University of Stirling, UK. From 2004 to 2009, he was professor for the study of the book at University of Erlangen-Nuremberg, Germany, and from 1992 to 2004, he held senior positions in digital publishing and strategic information management of various major German publishing houses. From 1989 to 1992, he served as an assistant professor / researcher (computational linguistics) at the universities of Heidelberg and Bielefeld, Germany. In 1991, he was a research fellow at the University of Pisa, I. He studied mathematics, German studies, linguistics, computational linguistics) at the universities of Freiburg, Germany and Sussex (Brighton, U.K.) from 1982 to 1989.

Martin Butler is Junior Professor of American Literature and Culture at the University of Oldenburg. He studied English and Social Sciences at the University of Duisburg, and received his PhD in 2007 with a study on the songs of Woody Guthrie (*Voices of the Down and Out: The Dust Bowl Migration and the Great Depression in the Songs of Woody Guthrie*). His main areas of research include the study of popular culture, particularly focusing on the history of political music, forms and figures of cultural mobility as well as cultures of participation. Among his publications are the co-edited volumes *Hybrid Americas: Contacts, Contrasts, and Confluences in New World Literatures and Cultures* (2008), *Sound Fabrics: Studies on the Intermedial and Institutional Dimensions of Popular Music* (2009), *EthniCities: Metropolitan Cultures and Ethnic Identities in the Americas* (2011) as well as a co-edited special issue of *Popular Music and Society* on *Musical Autobiographies* (2015).

Ralf Grüttemeier is Professor of Dutch Literature at the University of Oldenburg, where he was dean of the School of Linguistics and Cultural Studies from 2005 to 2007. In 2008/9 he was appointed as research-fellow at the Netherlands Institute for Advanced Study (NIAS) at Wassenaar. He is co-editor of the journal *Spiegel der Letteren*. With Maria Leuker, he edited and partly wrote a history of Dutch Literature (*Niederländische Literaturgeschichte*, 2006). With Gillis Dorleijn and Liesbeth Korthals Altes, he edited *The Autonomy of Literature* (2007) and *Authorship Revisited* (2010). His most recent monograph is a history of the concept of authorial intention (*Auteursintentie: Een beknopte geschiedenis*, 2011), the most recent book he co-edited is *Neue Sachlichkeit and Avant-Garde* (2013). A major line in his research focusses on law and literature, especially as regards literary trials (cf. Klaus Beekman / Ralf Grüttemeier: *De wet van de letter*, 2005). Currently (2010-2015) he is leading the DFG-project "Literature and Jurisprudence in South-Africa and Belgium."

Albrecht Hausmann is Professor of Medieval Studies at the University of Oldenburg. He studied Medieval German Language and Literature and Political Sciences in Munich. In 1997, he received his PhD with a dissertation on medieval love poetry (published as ‚Reinmar der Alte als Autor', 1999). From 2000 to 2006, he led the Junior Research Group "Voice – Sign – Scripture in the Middle Ages and Early Modern Times" at the University of Göttingen. His areas of research include courtly epic, historical narratology, the poetics of medieval poetry, and the mediality of medival literature. Among his publications are *Struktur, Autorisierung, Autorschaft: Untersu-*

chungen zur Poetik von 'Erec', 'Gregorius' und 'Tristan' (2009) as well as the volumes *Text und Handeln: Zum kommunikativen Ort von Minnesang und antiker Lyrik* (2004, as editor) and *Übertragungen: Formen und Konzepte von Reproduktion in Mittelalter und Früher Neuzeit* (2005, as co-editor).

Henry Jenkins was the founder and co-director of the MIT Program in Comparative Media Studies and now serves as the Provost's Professor of Communication, Journalism, Cinematic Arts, and Education at the University of Southern California. He has published more than seventeen books on various aspects of new media, popular culture, and public life, starting with *Textual Poachers: Television Fans and Participatory Culture* in 1992. His most recent books have included *Reading in a Participatory Culture: Remixing Moby-Dick in the Literature Classroom*; *Spreadable Media: Creating Meaning and Value in a Networked Culture*; and the forthcoming *By Any Media Necessary: The New Activism of American Youth*. In addition to his academic publishing, Henry blogs regularly at henryjenkins.org. He serves on the Jury of the Peabody Awards, as chief advisor to the Annenberg Innovation Lab, as a member of the MacArthur Foundation's Youth and Participatory Politics Network, and on the advisory board for Disney Jr.

Anton Kirchhofer is Professor of English Literature at the University of Oldenburg. He studied at Berlin, Dublin, Pittsburgh and Munich, earning his doctoral and postdoctoral degrees with studies on sex in the eighteenth century English novel and on criticism on the nineteenth century periodical market respectively. His chief research interests and areas of publication are literary theory and its relation with literary production; Anglophone Literature and Culture from the eighteenth century to the present, including the media, cultural settings and discursive environments of fiction and literary discourse; and most recently, the connections between literature and secular modernity, and between literature and science. He currently leads two projects in the interdisciplinary *Fiction Meets Science* research group funded by the VolkswagenStiftung. Previous co-edited volumes include *Psychoanalytic·ism: Uses of Psychoanalysis in Novels, Poems, Plays and Films* (2000), *Internet Fictions* (2009), and *Religion, Secularity and Cultural Agency* (2010).

Gun-Britt Kohler is Professor of Slavonic Literary Studies at the University of Oldenburg, Germany. Her primary research interests and topics of several articles are the typology, development and modernisms of 'small' Slavic literatures from a comparative field-theoretical perspective as well as questions concerning its historiographical reflection and canonizetion. Current areal foci covered by this research are Belarus, the Ukraine, and also Croatia. Other fields of interest include the literature and literary theory of Slavic, especially Russian Modernism in its cultural contexts. She co-edited *Gabe und Opfer in der russischen Literatur der Moderne* (2006), *Habsburg und die Slavia* (2008), *Blickwechsel: Perspektiven der slavischen Moderne für den internationalen literaturwissenschaftlichen Dialog* (2010) and *Kleinheit als Spezifik: Beiträge zu einer feldtheoretischen Analyse der belarussischen Literatur im Kontext 'kleiner' slavischer Literaturen* (2012) and regularly publishes on several Slavonic literatures.

Sabine Kyora has been Professor of Modern German Literature at Carl von Ossietzky University in Oldenburg, Germany, since 2002. She studied literature and history in Bielefeld and Hamburg and did her PhD on psychoanalysis and prose in the 20th century (*Psychoanalyse und Prosa im 20. Jahrhundert*). In 1999, she completed her Habilitation with a study on the poetics of modernity (*Eine Poetik der Moderne,* 2007). She has published widely on a different authors and texts, ranging from classical modernity to the present day, particularly on Arno Schmidt, Friederike Mayröcker, and Paul Wühr, as well as on methodological questions in literary studies and on literary figurations of the subject and authorship.

Ulrich Schmid is Professor of Russian Studies at the University of St. Gallen. His research interests include nationalism, popular culture, and the media in Eastern Europe. He studied German and Slavic literature at the Universities of Zürich, Heidelberg, and Leningrad. He held academic positions in Basel, Bern, Bochum and was visiting researcher at Harvard and in Oslo. Publications: *Technologies of the Soul: The Production of Truth in Contemporary Russian Culture* (2015); *Sword, Eagle and Cross: The Aesthetics of the Nationalist Discourse in Interwar Poland* (2013); *Tolstoi as a Theological Thinker and a Critic of the Church* (2013, with Martin George, Jens Herlth, Christian Münch); *Lev Tolstoi* (2010), *Literary Theories of the 20th Century* (2010); Russian Media Theories (2005); *Russian Religious*

Philosophers of the 20th Centure (2003); *The Designed Self: Russian Autobiographies between Avvakum and Herzen* (2000).

Arvi Sepp is Senior Lecturer in German Literature at the University of Antwerp, Guest Professor for German-Jewish literature at the Institute for Jewish Studies in Antwerp, and lecturer in Translation Studies at the Free University of Brussels (VUB). He published widely on German-Jewish literature, German popular culture, autobiography studies, translation theory, and literary theory. For his research on German-Jewish literature, he was awarded the Fritz Halbers Fellowship Award (Leo Baeck Institute), the Tauber Institute Research Award (Brandeis University), the Memorial Foundation for Jewish Culture Award, and the Prix de la Fondation Auschwitz for his PhD on Victor Klemperer's Third Reich Diaries.

Geoffrey Turnovsky is Associate Professor of French Studies at the University of Washington in Seattle, with an affiliation in the department of Comparative Literature, Cinema and Media and in the program for Textual Studies. In 2010, he published *The Literary Market: Modern Authorship in the Old Regime* (Penn). His current project investigates the history of reading in 17th- and 18th-century France and Europe, with a focus on spiritualized, uplifting ideals of reading and the relation of these ideals to commercial and typographic developments in the book trade. His publications on this topic can be found in *Modern Language Quarterly*, *Romanic Review* and forthcoming in *XVIIIe Siècle*.

Wil Verhoeven is Professor of American Culture and Cultural Theory and Chair of the American Studies Department at Groningen University, the Netherlands. In 2003-4 he was Charles H. Watts II Professor in the History of the Book at Brown University, where he is currently an invited research scholar at the American Studies Department. His publications include: *Americomania and the French Revolution Debate in Britain, 1789-1800* (C.U.P., 2013); *Gilbert Imlay: Citizen of the World* (Pickering and Chatto, 2008); Editor, *Revolutionary Histories: Transatlantic Cultural Nationalism, 1775-1815* (Palgrave, 2002); Co-editor, *Epistolary Histories: Letters, Fiction, Culture* (U of Virginia P, 2000); Co-editor, *Revolutions & Watersheds: Transatlantic Dialogues, 1775-1815* (Rodopi, 1999). His current book projects include: *The Revolution of America: The Ideological Origins of American Ex-*

ceptionalism and *Enemies of the State: Sedition and Resistance in the Trans-Allegheny West, 1776-1806.*

James L. W. West III is Edwin Erle Sparks Professor of English at Pennsylvania State University. He is a biographer, book historian, and scholarly editor. West is the author of *American Authors and the Literary Marketplace* (1988), *William Styron: A Life* (1998) and *The Perfect Hour: The Romance of F. Scott Fitzgerald and Ginevra King* (2005). His most recent book is a collection of essays called *Making the Archives Talk* (2011). West has held fellowships from the Guggenheim Foundation, the National Humanities Center, and the National Endowment for the Humanities. He has had Fulbright appointments in England (at Cambridge University) and in Belgium (at the Université de Liège) and has been a visiting fellow at the American Academy in Rome. West is the General Editor of the Cambridge Fitzgerald Edition.